VITAL
THEOLOGICAL
ISSUES

THE VITAL ISSUES SERIES

VOLUME ONE

Vital Ministry Issues:
Examining Concerns and Conflicts in Ministry

VOLUME TWO

Vital Contemporary Issues:
Examining Current Questions & Controversies

VOLUME THREE

Vital Biblical Issues:
Examining Problem Passages of the Bible

VOLUME FOUR

Vital Theological Issues:
Examining Enduring Issues of Theology

VITAL ISSUES SERIES

VITAL THEOLOGICAL ISSUES

*Examining Enduring
Issues of Theology*

ROY B. ZUCK
GENERAL EDITOR

Grand Rapids, MI 49501

Vital Theological Issues by Roy B. Zuck, general editor.

Copyright © 1994 by Dallas Theological Seminary.

Published by Kregel Resources, an imprint of Kregel Publications, P.O. Box 2607, Grand Rapids, MI 49501. Kregel Resources provides timely and relevant resources for Christian life and service. Your comments and suggestions are valued.

Cover Design: Sarah Slattery
Book Design: Alan G. Hartman

Library of Congress Cataloging-in-Publication Data
　Roy B. Zuck.
　Vital theological issues: examining enduring issues of theology / Roy B. Zuck, gen. ed.
　　　p.　　cm. (Vital Issues Series)
　　1. Christian life—1960. 2. Conduct of life—Biblical teaching. 3. Bible—Use. I. Zuck, Roy B. II. Series: Zuck, Roy B. Vital Issues Series.
BV4501.2.V55　　1994　　230'.046—dc20　　94-37863
　　　　　　　　　　　　　　　　　　　　　　　　CIP

ISBN 0-8254-4069-6 (paperback)

1 2 3 4 5 Printing / Year 98 97 96 95 94

Printed in the United States of America

Contents

Contributors 7
Preface 9
About *Bibliotheca Sacra* 10

1. Prayer and the Sovereignty of God
   John D. Hannah 11

2. Is Foreknowledge Equivalent to Foreordination?
   Edgar C. James 21

3. The Doctrine of Miracles
   John A. Witmer 26

4. The Importance of Inerrancy
   Charles C. Ryrie 34

5. The Role of the Holy Spirit in Hermeneutics
   Roy B. Zuck 42

6. The Image of God
   Charles Lee Feinberg 52

7. The Doctrine of the Conscience
   Roy B. Zuck 61

8. Untold Billions: Are They Really Lost?
   J. Ronald Blue 71

9. The Impeccability of Jesus Christ
   Joseph G. Sahl 83

10. For Whom Did Christ Die?
    Lewis Sperry Chafer 92

11. The Present Work of Christ in Hebrews
    David J. MacLeod 108

12. The Terms of Salvation
    Lewis Sperry Chafer 117

13. The Role of the Holy Spirit in Conversion
    Robert A. Pyne 140

14. Has Lordship Salvation Been Taught
     Throughout Church History?
     Thomas G. Lewellen 153

15. The Significance of Pentecost
     Charles C. Ryrie 165

16. The Purpose of the Law
     J. Dwight Pentecost 174

17. The Mediatorial Kingdom from the Acts Period to the
     Eternal State
     Alva J. McClain 181

18. The Theological Context of Premillennialism
     John F. Walvoord 187

     Chapter Notes 197

Contributors

J. Ronald Blue
   President, CAM International, Dallas, Texas

Lewis Sperry Chafer
   Late Founder and President, and Professor of Systematic
   Theology, Dallas Theological Seminary, Dallas, Texas

Charles Lee Feinberg
   Dean, Emeritus, and Professor of Semitics and Old
   Testament, Talbot School of Theology, La Mirada,
   California

John D. Hannah
   Chairman and Professor of Historical Theology, Dallas
   Theological Seminary, Dallas, Texas

Edgar C. James
   Professor of Bible and Theology, Moody Bible Institute,
   Chicago, Illinois

Thomas G. Lewellen
   Senior Pastor, Grace Countryside Church, Milford,
   Michigan

David J. MacLeod
   Dean of the Graduate Program, Emmaus Bible College,
   Dubuque, Iowa

Alva J. McClain
   Late President and Professor of Systematic Theology,
   Grace Theological Seminary, Winona Lake, Indiana

J. Dwight Pentecost
   Distinguished Professor of Bible Exposition, Emeritus,
   Dallas Theological Seminary, Dallas, Texas

Robert A. Pyne
   Assistant Professor of Systematic Theology, Dallas
   Theological Seminary, Dallas, Texas

Charles C. Ryrie
Professor of Systematic Theology, Emeritus, Dallas
Theological Seminary, Dallas, Texas

Joseph G. Sahl
Pastor, Believers Fellowship, San Antonio, Texas

John F. Walvoord
Chancellor, Minister-at-Large, and Professor of Systematic
Theology, Emeritus, Dallas Theological Seminary, Dallas,
Texas

John A. Witmer
Seminary Archivist and Associate Professor of Systematic
Theology, Emeritus, Dallas Theological Seminary, Dallas,
Texas

Roy B. Zuck
Chairman and Senior Professor of Bible Exposition, and
Editor of *Bibliotheca Sacra*, Dallas Theological Seminary,
Dallas, Texas

Preface

*Ivory tower . . . academic . . . irrelevant . . . impractical
. . . unnecessary.*

These are terms some people use to describe theology. And yet theology—the study of God and His relationship to the universe and mankind—is remarkably relevant and practical.

What could be more practical for believers than the question of how prayer relates to God's sovereignty? What could be more relevant to evangelism than the question of those for whom Christ died or the question of what one must do to be saved?

Numerous other theological issues vie for the attention of the thinking Christian. Does God perform miracles today? Is the Bible inerrant in its original manuscripts? How does the Holy Spirit help us interpret the Bible? Are the unsaved really lost eternally? Could Christ have sinned? What is the significance of the Day of Pentecost? Why did God give the Mosaic Law? Why is premillennialism essential?

Over the years the theological journal *Bibliotheca Sacra* has addressed numerous doctrinal subjects of concern not only to theologians but also to laypersons—to all individuals interested in knowing the teachings of Scripture, God's authoritative Word, and how those truths relate to life.

This volume assembles 18 pressing issues of theology so that as the Apostle Paul wrote, we may "encourage others by sound doctrine" (Titus 1:9), and, as the Apostle Peter wrote, we may "grow in the grace and knowledge of our Lord and Savior Jesus Christ" (2 Pet. 3:18).

ROY B. ZUCK

About *Bibliotheca Sacra*

A flood is rampant—an engulfing deluge of literature far beyond any one person's ability to read it all. Presses continue to churn out thousands of journals and magazines like a roiling, raging river.

Among these numberless publications, one stands tall and singular—*Bibliotheca Sacra*—a strange name (meaning "Sacred Library") but a journal familiar to many pastors, teachers, and Bible students.

How is *Bibliotheca Sacra* unique in the world of publishing? By being the oldest continuously published journal in the Western Hemisphere—1993 marked its 150th anniversary—and by being published by one school for sixty years—1994 marks its diamond anniversary of being released by Dallas Seminary.

Bib Sac, to use its shortened sobriquet, was founded in New York City in 1843 and was purchased by Dallas Theological Seminary in 1934, ten years after the school's founding. The quarterly's one-hundred-and-fifty-year history boasts only nine editors. Through those years it has maintained a vibrant stance of biblical conservatism and a strong commitment to the Scriptures as God's infallible Word.

I am grateful to Kregel Publications for producing a series of volumes, being released this year and next, commemorating both the journal's sesquicentennial (1843–1993) and its diamond anniversary (1934–1994). Each volume in the Kregel *Vital Issues Series* includes carefully selected articles from the thirties to the present—articles of enduring quality, articles by leading evangelicals whose topics are as relevant today as when they were first produced. The chapters have been edited slightly to provide conformity of style. As Dallas Seminary and Kregel Publications jointly commemorate these anniversaries of *Bibliotheca Sacra*, we trust these anthologies will enrich the spiritual lives and Christian ministries of many more readers.

ROY B. ZUCK, EDITOR
Bibliotheca Sacra

For *Bibliotheca Sacra* subscription information, call Dallas Seminary, 1–800–992-0998.

CHAPTER 1

Prayer and the Sovereignty of God

John D. Hannah

I f God is sovereign, why should Christians pray? This is one of the perennial questions inquiring Christian minds often reflect on or by which they are troubled. If God is sovereign, is not prayer a superfluous activity, or at best an exercise in meditation or some form of inspiring soliloquy? The question of the tension between solicitations to prayer and the presupposition of absolute sovereignty is but a harbinger of numerous other difficulties with the doctrine of prayer. Does prayer limit sovereignty? Does God change His mind? Is it possible that one's will can prevail over God's will? Is God obligated to answer prayer?

Prayer is so repeatedly commanded in the Scriptures that its necessity is unquestioned (e.g., 1 Tim. 2:8); it is manifestly evident as that of divine sovereignty. The initial step in resolving the apparent conflict is to define prayer. In the Reformed tradition prayer is viewed as an act of spiritual intercourse of the creature with the Creator. According to Dabney, the brilliant Southern Presbyterian theologian, prayer is "the natural homage due from the creature to his heavenly Father."[1] Charles Hodge states that prayer is "the converse of the soul with God."[2] He adds, "It is not therefore prayer as the mere uttering of words, nor prayer as the uttering of natural desires of affection, as when one prays for his own life or the life of those dear to him; but it is prayer as the real intercourse of the soul with God, by the Holy Spirit, that is, the Holy Spirit revealing truth, exciting feeling, and giving appropriate utterance."[3] Calvin's discussion of prayer is located in an unusual place in his systematic theology; he prefaced the treatment of election and predestination with a lengthy treatment of the nature and significance of prayer. To Calvin prayer is the vehicle of spiritual exercise whereby the promises of blessing and comfort seen faintly by the eye of faith are actualized in sight.

To prayer, then, are we indebted for penetrating to those riches which are treasured up for us with our heavenly Father. For there is a kind of intercourse between God and men, by which, having entered the upper sanctuary, they appear before Him and appeal to His promises, that when necessity requires, they may learn by experience, that what they believed merely of the authority of His word was not in vain. Accordingly, we see that nothing is set before us as an object of expectation from the Lord which we are not enjoined to ask of Him in prayer, so true it is that prayer digs up those treasures which the Gospel of our Lord discovers to the eye of faith.[4]

Prayer can be delineated as an act of faith and worship whereby the precious promises of God are brought home to the mind of the believer. In a formal definition the Westminster Shorter Catechism stated, "Prayer is an offering up of our desires unto God, for things agreeable to His will, in the name of Christ, with confession of our sins, and thankful acknowledgment of His mercies."[5] Charles Hodge defines the action of prayer as that wherein we manifest or express to Him our reverence, and love for His divine perfection, our gratitude for all His mercies, our penitence for our sins, our hope in His forgiving love, our submission to His authority, our confidence in His care, our desires of His favor, and for the providential and spiritual blessings needed for ourselves and others."[6] Again Hodge discussed elsewhere the meaning of prayer in this way:

It is not simply petition, but converse with God, including therefore, 1. The expression of our feelings in view of His greatness and glory, i.e., adoration. 2. The expression of our feelings in view of His goodness, i.e., thanksgiving. 3. The expression of our feelings in view of our sins and sinfulness, i.e., confession. 4. The expression of our feelings in view of our wants, i.e., supplication.[7]

As the believer approaches the knotty problem of prayer and sovereignty, he does not conceive of them as opposites. Indeed, prayer is valid only when it is based on the sovereignty of God. Prayer is primarily, though not exclusively, an act of communication through worship whereby the "treasures" of God's promises come to the believer. Prayer is not so much the vehicle of benevolent acquisition as that of worship, adoration, and praise.

The Function of Prayer

While prayer is the subjective response of the rational creature to the benevolent Deity, the question must be asked, What is the purpose for which God instituted it? It is understood that believers are to pray because He ordered them in His infinite wisdom to do so, thus making prayer a wise function for believers, but for what purpose did He leave these instructions? In the Reformed tradition prayer is conceived under the rubric of the "means of grace," which are "those means which God has ordained for the end of communicating the live-giving and sanctifying influences of the Spirit to the souls of men."[8] By this means, as well as the Word of God and the ordinances, the saint is drawn to God and matured in spiritual experience. Prayer is a means of the self-disclosure of the great condescending God whereby His creatures are permitted to gain insight and understanding of His ways. A. A. Hodge views prayer as an educational vehicle.

> The great design of God in this relation is to effect our education and government as rational and spiritual beings. He accomplishes these ends by revealing to us His perfections, by training our intellects to follow the great lines of thought developed in His plans and revealed in His works, and by training us to action in the exercise of all our faculties as coworkers with each other and with Him in the execution of His plans.[9]

Thus prayer has been ordained of God as a means of "man's receiving His spiritual influences."[10] In what sense then is prayer a means of conveying God's gracious influences to the soul? The answer is twofold: first, by changing the saint inwardly without changing the saint's immediate circumstances, and second, by changing external circumstances.

Before delineating the two foci of prayer as a means of grace to the believer, a secondary yet important question should be raised regarding prayer. Does the believer obligate God to answer his requests if he sincerely, honestly, and selflessly pleads? If believers subscribe to the biblical conditions for answered prayer, are God's promises that He will answer to be considered absolute? Charles Hodge answers this question rather bluntly.

> A false doctrine has been deduced from these passages, viz.: that every specific request made with the assurance of its being granted, shall be granted. This cannot be true.
> 1. Because it would be to submit the divine government to the erring wisdom of men.
> 2. Because it would lead to undesirable or disastrous consequences. Men might pray for things which would be their own ruin and the ruin of others.
> 3. It is contrary to all experience.
> 4. It is contrary to the desire of every pious heart, as every Christian would rather that God's will than his own should be done.[11]

Hodge concluded by affirming that the great promises of God do not apply to every case, but "assert the general course of providence. And this is enough for encouragement and direction."[12]

PRAYER AND THE BELIEVER

Prayer, as a means of sanctifying grace, results in the alteration of the saint, that is, it effects his spiritual maturity. Calvin is eloquent in arguing that prayer changes the one who prays.

> The necessity and utility of this exercise of prayer no words can sufficiently express. Assuredly it is not without cause our heavenly Father declares that our only safety is in calling upon His name, since by it we invoke the presence of His providence to watch over our interests, of His power to sustain us when weak and almost fainting, of His goodness to receive us into favor, though miserably loaded with sin, in fine, call upon Him to manifest Himself to us in all His perfections. Hence, admirable peace and tranquillity are given to our consciences; for the straits by which we were pressed being laid before the Lord, we rest fully satisfied with the assurance that none of our evils are unknown to Him, and that He is able and willing to make the best provisions for us.[13]

Dabney simply writes, "Prayer is not intended to produce a change in God, but in us."[14] Calvin continues, "It was not so much for His sake as for ours. He wills indeed, as is just, that due honor be paid Him by acknowledging that all which men desire or feel to be useful, and pray to obtain, is derived from Him. But even the benefit of the homage which we thus pay Him redounds to ourselves."[15] To say that prayer changes the one who prays is unquestioned. It is readily apparent that people change as they spend time with God. But what about the thorny question about the kind of prayer designated as supplication or intercession?

PRAYER AND CIRCUMSTANCES

A second facet of prayer as a means of grace whereby the knowledge and worth of God is brought safely home to the saint's experience is that of the providential alterations of circumstance. These, like the comforting of the believer's soul and mind in the context of sorrow or humiliation, function to cause the believer to experience the reality of faith's profession. God changes not only the invisible and internal, but also He most certainly changes the visible and external. A. A. Hodge confesses:

> The Scriptures assure us, and all Christians believe, that prayer for material as well as for spiritual good is as real a means effecting the end sought as is sowing seed a means of getting a crop, or as is studying a means of

getting learning, or as are praying and reading the Bible a means of sanctification. But it is a moral, not a physical, cause. Its efficiency consists in its power of effecting the mind of God and disposing Him to do for us what He would do if we did not pray.[16]

The Reformed tradition argues strongly for the God of history, who sovereignly directs the course of all events. Similarly it is understood that the New Testament finds no conflict between the sovereignty of God and the effectual power of supplication by His people. Charles Hodge notes:

> This Supreme Power is roused into action by prayer, in a way analogous to that in which the energies of a man are called into action by the entreaties of his fellow men. This is the doctrine of the Bible; it is perfectly consistent with reason, and is confirmed by the whole history of the world, and specially the Church. Moses by his prayer saved the Israelites from destruction; at the prayer of Samuel the army of the Philistines was dispersed. . . . This of course supposes that prayer is a power. Queen Mary of Scotland was not beside herself, when she said she found the prayers of John Knox more than an army.[17]

Thus Calvin's conclusion at this point is entirely appropriate: "It is very absurd, therefore, to dissuade men from prayer, by pretending that Divine Providence, which is always watching over the government of the universe, is in vain importuned by our supplications, when, on the contrary, the Lord himself declares, that He is 'nigh unto all that call upon Him, to all that call upon Him in truth' (Ps. 145:18)."[18]

While Calvinists extol, even celebrate, the power of prayer, it must not be conceived that the power of prayer is unlimited. It is not conceived as valid that Christians can do or receive anything by simply praying correctly. To bring the problem into a sharper focus, this question may be posed: Does prayer change God's mind? Sproul writes, "When we are talking about God's sovereignty, do we think for a moment that if there is a conflict of interests between the will of God and my will, that my will could possibly prevail?"[19] Prayer then functions as a moral not a physical stimulus to God; it is limited by the will of God, which always takes precedence over the will of His creatures. Sproul concludes, "You cannot manipulate God. You cannot manipulate Him by incantations, repetition, public utterances, or your own predictions. God is sovereign. So when you bring your requests to God He may say yes, and He may say no."[20]

Thus prayer is viewed as an action of the believer wherein God has ordained to reveal Himself by internal and external comfort with the result that the one who prays is encouraged to deepen his walk with God. Prayer, like the Word of God and the ordinances, is a means of grace, that is, a vehicle by which God so condescends to the mind of the believer as to reveal His Person. God's intent in prayer is ultimately the strengthening of the saint and the extension thereby of His will on the earth.

The Tensions in Prayer

While it might safely be affirmed that prayer is a means of the believer's sanctification, that is, it changes both the believer and his circumstances, the doctrine of prayer is not without difficulties related to the character of God. Granted, "He commands it because He has seen fit to ordain it as the appointed means for reception of His blessings,"[21] yet the finite mind is perplexed to answer some of the issues that can be raised. One argument emerges from the infinitude of God: it would seem inconsistent with His dignity to suppose that He concerns Himself with the trifling affairs of mankind. Hodge replies, "It assumes that His knowledge, power, or presence is limited; that He would be distracted if His attention were directed to all the minute changes constantly occurring throughout the universe. This supposes that God is a creature like ourselves, that bounds can be set to His intelligence or efficiency."[22]

Does infinitude dispense with prayer? No, instead infinitude establishes prayer. Another argument of the same type deals with the relationship of God's omniscience to prayer. If God is all-knowing, then why should believers inform Him? Calvin argues that Christians pray because it is a commanded means of grace.

> But someone will say, Does He not know without a monitor both what our difficulties are, and what is meet for our interest, so that it seems in some measure superfluous to solicit Him by our prayers, as if He were winking, or even sleeping, until aroused by the sound of our voice. Those who argue thus attend not to the end for which the Lord taught us to pray. It was not so much for His sake as for ours.[23]

Thus these objections to pray are not so difficult that an immediate reply cannot be marshaled. But what about the problem theologians call concurrence, the relationship between the ultimate providence of God and one's desires and activities. While it can and should be argued that prayer is a wonderfully powerful instrument, that it changes outward circumstances and inward turmoil, what is the relationship of the prayers of the saints to the determinate counsel of God? What is the fundamental relationship between secondary and primary causality?

PRAYER AND THE FIXITY OF NATURAL LAW

To approach an intelligent consideration of the relationship of secondary cause (i.e., prayer) to primary actualization, it must be understood that God has sovereignly, and without conflict or incongruity, established both. A. A. Hodge writes:

> In order to accomplish both these ends at once, the education of our thought and the training of our faculty by active exercise, God has established a comprehensive and unchangeable system of laws, of second causes working uniformly, of fixed consequences and established methods, by which He works, and by which He can train us to understand His working and to work with Him. This careful adherence to the use of means, to the slow and circuitous operational second causes and established laws, is surely not for God's sake. It cannot be necessary to Him. It is ordained and rigidly adhered to only for our sake.[24]

The argument has been raised that if God has constructed a machine which is so perfect and so completely His, then to modify that perfect machine (i.e., the natural laws) would be to break it. Therefore prayer cannot be even a secondary cause or natural change because God's creation cannot be altered even by Himself. To so argue would imply that God established such laws as to exclude Himself and His own purposes. Dabney is more specific when he writes:

> Now only postulate that desire, prayer, and the answers to prayer are among these general laws, which as a complex whole, have been assigned to regulate nature, and the uniformity of nature only confirms the hoped answers to prayers. Has the philosopher explored all the ties of natural causation made by God? He does not pretend so. Then it may be that among the unexplored ties are some subtle and unexplained bonds which connect prayer with their answers as natural causes and effects.[25]

Does natural law govern the universe? Does God govern the universe by natural law? The answer to these questions must be that people err with the idea that law is a power, whereas it is simply the method of power.[26] As A. A. Hodge concludes:

> This great permanent framework of second causes and natural law is, of course, incomparably more flexible in the hands of God than it can be in the hands of man. We know these laws partially and imperfectly: God acts upon them internally. We act upon them at a few isolated points: God acts upon every point of the infinite system at the same time. Surely, therefore, while God can act through nature in a supernatural manner, He

can also, like us, only infinitely more perfectly, act through nature and in accordance with natural law in accomplishing His purposes.[27]

Thus with regard to the accomplishment of God's purpose through the agency of natural law, He not only wills an end but also the proper secondary causes productive of that effect. God does not violate natural law but natural law is not an immutable god; God alone, not His creation, is God. To effect an end God also ordains the proper arrangement of secondary causes (i.e., prayer).

PRAYER AND THE DOCTRINE OF SOVEREIGNTY

The relationship between divine sovereignty as primary cause and prayer as a secondary cause raises the tempo of the question of the relationship of causes. While one might agree that prayer is a divinely given constituent of natural law, it may be more difficult to conceive the direct relationship of absolute sovereignty to human petitioning. If God has absolutely decreed all that can and will come to pass to the smallest detail in the lives of every human being, does prayer change things? Or do believers pray because God has yet to determine His will for them? To state the issue theologically in the words of Turrettine, the famous professor of theology at the Academy of Geneva, "How can the concourse of God be reconciled with the contingency and liberty of second causes?"[28] Turrettine discusses the difficulty of this question.

> The providence of God concurs with all second causes and especially with the human will, and yet its own contingency and liberty remain unimpaired. But how these two things can consist with each other no mortal can in this life perfectly understand. Nor should it seem wonderful since He has a thousand ways, to us incomprehensible, of concurring with our will, insinuating Himself into us, and turning our hearts, so that by acting freely what we will, we still do nothing besides the will and determination of God.[29]

One Calvinist who has most recently raised the issue of primary and secondary causality concludes with the answer, "I do not know! I have not a clue."[30] While this answer is blunt, it does speak to the inadequacy of finitude when confronted by infinitude. Dabney, however, adds these comments.

> The familiar old answer applies here, that God's decree embraces the means as much as the end. Whenever it was His eternal purpose that anyone should receive certain graces, it was His purpose equally that he should ask. In a word, these objections are just the same with those of the vulgar fatalists, who object that "what is to be will be," therefore it is of

no use to make any effort. . . . To be consistent, these rationalists who refuse to pray should also refuse to plow, to sow, to cultivate, to take medicine when sick, to watch against danger, etc.[31]

A. A. Hodge speaks to the same point.

Prayer is only one means appointed by God for attaining our ends. In order to educate us, He demands that we should use the means, or go without the ends which depend upon them. There are plenty of fools who make the transcendental nature of eternity and of the relation of the eternal life to God to the tome-life of man an excuse for neglecting prayer. But of all the many fools in the United States, there is not one absurd enough to make the same eternal decree an excuse for not chewing his food or for not voluntarily inflating his lungs.[32]

The Calvinist would argue for the truly effectual character of both primary and secondary causation, yet the exact relationship of the causative agencies is blurred in the complexities of conceiving infinitude from the vantage point of finiteness. Turrettine explains,

God so concurs with second causes that although He previously moves and predetermines them by a motion, not general only, but also special, still He moves them according to their own nature, and does not take away from them their own proper mode of operating. The reason is because the decree of God is occupied not only about the determination of things which ought to be done, but also the means according to which they are to be, relatively to the nature and condition of each; so actual Providence, which is the execution of this decree, not only secures the infallible futurition of the thing decreed, but also its taking place in the very manner decreed, to wit, consentaneously with the nature of each, that is, necessary things take place necessarily, free and contingent things, however, freely and contingently.[33]

Conclusion

Thus prayer is understood as primarily a means of grace, a vehicle of progressive sanctification. Prayer is essentially an act of worship wherein homage is given to God alone through praise, adoration, confession, or request. The purpose of prayer, while it points alone to God as the source of all benevolences, is a help for the saint to strengthen Christian experience. Calvin wrote of prayer as a Christian necessity.

Wherefore, although it is true that while we are listless or insensible to our wretchedness, He wakes and watches for us, and sometimes even assists us unasked; it is very much for our interest to be constantly supplicating Him: first, that our heart may always be inflamed with a serious and ardent desire of seeking, loving, and serving Him, while we accustom ourselves to have recourse to Him as a sacred anchor in every necessity; secondly, that no desire, no longing whatever, of which we are ashamed to make Him the witness, may enter our minds, and thus pour out our heart before Him; and, lastly, that we may be prepared to receive all His benefits with true gratitude and thanksgiving, while our prayers remind us that they proceed from His hand. Moreover, having obtained what we ask, being persuaded that He has answered our prayers, we are led to long more earnestly for His favor, and at the same time have greater pleasure in welcoming the blessings which we perceive to have been obtained by our prayers.[34]

Prayer then is not so much asking favors as it is a worshipful intercourse that includes request. The fruit of answered prayer is most importantly the deepening of one's spiritual life. This is accomplished as God graciously quiets the turbulent saint without altering external circumstances, or as He changes the course of history, or as He does both. The end of prayer is not so much tangible answers as a deepening life of dependency and love that can come to the saint only through this means of grace. While the present age is both materialistic and narcissistic, it would be a mistake to conceive of prayer in such a denigrating fashion. The call to prayer is a call primarily to love, submission, and obedience; it is a call to God who entreats the believer to a life of adoration.

While prayer has paradoxes, it should not drive the believer to uncertainty. It is because God is absolutely sovereign that the believer for his own sake must heed God's invitation to bring his petitions and praises to Him. Not only does God invite the child of God to His presence in prayer; He also has provided a Mediator who constantly carries the believer's weak, stuttering petitions to His throne of grace (Heb. 7:25). Furthermore with the invitation comes the assistance of God's Spirit, who knows the secret counsels of the Father and who aids the saint in prayer (Rom. 8:26–27). While the relationship of prayer to the sovereignty of God cannot be fully comprehended by the finite mind, prayer can assuredly be enjoyed by the saint as the avenue of sweet, intimate, and intense fellowship of the soul with the infinite Creator.

CHAPTER 2

Is Foreknowledge Equivalent to Foreordination?

Edgar C. James

F
ew biblical words have more theological significance than the word 'foreknowledge." That the meaning of the word is "knowledge beforehand without predetermination" is the basis of the Arminian view of election. As Boettner says, "Some [Arminians] acknowledge that God foreknows all things. Others say that He foreknows all events that are knowable, but that the acts of free agents by their very nature are uncertain."[1] However, Calvinists hold that the biblical meaning of foreknowledge in some sense approaches that of foreordination.[2] Actually Arminianism has not solved the problem for if God's foreknowledge of all things is acknowledged, the acts of men then become as certain as if foreordained. Nonetheless the meaning of this word determines one's view of God, for election is rightly an aspect of God's decree. It seems that one's view of man and his view of God are on opposite ends of a seesaw. When one view is elevated, the other must be lowered.

Of significance also is that the view one holds in this area determines his message, methods, and motives of proclaiming the gospel of Christ. Will he try to persuade or make clear? Will he be speaking from God's viewpoint or his own? The question is not a matter of results but rather of veracity for if the end does not justify the means elsewhere, why should it here? The purpose of this chapter therefore is to determine the biblical meaning of foreknowledge (πρόγνωσις and προγινώσκω) in its New Testament contexts.

The Meaning of the Terms

Before considering the passages involved, one may well ask, What is the meaning of foreordination and foreknowledge? There does not seem to be much disagreement among lexicographers on the meaning of προορίζω (foreordination or predestination). Bauer, Arndt, and Gingrich give the meaning as "decide upon beforehand, predestine."[3] It is used in Acts 4:28; Romans 8:29–30, 1 Corinthians 2:7; and Ephesians 1:5, 11. A related word is ὁρίζω which means to "determine, appoint, fix, set."[4] It is used in Luke 22:22; Acts 2:23; 10:42; 11:29; 17:26, 31; Romans 1:4; and Hebrews 4:7.

However, the real problem is not with προορίζω and its cognates but rather with πρόγνωσις and προγινώσκω, which the King James Version renders as "foreknowledge," "foreordination," and "to know" or "to know before." The word "foreknowledge" in English means "knowledge of something before it happens or exists; presence."[5] All are agreed that this word does have such a theological meaning and as such is related to the omniscience of God.[6] God's omniscience is His knowledge of all things both actual and possible, while foreknowledge in this sense is His knowledge of those things that are actual. However, such a theological meaning is not the biblical meaning of the word, and the biblical meaning must be determined from its context and usage.

An illustration of this same problem is the word "atonement," an Old Testament word with the biblical meaning of "to cover."[7] However, theologically it has come to mean all that has been accomplished in the death of Christ on the cross.[8] When one reads into the biblical meaning the theological meaning, difficulties can result. Likewise this is true with πρόγνωσις, and thus one must determine its biblical meaning from the passages employed.

A Consideration of the Passages

Πρόγνωσις and προγινώσκω are used seven times in the New Testament, the noun πρόγνωσις being employed in Acts 2:23 and 1 Peter 1:2 and the verb προγινώσκω in Romans 8:29; 11:2; 1 Peter 1:20; Acts 26:5; and 2 Peter 3:17. The last two passages are not related to this study since they concern person-to-person relationships and not divine activity. The most important passages are Acts 2:23; Romans 8:29; and 1 Peter 1:2 since in these three passages πρόγνωσις or προγινώσκω is used with ὁρίζω, προορίζω, or ἐκλεκτος.

ACTS 2:23

In Acts 2:23 the Apostle Peter employed the noun πρόγνωσις in his great Pentecostal address. Speaking of Jesus, he described Him as τῇ ὡρισμένῃ βουλῇ καὶ προγνώσει τοῦ θεοῦ ἔκδοτον, "delivered up by the predeterminated plan and foreknowledge of God." It is evident that προγνώσει here is in the instrumental case.[9] The question is, Was it possible for Christ to be delivered over to His enemies "by the foreknowledge of God?" Certainly in foreknowledge one knows, but he does not perform an act like the delivering of Jesus to His enemies. Are not those who contend otherwise reading something more than the English meaning of foreknowledge into this passage? However, if one translates the verse that Christ was delivered over by the determinate counsel and forethought of God, that is, by His decision reached in eternity, then the thought is both intelligible and satisfying. Thus it is that "determinate counsel and forethought are synonymous expressions, both describing one and the same act, one stressing the element of will and the other that of knowledge."[10]

1 PETER 1:2

In this verse Peter used πρόγνωσις of the "strangers scattered throughout Pontus, Galatia, Cappadocia, Asia, and Bithynia" (v. 1). He told them they were elect or chosen κατα πρόγνωσιν θεους πατρός, "according to the foreknowledge of God the Father." Certainly here πρόγνωσις has the same meaning as in Acts 2:23. If the word here is taken in the sense of prescience, the whole phrase is rather meaningless. Certainly they were elect strangers according to the foreknowledge of God because God knows everything from eternity. No one who believes in the existence of an omniscient God could dispute that fact. So it is difficult to see why there would have been any special point for Peter to refer here to the omniscience of God. Another reason for this consideration is that many biblical scholars support such a rendering in this verse. Bauer, Arndt, and Gingrich translate this, "according to the predestination of God the Father."[11] Thayer renders it as "forethought, pre-arrangement."[12] Moffatt translates, "Peter an apostle of Jesus Christ, to the exiles of the Dispersion . . . whom God the Father has predestined and chosen."[13] Certainly the opinions of exegetes are not decisive but nevertheless these translations of the word as "predestination," "forethought," "prearrangement" strengthen the position.

1 PETER 1:20

Here Peter spoke of Christ as the lamb προεγνωσμένου by God before the foundation of the world. Certainly foreknowledge cannot act, and since the act of redemption is in view (v. 18), it is evidently "God's foreordination of Jesus as Savior which Peter has in mind."[14] Even the King James Version translates it "foreordain."

ROMANS 11:2

This verse employs the verb προγινώσκω. Speaking of the Jews, Paul said, "God has not rejected His people whom He foreknew." It is impossible to make this mean that God had a mere prescience or prevision of some quality in Israel that determined His choice of them. Such a view would be in direct opposition to what the apostle taught in Romans 9. There he pointed out that God's selection of Israel was not according to natural generation (vv. 7–9) or human merit (vv. 10–13) but rather according to His mercy (vv. 14–18) and power (vv. 19–24). Having therefore discussed God's sovereign election of Israel, the apostle then turned to its future (chap. 11). God had made certain unconditional promises to this nation (Gen. 12; 15; 17; Deut. 28–30; 2 Sam. 7:12–16; Jer. 31:31–34), and as yet these had not been fulfilled. However, Israel had failed: the people had disobeyed, apostatized, and had been unfaithful. Would God therefore discontinue His promises to them? Romans 11:2 gives the reason God has not cast them away. It is because He προέγνω them. Certainly if this means only a mere prevision here, then in view of their unfaithfulness this would be reason for God to discontinue His promises—not to continue them. Thus the meaning here must be the same as in Acts 2:23 and 1 Peter 1:2, 20.

ROMANS 8:29

The context of this verse has to do with God's predestination of the objects of salvation. Certainly if προγινώσκω has the meaning of forethought, prearrangement, or predetermination in Romans 11:2, it is imperative that it have the same meaning here unless cogent reasons should forbid it, and such reasons are lacking. In 8:28 the apostle offered his readers encouragement for their troubles, including their own inward weakness. He told them that all things work together for good to those who love God, and those who love God are defined as those whom God has called in accord with His purpose. Thus they have not come within the sphere of God's love by their own choice, but rather have been called into this relationship in accord with God's eternal purpose.[15]

Conclusion

From an examination of the passages where πρόγνωσις and προγινώσκω are used of divine activity, the biblical meaning must be forethought, prearrangement, or predetermination. Thus the biblical meaning of foreknowledge is equivalent to foreordination, both describing the same act, one stressing the element of knowledge and the other that of will. To say that God made a decision based on His prevision would mean that there was a time of indecision. This of course would be contrary to the nature of God and to the biblical fact that God's decree is eternal. Thus His decree is from eternity past and is the product of His knowledge and will.

CHAPTER 3

The Doctrine of Miracles

John A. Witmer

A ffirmation of belief in miracles is an essential ingredient in biblical, historic Christianity. It is inseparably joined to the biblical doctrine of God as Creator and Ruler of all things. Miracles are woven into the fabric of Scripture, and belief in them is a concomitant of the historic Christian doctrine of the Bible as God's Word to mankind. C. S. Lewis rightly calls Christianity "the story of a great miracle."[1]

Reactions to Miracles

This historic Christian affirmation of belief in miracles faces two differing reactions in contemporary thought. The first is bemused silence, which grows out of the fact that the word "miracle" is used in such loose ways today that it has been robbed of much of its historic meaning. For example, *Miracle on Thirty-Fourth Street* is a fantasy for youth by Valentine Davies, but it serves to identify the word "miracle" for many with the imaginary world of fiction or myth. Miracles, it is thought, like the adventures of Hercules and Sinbad the sailor, never take place in real life. Again, when Roger Staubach led the Dallas Cowboys to two touchdowns in less than two minutes to win the 1972 NFC Championship over the San Francisco '49ers, the feat was called "the miracle victory." This ties the word "miracle" to unusual human exploits and what Mary Hesse calls "the remarkable, unpredictable, coincidental, nature of the events." She points out that in most such cases "there would probably not be any implication of a divine or providential act in the events described."[2]

Still another use of the word "miracle" is found in the popular radio and television evangelist's challenge to his audience, "Expect a miracle today." In this case a "divine or providential act" is implied, because the challenge is frequently coupled with the evangelist's promise, "Something good is going to happen to you." Here miracles are equated with the providential blessings of life. The implication is that miracles occur day after day in the lives of the evangelist and his associates and anyone who responds to this challenge. Little wonder that when historic Christians' belief in miracles is proclaimed people wonder what is meant.

Denial of Miracles

The second response to the Christian affirmation of belief in miracles is the dogmatic denial of the possibility of miracles. This is made by the person, whether professedly religious or not, who in reality embraces a philosophy of naturalism. In his judgment nature is supreme and nothing can conceivably interrupt its steady operation, not even God. As Einstein said, "the idea of a Being who interferes with the sequence of events in the world is absolutely impossible."[3]

Such denial of miracles is frequently thought to be scientific. For example Van Buren declares, "the idea of the empirical intervention of a supernatural 'God' in the world of men has been ruled out by the influence of modern science in our thinking."[4] It is not scientific, however, but rather metaphysical, the result of the person's philosophy or beliefs, not of the facts of science.

Underlying such dogmatic denial of miracles is acceptance of the uniformity of nature and its operation in orderly fashion according to the laws of nature. This concept began with the laws of motion of Isaac Newton, whose mechanistic physics was applied to nature by LaPlace. As a result, "the whole process of nature is unique and rigidly determined."[5] Such a point of view is expressed in Hume's definition of a miracle as "a transgression of a law of nature by a particular volition of the Deity or by the interposition of some invisible agent."[6] Elsewhere Hume explains, "A miracle is a violation of the laws of nature; and as a firm and unalterable experience has established these laws, the proof against a miracle, from the very nature of the fact, is as entire as any argument from experience can possibly be imagined."[7] For many, Hume succeeded in eliminating miracles by definition. Who would possess the temerity to give credence to something identified as a "transgression" and a "violation" of such an inviolable entity as "the laws of nature"?

Ironically in the 20th century the mechanistic view of the universe based on Newton's laws of motion has been largely abandoned in favor of the quantum theory. This considers the universe "in essence indeterministic"[8] and its laws merely statistical in nature, "that is, they do not determine occurrences of single events, but only proportions in large classes of events."[9] In other words science itself has now ruled out the point of view which for so long eliminated the possibility of miracles by definition. The new theories of science, however, are no friendlier to the recognition of miracles than the old. Furthermore "undoubtedly a great deal of popular reaction to the notion of miracle is still conditioned by this view,"[10] that is, the Newtonian. But at least the point has been made that the uniformity of nature is a metaphysical assumption of science, part of its theoretical framework, not of its factual evidence. This is what Christians have argued all along.

The Christian Point of View

The Christian position is not that the universe is capricious and erratic. Christians expect the sun to rise in the east each morning as it always has. Christians recognize that this world is a cosmos, an orderly system, not a chaos. More than that, Christians agree that the regularity of the universe is observable and is expressible in principles or laws. As a result Christians do not deny the existence of what are called laws of nature. Nor do they think that the occurrence of miracles destroys these laws or makes them inoperative. What Christians reject is the idea that the universe is a self-contained, closed system with laws that are inviolable. Such a view is a metaphysical concept related to a philosophical system such as deism, materialism, or naturalism. Such a position rules out God and His relationship to the world and to men as believed by Christians on the basis of biblical revelation.

The Christian position is that God is the self-existent Creator of all things (Gen. 1:1; Isa. 44:24; Acts 14:15; Eph. 3:9). But for Christians God is more than a cosmic watchmaker who has brought into being a giant machine that continues to run its prescribed course without intervention, even by its Creator. That is the view of deism, which accepts the transcendence of God over the world as Creator but denies His immanence. On the basis of biblical witness Christians believe that God is also the self-existent Sustainer and Governor of all things (Acts 14:16–17; 17:24–28). The eternal Son of God, who became incarnate as the Lord Jesus Christ, is described as the One who "upholds all things by the word of His power" (Heb. 1:3) and the One in whom "all things hold together" (Col. 1:17). As a result the regularity of the universe which people call "the laws of nature" is in reality the normal pattern of the cosmos-sustaining power of God; for as Paul wrote, "God is not a God of confusion" (1 Cor. 14:33; cf. v. 40).

At this point the extreme on the other side of the Christian position demands consideration. In contrast to the scientific, rationalistic denial of the possibility of miracles, this romantic, mystical view insists that "all is a miracle." Voltaire wrote, "The stupendous order of nature, the revolution of a hundred millions of worlds around millions of suns, the activity of light, the life of animals, all are grand and perpetual miracles."[11] In a similar vein Walt Whitman exclaims, "To me every hour of the light and dark is a miracle, every cubic inch of space is a miracle."[12]

According to this view, if God is acknowledged at all, He is related to nature so closely that He is equated with it. This is pantheism, which denies the transcendence of God and stresses His immanence in the world to the point of identity. Such a view eliminates miracles as effectively as their denial does. By making the whole course of nature miraculous, no place is left for what is truly miraculous according to the meaning of the word itself. As Lewis says in speaking about the normal course of nature, "A miracle is by definition an exception."[13] A miracle is a special application of the power of God to accomplish an unusual event.

As a result, the Christian position on God's relationship to the world involves a third point. The living God is not only the self-existent Creator and Sustainer of all things but also the Sovereign Ruler who is executing an eternal plan in His creation of the greater glory of His own name (Rom. 11:33–36; Eph. 1:3–14; 3:11). Everyone needs to learn the lesson God taught Nebuchadnezzar "that the most High ruleth in the kingdom of men, and giveth it to whomsoever he will" (Dan. 4:18, 25, 34–35). In the carrying out of His program God from time to time steps into the normal course of nature and of history in extraordinary deeds. Such deeds are miracles and are a logical and necessary part of the biblical, Christian faith in God. As Trueblood writes, "If the world is really the medium of God's personal action, miracle is wholly normal."[14]

For the biblical Christian miracles are not expendable; they are not incidental but are an essential part of his theistic world view. Miracles are a benchmark of historic biblical Christianity that distinguishes it from its counterfeits. Lewis explains, "The popular 'religion' excludes miracles because it excludes the 'living God' of Christianity and believes instead in a kind of God who obviously would not do miracles, or indeed anything else."[15] Elsewhere he elaborates,

> But in Christianity, the more we understand what God it is who is said to be present and the purpose for which He is said to have appeared, the more credible the miracles become. This is why we seldom find the Christian miracles denied except by those who have abandoned some part of the Christian doctrine.[16]

Belief in miracles can serve as a touchstone of genuine Christian faith.

A Proper Definition

In developing an accurate definition of a miracle in accord with Scripture the first point is that a miracle is an extraordinary work of God, an exercise of supernatural divine power. As such it produces amazement, if not fear, in its observers. For example as Israel stood at the shore of the Red Sea with Pharaoh's army in pursuit, Moses said, "Do not fear! Stand by and see the salvation of the Lord, which He will accomplish for you today" (Ex. 14:13) and, in the words of Rahab, "the Lord dried up the water of the Red Sea before you" (Josh. 2:10). In connection with one of the miracles of the Lord Jesus, Luke wrote, "And they were all amazed at the greatness of God" (Luke 9:43). In performing miracles God usually worked through individuals as His agents, but what was done was recognized as ultimately the work of God (Acts 2:22; 19:11). Booth emphasizes this point in his definition of a miracle as "an observable phenomenon effected directly or indirectly by supernatural power."[17]

In a proper understanding of miracles it is also important to recognize that a miracle is a revelatory event. Because of their astounding character miracles are a "special revelation of the presence of God."[18] But they are also related to the revelation of God's purposes and His program in the world by identifying God's servants as His messengers. Nicodemus told Jesus, "Rabbi, we know that You have come from God as a Teacher; for no one can do these signs that You do unless God is with him" (John 3:2).

A study of the Hebrew and the Greek words used in connection with the miracles of Scripture helps in understanding the nature of these special events and in formulating a definition. On the basis of the four Greek words, all of which are translated in English by the word "miracle," Thiessen defines a miracle as "a unique and extraordinary event awakening wonder (τέρας), wrought by divine power (δύναμις), accomplishing some practical and benevolent work (ἔργον), and authenticating a messenger and his message as from God (σημεῖον)."[19] Such a biblical definition aids in distinguishing genuine miracles from the spurious and satanic ones.

Miracles in the Bible

Since miracles relate to the revelation of God and His communication and execution of His program in the world, their focal point is the Lord Jesus Christ, the incarnate Son of God. Lewis says, "The central miracle asserted by Christians is the Incarnation. They say that God became Man. Every other miracle prepares for this, or exhibits this, or results from this." He calls the incarnation "the Grand Miracle."[20] Jesus' birth was indeed a miracle—conceived by the Holy Spirit in the womb of the virgin Mary (Luke 1:35). He was the supreme miracle worker (John 20:30–31). The Lord Jesus Christ is the miracle Person—God "manifest in the flesh" (1 Tim. 3:16). His miraculous resurrection (Acts 2:24; 1 Cor. 15:4) is the guarantee of victory over sin and death (1 Cor. 15:5–57) and of the miracle of life to all who trust in Him (2 Cor. 5:17).

Though miracles cluster around the Lord Jesus Christ like steel shavings to a magnet, they are found throughout the Bible. However, even a casual reading of Scripture reveals that miracles occur with greater frequency at special times. Israel's deliverance from Egypt and entrance into Canaan provided one great concentration of miracles. So did the ministries of Elijah and Elisha when God sought to stem the tide of apostasy among His people Israel. Related to the earthly life and miracles of Jesus are the miracles of the apostolic church. As Lewis explains, "God does not shake miracles into Nature at random as if from a pepper-caster. They come on great occasions: they are found at the great ganglions of history—not of political or social history, but of spiritual history which cannot be fully known by men."[21]

A form of miracle not to be overlooked is prophecy. For a human being to predict in detail what will occur in the future, near or far, and have it take place requires supernatural revelation and supernatural action. Prophecy looms large in the Bible. Chafer states that "over one-fourth of the books of the Bible are avowedly prophetic, and, in the actual text of all the Scriptures, at least one-fifth was prediction at the time it was written."[22] Furthermore, "A portion of the Bible prediction has now been fulfilled, and . . . its fulfillment has been . . . precisely as predicted."[23] Hume did not accept the possibility of prophecy any more than that of miracles, but he recognizes the logical conclusion that "all prophecies are real miracles."[24]

From time to time in the Bible miraculous things were done by others than the servants of God. Examples are "the magicians of Egypt" (Ex. 7:11, 22), Simon the sorcerer of Samaria (Acts 8:9–11), Bar-Jesus or "Elymas the sorcerer" (Acts 13:6, 8, KJV) and the "seven sons of Sceva" (Acts 19:13–14). Some of these spectacles are mere trickery, that is, spurious miracles. Others of them are truly supernatural events, but satanic in origin and power, not divine. The devil, who showed the Lord Jesus "all the kingdoms of the world in a moment of time" (Luke 4:5), is able to disguise himself as "an angel of light" (2 Cor. 11:14). Satan's great miracle worker will be the man of sin of the great tribulation whose presence will be in accord with the activity "of Satan with all power and signs and false wonders" (2 Thess. 2:9). Believers need to be careful they are not deceived by satanically inspired miracles, and to remember that his power, although superhuman, is finite and his conqueror is the Lord Jesus Christ. God's final miracles are yet to come with the rapture of the church, the establishment of the Messiah's kingdom, and the creation of the new heavens and the new earth.

Miracles Today

Since miracles in the Bible are tied to God's special revelation of Himself and of His program, centering in the Lord Jesus Christ as God incarnate "who was delivered, and was raised because of our justification" (Rom. 4:25), miracles in the biblical pattern do not occur today. The gift of miracles provided by God for the apostolic church (1 Cor. 12:28–29) is undoubtedly among those temporary gifts of the Holy Spirit that passed away with the apostles. Just as God has spoken climactically "in His Son" (Heb. 1:2), so He has acted in revelatory miracles.

This does not mean that God is not at work supernaturally in the world today. A supernatural work of God takes place each time another human being is regenerated by the Holy Spirit (2 Cor. 5:17). Many times regeneration is followed by almost immediate extraordinary transformation of personality and lifestyle that is truly miraculous. Furthermore, in answer to believing prayer by His children God provides many things that defy human explanation—healings that are medically inexplicable, deliverances from danger that seem impossible, provision of money, food, clothing, shelter from untraceable sources. As the psalmist wrote, "Thou art the God who workest wonders" (Ps. 77:14). Christians properly call such mighty works of God miracles, but they are in a different class from the miracles of Scripture.

Christians affirm their belief in miracles because of the witness of the Bible as God's infallible message to mankind. And believers believe in miracles because of God's work of regeneration and His working in answer to prayer. However, John Peterson summed up Christian faith in miracles best in these words from his son, "I believe in miracles, for I believe in God."

CHAPTER 4

The Importance of Inerrancy

Charles C. Ryrie

E very generation has its doctrinal problems and this one is no exception. Sometimes those problems develop within the circle of conservatism, a fact which is also true of this day. The discussions that have arisen among conservatives in the field of eschatology are well known, but the debates and sometimes defections in the area of bibliology are less evident. However, they are more serious, since they touch the heart of the authority—to say nothing of the truth—of Christianity.

One of these contemporary problems concerns the inerrancy of the Scriptures. "Inerrant" means "exempt from error," and dictionaries consider it a synonym for "infallible" which means "not liable to deceive, certain." Actually there is little difference in the meaning of the two words, although in the history of their use in relation to the Bible, "inerrant" is of more recent use. If there is any difference in the shade of meaning it is simply this: "Infallible" includes the resultant idea of trustworthiness while "inerrant" emphasizes principally the truthfulness of the Scriptures.

History of the Doctrine

A survey of the history of the doctrine of inerrancy shows that the discussions concerning its importance belong to the modern period. The church fathers accepted the inspiration and authority of the Scriptures as an assumed and self-evident fact. Scripture was used to prove the deity of Christ, for instance, in the early debates over this doctrine. Origen constantly referred to the Scriptures as final authority in his controversy with Celsus. Augustine has a clear statement concerning inerrancy: "For I confess to your charity that I have learned to defer this respect and honor to those scriptural books only which are not called canonical, that I believe most firmly that no one of those authors has erred in any respect in writing."[1]

The medieval period saw little development in this area of

doctrine. Indeed, sterility was the characteristic of the time. Interest was centered "in defining the status of the Bible in relation to that of other authorities in the Church."[2] Abelard expressed doubt as to the inerrancy of the text, though generally a high view of inspiration was held by most.

It was the Reformers who gave proper emphasis to the doctrines of inspiration and infallibility. And yet these did not occupy a large place in their writings. It seems that they realized the importance of these truths as the basis for true authority against the claim to authority of the Roman Catholic Church, and yet they were so convinced of these truths that they could take them for granted rather than spending time in a systematic development of these doctrines. Calvin referred to the Scriptures as the "sure and infallible record"[3] and the "unerring standard."[4] Luther declared in no uncertain terms: "I have learned to ascribe this honor i.e., infallibility only to books which are termed canonical, so that I confidently believe that not one of their authors erred."[5]

In the modern period the doctrine has of necessity had to be developed. The rationalistic attacks on the reliability of historical matters with a subsequent questioning of the authenticity of the text of Scripture were a denial of inerrancy and rejection of inspiration. It is important to notice that the two doctrines—inerrancy and inspiration—fell together under these attacks. Thus a new theory of inspiration arose which recognized the inspiration of certain truths in general and insofar as they conformed to natural reason. The doctrines of human fallibility in the production of Scripture and the infallibility of human reason in the interpretation of Scripture had gained the day.

But God had prepared others to expound and defend the truth. What the church owes to men like Hodge and Warfield can scarcely be measured. Their writings on these matters concerning inspiration are still classics. More recently, and in their train, *Thy Word Is Truth*, by Edward J. Young[6] presents and defends verbal inspiration and inerrancy.

Modern Views of the Doctrine

The liberal attack, which substituted an inspired experience for an inspired text, was soon followed by the neoorthodox attack. Neoorthodoxy was in turn followed (but not supplanted) by neoliberalism. There are similarities between these schools of thought particularly in relation to their views of the Scriptures.

Both believe that the Scriptures are at best a fallible witness to revelation (which may have been infallible when it was given by God but which certainly was corrupted by the time it was recorded in the Bible). Obviously what a person chooses to guide his or her life from this fallible record is up to the individual, and the entire approach to the worthwhileness of the Scriptures becomes completely subjective. Both believe that revelation cannot be given in propositional truth but only in one's personal encounter with God. The Barthian attempts to rescue from this maze of subjectivity some remnant of authority for the Bible in that it does witness (however fallibly) to Christ, who is the revelation of God. But how can one expect to have a true encounter based on or at least aided by a false witness? Authority, under these conditions, not only does not reside in the Bible but in reality does not even reside in Christ (the biblical witness to Him may be mistaken). Actually the authority comes to reside in the individual reader's opinion of the particular portion of the Bible he is reading at the time. The attacks of both neoorthodoxy and neoliberalism have been against verbal inspiration and what is included in it, namely, inerrancy, for the proponents apparently realize that the two stand together.

With great sorrow one notices a tendency among conservatives to attempt to divorce inerrancy from verbal inspiration. Harrison accurately states the situation.

> Unquestionably the Bible teaches its own inspiration. It is the Book of God. It does not require us to hold inerrancy, though this is a natural corollary of full inspiration. The phenomena which present difficulties are not to be dismissed or underrated. They have driven many sincere believers in the trustworthiness of the Bible as a spiritual guide to hold a modified position on the non-revelation material. Every man must be persuaded in his own mind. . . . It is possible that if our knowledge were greater, all seeming difficulties could be swept away.[7]

In other words because of apparent difficulties in the Bible (such as historical and chronological problems) some are concluding that these sections, though inspired, are not inerrant. One hears more and more these days, "I believe the Bible is inspired, but I cannot believe it is without error." Inspiration, yes; verbal inspiration, no.

Why is this view taken? One cannot see motives, but for some, honest wrestling with problems has shaken their faith. For others, one cannot help but feel that it is part of the current worship of intellectualism as a sacred cow and a necessary step in achieving the approbation of godless so-called "intellectuals." Is inerrancy important or must it be abandoned in this enlightened age?

The Importance of the Doctrine

The importance of biblical inerrancy can best be seen in its relationships.

IN RELATION TO THE CHARACTER OF GOD

God's Word is infallible simply because God Himself is infallible. God is true (John 3:33; 17:3; Rom. 3:4; 1 Thess. 1:9), and this true God speaks in the true Scriptures. "What Scripture says is to be received as the infallible Word of the infallible God, and to assert biblical inerrancy and infallibility is just to confess faith in (i) the divine origin of the Bible and (ii) the truthfulness and trustworthiness of God."[8] But, the critics say, fallible men have corrupted what originally came from God in perfect form. Certainly, this *need* not be true, for God is fully *able* to preserve the record of His revelation inerrant. Only an examination of the biblical evidence itself can determine whether there are errors, but not only is it not necessary that there be errors, but it is more plausible that the God of truth and power would preserve the record without word. "Revelation is but half revelation unless it be infallibly communicated; it is but half communicated unless it be infallibly recorded."[9] Men were used but they were used by being borne along by the Holy Spirit (2 Peter 2:21). This is what kept the record from error even though fallible men were used in producing it.

IN RELATION TO INSPIRATION

A full and high view of inspiration requires inerrancy as a natural and necessary part of it. Errancy and inspiration are incompatible.

> The real reason why men oppose the doctrine of an infallible Scripture is that they are not willing to embrace the Biblical doctrine of inspiration. There is no such thing as inspiration which does not carry with it the correlate of infallibility. A Bible that is fallible—and we speak of course of the original—is a Bible that is not inspired. A Bible that is inspired is a Bible that is infallible. There is no middle ground.[10]

Sometimes in an attempt to preserve inspiration without infallibility, the latter is limited to matters of "faith and practice."

In other words the Bible is infallibly inspired in doctrinal areas that concern the Christian's faith and life, but in "lesser" matters it is only inspired but not inerrant. It is popular, for instance, to exclude the area of scientific matters from infallibility. "The Bible is not a textbook of science" is the cry. While this is true, such a statement should not be used to deceive people into thinking that when the Bible speaks on a matter in the area of science it may be in error. Though the Bible is not a textbook of science, when it records a scientific fact it speaks of that fact with infallible authority just the same as with matters of "faith and practice." If parts of the Bible are not inerrant, then the question properly arises, Who decides which parts are true and which parts are erroneous? One cannot hold to inspiration and infallibility of certain parts and only the inspiration of other parts.

IN RELATION TO THE BIBLE'S WITNESS CONCERNING ITSELF

The Bible witnesses to its own infallibility. Obviously if it is not infallible, it bears a false witness, and cannot be surely trusted in any of the matters on which it speaks. Its inerrancy therefore is vital to its own claims.

IN RELATION TO AUTHORITY

As stated, the authority of the Bible is under attack by those who charge that such authority is the authority of a "paper pope." Instead, they say, authority is in Christ, not the Bible, for God's Word must not be "petrified in a dead record."[11] This is such a superpious statement that it apparently cannot be questioned. But questioned it must be, for how can Christ have any authority if the witness to Him (the Bible) is not infallible? And if it is infallible, then it has authority too. (And of course the fundamentalist does not say the Bible has authority and Christ does not, though the Barthian tries to make the evangelical position appear thus.)

There is no other way of knowing about Christ and His authority except through the Bible. If the Bible is subject to error, then conceivably and very likely one of those errors concerns mankind's knowledge of Christ. It may concern His supernatural origin, or His deity, or His teachings, or His resurrection. And if in every detail He is not all He claimed to be (and one would have doubts if the witness to His claims is not inerrant), then what authority does that kind of person have?

Both the authority of Christ and the authority of the Scriptures depend on the inerrancy of the Scriptures, for statements that are not completely true cannot be absolutely authoritative. Furthermore parts of the Bible cannot be true and thus authoritative while other parts are not. It is not a book that is authoritative only in matters of "faith and practice." As Warfield correctly observed, "The authority which cannot assure of a hard fact is soon not trusted for a hard doctrine."[12]

The Proof of the Doctrine

Briefly summarized, the proof of the doctrine of inerrancy involves four concepts.

IT INVOLVES THE WITNESS OF SCRIPTURE TO ITS OWN INERRANCY

Is this a valid witness? Yes, for everyone has the right to speak for himself, and indeed there are some things that would never be known if the one involved did not speak for himself.[13]

Three classes of scriptural references testify to inerrancy. The first is the class of verses that affirm the truthfulness of God. These testify to the truthfulness of the communication of His revelation. The second involves verses that emphasize the abiding character of the complete Scriptures. Two principal passages relate to this point. The first guarantees the abiding character of the letters that make up words and the parts of letters that distinguish them from each other. In Matthew 5:18 (KJV) the Lord referred to the jot (the smallest Hebrew letter) and the tittle (the minor stroke that distinguishes certain Hebrew letters from one another). Of course this statement by Jesus has no meaning if the Scriptures are subject to errancy. The other passage is John 10:33–36, which records the Lord's words that the Scripture cannot be broken. This is an assertion that the entire Scripture cannot be broken and that the particular words being quoted on that occasion cannot be broken. This is only possible because the Bible is true in each particular and in all its parts.

The third class of passages are those in which an argument is based on a word or a form of a word. Of course, if the Bible is not inerrant, such arguments cease to be of any weight. When answering the Sadducees the Lord based His argument on the present tense of the verb "to be" (Matt. 22:32). In questioning the Pharisees He set His trap on the single word "Lord" (Matt. 22:43–

45). Paul's argument in Galatians 3 is based on the singular form of the word "seed" in contrast to the plural (v. 16). None of these arguments is valid unless tenses, words, and singulars and plurals are to be trusted. And they cannot be trusted apart from inerrancy.

IT INVOLVES A PROPER CONCEPT OF COMMUNICATION

Hodge has best stated this argument as follows: "Men think in words, and the more definitely they think the more are their thoughts immediately associated with an exactly appropriate verbal expression. Infallibility of thought cannot be secured or preserved independently of an infallible verbal reading."[14]

IT INVOLVES THE ANALOGY OF CHRIST

Frequently the objection is raised, How can the Bible be without error since all the writings came through men who are fallible? The answer to this involves an analogy with the Person of Christ. It might be objected that the Person of Christ cannot be sinless because humanity is sinful. But Christ is sinless because humanity is not necessarily per se sinful. The first man was created sinless and Jesus took on Himself the form of sinful flesh (Phil. 2:7), but not sinful flesh itself. Sinfulness is not necessary to humanity; in fact the pattern of real humanity is not to be found in the universal examples of fallen individuals. Likewise fallibility is not a necessary part of the result of a person being used to convey God's revelation. Usually man does corrupt whatever he touches, but this need not be so, and it was not so in the giving of the Scriptures.

IT INVOLVES FAITH

No one who holds to inerrancy denies that there are problems. Nor does he deny that fully satisfactory solutions have not been found to all the problems. But, accepting the witness of Scripture to its inerrancy, when he meets a problem for which he presently has no solution, he places his trust in the Scriptures rather than in his fallible mind. After all, the Bible has proved its reliability in many ways and in many areas, and it is worthy of trust. Human knowledge has often proved unreliable and at best it is limited. "It is indeed true that we should not close our minds and researches to the ever-progressing resolution of difficulties under the illumination of the Spirit of truth, but those whose approach to faith is that of resolution of all difficulty have deserted the very nature of faith and of its ground."[15] Even though the problems connected with apparent discrepancies, parallel passages, manner of quotations, and absence of original autographs may not yet have been fully solved, neither have they ever been conclusively demonstrated to contain errors. In the meantime they are proper subjects for reverent, scholarly investigation—reverence that includes a proper faith in the God of truth and His inerrant record of that truth.

CHAPTER 5

The Role of the Holy Spirit in Hermeneutics

Roy B. Zuck

ermeneutics, the science and art of biblical interpretation, is of primary concern to evangelicals because of their commitment to the inerrancy and authority of the Bible. The task of Bible interpreters is to seek to ascertain the meaning of Bible passages to their original hearers and readers and to determine how that meaning relates to readers today.[1] Biblical scholars have wrestled and are wrestling with serious hermeneutical issues but comparatively little attention has been given to the Holy Spirit's role in hermeneutics.

Since inaccurate interpretation of Scripture can lead to improper conduct, one must be sure he is interpreting properly. Adequate application of truth builds on an adequate understanding of truth. A distorted meaning of a Bible verse or passage may result in misguided living.

The Holy Spirit, as the παράκλητος ("Helper"; John 14:16, 26; 15:26), is available to help believers ascertain the correct meaning of the Bible's statements, commands, and questions. He is involved in the hermeneutical process because He is "the Spirit of truth," who, Jesus said, "will guide . . . into all truth" (John 16:13). And as Paul wrote, "We have . . . the Spirit who is from God, that we may understand what God has freely given us" (1 Cor. 2:12). John wrote, "His anointing teaches you about all [spiritual] things" (1 John 2:27). Probably "anointing" refers to the Holy Spirit; by metonomy the act of anointing stands for what is given in the anointing, namely, the indwelling Holy Spirit.

However, the Holy Spirit's involvement in teaching believers and guiding them in the truth raises some thorny questions. If true learning comes by the Spirit's inner working, does this mean that one's understanding of Scripture is ultimately a subjective matter? If a person senses the work of the Holy Spirit in his heart, does he automatically know the correct view of a Bible verse? If the Spirit interprets the Word privately to individual believers, how can one determine the correct view among several conflicting interpretations? If two people profess to be taught by the Spirit and yet hold differing views on some scriptural passage or issue, which view is valid?

As Moule put it, "the blessed Spirit is not only the true Author of the written Word but also its supreme and true Expositor."[2] But the question remains as to how the meaning of God's authoritative Word can be accurately discerned amid conflicting interpretations. If human interpretations confuse the clarity of the Word, is the Bible no longer authoritative? Is a person inconsistent if he allows the right of private judgment and at the same time claims that his interpretations are right and another's wrong?

Is the Bible not clear in its meanings? Can only a select few have insight into the meaning of Scripture? Are the "deep things of God" and His "thoughts" (1 Cor. 2:10–11) understood only by some Christians? Can a Christian claim infallibility for his interpretation of a Bible passage simply by affirming that the Holy Spirit "taught" him that meaning?

In what sense does the Holy Spirit give insight into the Bible's meaning? Does such "light" come suddenly? Or is it the result of study? If insight comes from study, can the Bible's meaning be ascertained by rational processes apart from the Holy Spirit?

How does the Spirit's role in interpretation relate to His work in illumination? Are the two functions the same? If not, how do they differ?

These are vital issues because, as Parker explains, "there is no function assigned to the Spirit more important for us to understand than that by which He assures to the church a profound and correct interpretation of Scripture."[3] Eternal truth must be understood and correctly interpreted.

How does the Holy Spirit "guide and direct"[4] believers in their involvement in the interpretive process? What does that guidance mean? Fourteen propositions are suggested as a means of speaking to some of these issues.

1. *The Spirit's ministry in Bible interpretation does not mean He gives new revelation.* His work is always through and in association with the written Word of God, not beyond it or in addition to it. The Holy Spirit and the Word operate together. The Bible, being God-breathed (2 Tim. 3:16), has power to *generate*

faith (Ps. 19:7; Rom. 10:17; 2 Tim. 3:15; James 1:18; 1 Peter 1:23), to *sanctify and nurture* (John 17:17–19; Acts 20:32; Eph. 5:26; 1 Peter 2:2), and to *enlighten* (Ps. 119:105, 130; 2 Tim. 3:16). The Holy Spirit, along with the Word, is said to *regenerate* (John 3:5–7; Titus 3:5), to *sanctify* (2 Thess. 2:13; 1 Peter 1:2) and to *enlighten* (John 14:26; 16:13; 1 Cor. 2:10–15). "The written Word . . . is always indissolubly joined with the power of the Holy Spirit."[5] The Bible, God's Word, is "living," (ζῶν) and "active" (ἐνεργης), "operative or effective" (Heb. 4:12; cf. 1 Thess. 2:13; 1 Peter 1:23). But its effectiveness is evident only when the Holy Spirit is at work in connection with the Word. "The Word of God can have no efficacy unless at the same time the Holy Spirit works in the hearts of the hearers, creating faith and making men's minds open to receive the Word."[6] In relation to man's receptivity, Calvin wrote, "The heavenly doctrine proves to be useful and efficacious to us in so far as the Spirit both forms our minds to understand it and our hearts to submit to its yoke."[7]

2. *The role of the Spirit in interpreting the Bible does not mean that one's interpretations are infallible.* Inerrancy and hence infallibility are characteristics of the Bible's original manuscripts, but not of the Bible's interpreters. The manuscripts were inerrant because of the Holy Spirit's guarding and guiding the writers to record what He wanted recorded, word for word. But such a superintending work cannot be claimed for interpreters of the Word. In *inspiration* the Holy Spirit superintended the authors in order to override any human error. In *interpretation* the Holy Spirit guides but He does not guard against infallibility. To elevate one's interpretations to the level of infallibility would blur the distinctions between inspiration (a past, now completed work of the Spirit in the recording of Scripture) and interpretation (a present, ongoing work of the Spirit in helping interpreters in the comprehending of Scripture). Also it would ascribe to Protestants a level of infallibility for human leaders which evangelicals reject in Roman Catholicism.

Therefore allowing the right of private (individual) judgment in interpreting the Bible does not mean that all the results of private interpretation are accurate.

3. *The work of the Spirit in interpretation does not mean that He gives some interpreters a mental acuity for seeing truths under the surface that are not evident to any other dedicated Bible students.* The interpreter, then, if he thinks he finds a "hidden"

meaning divergent from the normal, literal meaning of the passage, cannot claim the Holy Spirit's help.

4. *The role of the Holy Spirit in Bible interpretation means that the unregenerate do not welcome and apply God's truth, though they are able to comprehend many of its statements cognitively.* Obviously unsaved people can mentally grasp something of the objective data of the Bible. Many unbelievers have understood many of the historical facts presented in the Word of God. Some have even followed the logic of certain portions of the Bible. They have cognitively grasped certain objective biblical facts that certain Bible personalities performed certain tasks, said certain words, went to certain geographical locations, argued with certain points of logic, and so on, and yet they do not personally know the God of the Scriptures. "The world through its wisdom did not know him" (1 Cor. 1:21). Even with determined and diligent research on a high scholarly level, they are unable to respond to the true divine sense of the Scriptures.[8] The Spirit's illuminating of Christians, then, must include something more than mental apprehension of the Bible of which non-Christians are capable.

Though the unsaved may mentally observe objective data of the Bible, it remains foolishness to them (1 Cor. 1:18; 2:14). Though perhaps able to follow the logic of Paul's reasoning in his epistles, unbelievers do not "take to heart" the truth involved. The grammar of John 3:16 may be clear to the unsaved, but this does not mean that they receive to their hearts the truth of the verse. The unsaved do not welcome God's truth, because it strikes at the very core of their sinfulness.

Only the saved are able to welcome God's truth. When Paul stated in 1 Corinthians 2:14 that "the man without the Spirit [ψυχικὸς ἄνθρωπος, 'soulish, unsaved man'] does not accept the things that come from the Spirit of God," he did not mean that an unsaved person is totally incapable of comprehending any of the grammatical data of the Bible. Rather, Paul meant that a non-Christian does not welcome its truth! The Greek word translated "accept" (δέχομαι) means "welcome." If "receive" were intended, a different Greek word (λαμβάνω) would have been used. The verse does not mean that an unsavd person, who is devoid of the Holy Spirit, cannot understand mentally what the Bible is saying; instead it means that he does not welcome its message of redemption to his own heart.[9] He rejects the message, refusing to appropriate it and act on it. By contrast, people in Berea "received [from δέχομαι] the messsage with great eagerness" (Acts 17:11), and the Thessalonians "received [from δέχομαι] the Word . . . with the joy of the Holy Spirit" (1 Thess. 1:6).

The statement in 1 Corinthians 2:14 that the things of the Spirit of God are "foolishness" to an unbeliever would indicate that he has some understanding of what the Bible says. Otherwise, if nothing were communicated to him, how could he judge such a communication to be foolish? He could not call something foolishness unless he had some cognitive awareness of it.

"But," someone may argue, "this verse also states that an unsaved person cannot even know the things of the Spirit. Does not this argue against the point being made that the unsaved can be cognizant of Bible facts?" No, because the Greek word that is used means "know by experience" (γινώσκω), as opposed to οἶδα which means "know intuitively or intrinsically." An unbeliever does not know God's truth experientially. He may grasp portions of it mentally, but he does not discern it spiritually nor experience it personally. Virkler summarizes this point well when he writes:

> Thus unbelievers do not know the full meaning of scriptural teaching, not because that meaning is unavailable to them in the words of the text, but because they refuse to act on and appropriate spiritual truths for their own lives. Furthermore, the psychological results of such refusal make them less and less able (and willing) to comprehend these truths.[10]

In illumination the Holy Spirit's work is not only to show what the Bible means, but also to persuade Christians of its truth. Illumination is the Spirit's work, enabling Christians to discern the meaning of the message and to welcome and receive it as from God. Hodge states that obedience in the believer's life is the inevitable result of the illuminating work of the Spirit.[11]

To receive God's truths fully, one must first understand them and then appropriate them. Bromiley expresses this fact when he says that the Holy Spirit, who has given the Word of God, seeks to "open the eyes of the readers to *perceive* its truth and *receive* its light."[12] Klooster puts it this way: "Understanding Scripture requires more than an intellectual grasp of the historical setting of the text or the literary structure of the passage. . . . Heart-understanding demands the heart response in the totality of one's being to the living, triune God."[13]

5. *The Spirit's role in hermeneutics does not mean that only Bible scholars can understand the Bible.* The Bible was given to be understood by all; hence its interpretation is not in the hands of

an elite few (cf. 1 John 2:20, 27). And yet believers ought not neglect the interpretive helps that can be afforded by biblical scholars.

6. *The Holy Spirit's role in interpreting Scripture requires spiritual devotion on the part of the interpreter.* Thomas "Aquinas used to pray and fast when he came to a difficult passage of Scripture. Most of the scholars whose Biblical studies have blessed the church have mixed prayers generously with their studies."[14] "A deep religious experience has enlightened many an otherwise ill-instructed mind as to the meaning of much of the Holy Writ."[15] "Apart from the quickening of the Spirit, the interpreter will have only words and phrases. Only through the Holy Spirit can he enter into the meaning of the biblical writers. . . ."[16]

However, this is not to say that prayer automatically guarantees that a person's interpretations will be accurate. Spiritual devotion, depth, and sensitivity make correct interpretations more possible, but do not assure their accuracy. More is involved, as other propositions indicate.

7. *The Holy Spirit in interpretation means that lack of spiritual preparedness hinders accurate interpretation.*[17] A worldly Christian, one who is not obeying the truth and is not yielded to the Lord, is unable to understand the Word fully (1 Cor. 3:1–3) and "is not acquainted with the teaching about righteousness" (Heb. 5:13). A Christian who is in sin is susceptible to making inaccurate interpretations of the Bible because his mind and heart are not in harmony with the Spirit. As Chafer wrote, "Carnality of life excludes [believersl from understanding, or progressing in, the deep things of God."[18] God reveals His truths by the Spirit only to spiritual Christians. "The spiritual man" has greater depth in his discernment of spiritual truths (1 Cor. 2:15).

8. *The role of the Spirit in interpretation is no substitute for diligent study.* With a heart sensitive to the Spirit, the interpreter must study the Word intensely. The point here is that the Spirit does not make study superfluous. "The more self-consciously active the interpreter is in the process, the more likely is the Spirit's illumination."[19] The Holy Spirit works through the efforts of the individual as he reads the Bible, and studies it, meditates on it, and consults other works about it. In the inspiration of the Bible the Holy Spirit was working but so were the human authors. In a similar way in the interpretation of the Bible, human work is involved.

9. *The Spirit's work in biblical interpretation does not rule out the use of study helps such as commentaries and Bible dictionaries.* "It is often asserted by devout people that they can know the Bible competently without helps."[20] They assume they can go to the Bible and that the Holy Spirit interprets it for them directly. This seems to them more spiritual than relying on man's writings. Ramm answers this view by stating that no one has "either the right or the learning to by-pass all the godly learning"[21] of other Bible scholars both past and present. He suggests that such an affirmation is "a veiled egotism."[22]

Of course commentaries can come between a person and the Bible. It is possible to rely on others' interpretations to the neglect of one's own personal study of the Scriptures. Rather than using commentaries and other study helps as a crutch and accepting others' views unquestioningly, one should consult them and evaluate the views suggested in the light of his own study of the Scriptures (cf. Acts 17:11). This should be done prayerfully and humbly in dependence on the Spirit's guidance.

Chafer addresses this point well.

> No student of the Scriptures should be satisfied to traffic only in the results of the study of other men. The field is inexhaustible and its treasures ever new. No worthy astronomer limits his attention to the findings of other men, but is himself ever gazing into the heavens both to verify and to discover; and no worthy theologian will be satisfied alone with the result of the research of other theologians, but will himself be ever searching the Scriptures.[23]

10. *The ministry of the Holy Spirit in Bible interpretation does not mean interpreters can ignore common sense and logic.* Since the Spirit is "the Spirit of truth" (John 14:17; 15:26; 16:13), He would not teach concepts that failed to meet the tests of truth. (In a correspondence theory of truth, truth is what corresponds to the actual state of affairs.[24]) The Holy Spirit does not guide into interpretations that contradict each other or fail to have logical, internal consistency.

Two believers may be spiritual, but one or both may be wrong in their understanding of a Bible passage because of failure to think through the Bible logically. Two contradictory views may both be wrong, or one may be wrong, but they cannot both be correct. The Spirit seeks to aid the Spirit-filled learner to think clearly and accurately. The interpreter "must employ principles of reasoning in making inductions, deductions, analogies, and comparisons."[25]

Bible students recognize that while the Bible is a unique book—inspired by the Holy Spirit and therefore infallible and authoritative—it is a written means of communication (from God to man), which suggests that it must be understood in that light. As with any written communication the interpreter seeks to expose the meaning of the passage in its original setting, as it was understood by its original hearers. The Bible was written in languages unknown by most modern readers today, in cultural environments that differ from those in Western culture, in geographical settings that are distant from most present-day readers of the Bible, and in literary styles unlike many common literary forms today. These gaps—linguistic, cultural, geographical, and literary—are often hindrances to communication. Removing these hindrances or closing the gaps is much of what is involved in properly interpreting the Bible.[26]

Just as one uses common sense in seeking to bridge communication gaps within his own culture, so he should use common sense in interpreting the Bible. A reader normally gives an author the benefit of doubt if the author makes a statement that seemingly conflicts with a previous statement. The same should be granted the Bible. Also a reader normally uses principles of logic in seeking to understand an author's writing. He does not read into the writing a meaning that is foreign to the material. The same should be granted with regard to the Bible.

Though spiritual truths often supersede man's reasoning ability, they do not contradict or conflict with reason. Clear thinking, then, along with normal procedures followed in comprehending written communications is essential in Bible interpretation and harmonizes with the Holy Spirit's role.

11. *The place of the Holy Spirit in interpreting the Bible means that He does not normally give sudden intuitive flashes of insight into the meaning of Scripture.* Though many passages are readily understood, the meaning of others may come to light only gradually in the arduous process of careful study (as stated earlier in proposition 8). Still other times an interpreter may concentrate on a passage a long time with its meaning still eluding him. But later, after leaving the passage for awhile, the meaning may seem to jump to his mind suddenly. "The interpreter's struggle to understand always precedes that . . . experience, it does not occur in connection with a text on which one has expended no effort."[27] This sudden insight, if it occurs, does not come without his having studied the passage earlier.

To speak of the Spirit's part in hermeneutics is not to suggest some mysterious work that is beyond verification or validation. Lee argues against the view that the role of the Holy Spirit in interpretation and religious instruction means that His activity is a "mysterious and unfathomable" work[28] so that learning activity is unexplainable, unpredictable, or unverifiable,[29] or that teaching and learning are "miracles magically wrought by . . . zaps of the Holy Spirit."[30] Though Lee stresses this valid point about learning not coming by sudden impulses of the Holy Spirit, he then goes too far in ruling out the Holy Spirit's work altogether.[31] To depend on the Holy Spirit is, Lee says, to "spookify" religious instruction as if it were "an ethereal, mysterious, nonterrestrial affair which is fundamentally beyond the regular workings of nature."[32] But while some educators may seek to overemphasize the Holy Spirit, an equally dangerous direction is to neglect His work completely.

12. *The Spirit's ministry in interpreting the Bible is included in but not identical with illumination.* Illumination, as stated earlier, is the Spirit's work on the minds and hearts of believers that enables them not only to discern the truth but also to receive it, welcome it, and apply it. In interpretation a believer is aided by the Spirit to ascertain the meaning of a passage. This is the first step in illumination. But illumination is not complete until one has appropriated it to his life. Interpretation involves perception; illumination includes it but also involves reception.

13. *The role of the Spirit in scriptural interpretation does not mean that all parts of the Bible are equally clear in meaning.* Some scholars claim that all the Bible is equally perspicuous, that its meaning is clear and plain. However, perspecuity does not mean that all parts of the Bible are equally clear. Even Peter said that Paul's epistles "contain some things that are hard to understand" (2 Peter 3:16). Perspecuity means, instead, that the central message of the Bible, the message of salvation, is clear to all.

14. *The Spirit's work in interpretation does not result in believers having a comprehensive and completely accurate understanding of the entire Scriptures.* The exact meaning of many passages still eludes many Bible scholars, even after a lifetime of study in the Scriptures. The precise meaning of some verses will not be known until believers see the Savior "face to face" (1 Cor. 13:12). Students of the Bible, even though they are devout and are Spirit-taught, must admit that the correct interpretation of at least some passages simply cannot be fully ascertained this side of heaven.

These propositions suggest that at least five elements are necessary for properly interpreting the Bible: salvation, spiritual maturity, diligent study, common sense and logic, and humble dependence on the Spirit of God for discernment. Clearly the Holy Spirit needs to be much involved in the process of a believer's efforts to comprehend and interpret the Bible.

CHAPTER 6

The Image of God

Charles Lee Feinberg

It is true beyond cavil or dispute that the focus of interest today is upon man, his life, his actions, his feelings, his struggles, and his potentialities.[1] In fact some theologians have so occupied themselves with the study of man, that they have left little or no time for a discussion of supernatural themes, an interesting reversal of the emphasis manifest in theological realms in the Middle Ages. Zabriskie has correctly stated: "At no time in the history of theology has the doctrine of the *imago Dei* had a more challenging pastoral relevance or more provocative theological implications than it does within the current of contemporary theology."[2]

Henry acquiesces in the significance of the subject. After asking in what way man reflects God, since he is the resemblance of God, he presses the questions, "What of the vitiating effects of his fall into sin? Is the NT concept of the *imago* in conflict with the OT conception? Is it in conflict with itself? These questions are among those most energetically debated by contemporary theology."[3] The heated discussions and debates relative to the image of God reveal somewhat the weighty character of the subject.[4] One has only to delve into the almost interminable battle on the doctrine of the *imago Dei* to realize before long how complex and at times abstruse the factors are. Moreover, the biblical doctrine has wide ramifications that touch every area of theology with the possible exceptions of bibliology and ecclesiology. The doctrines of God, angels, man (the Fall, sin), salvation (atonement, sanctification), and future things (glorification, resurrection) are directly involved.[5] The concept of the image of God, implied or expressed, underlies all revelation.[6] Thus it is not too much to maintain that a correct understanding of the image of God in man can hardly be overemphasized. The position taken here determines every area of doctrinal declaration. Not only is theology involved, but reason, law, and civilization as a whole, whether it views regenerate or unsaved humanity from its origin to eternity.[7]

Any treatment of this vital theme must address three questions: (1) In what specifically does the image of God consist? (2) What effect did sin and the Fall have on this image? (3) What results accrued to the image of sinful humanity because of the redemptive work of the Lord Jesus Christ?[8]

Relevant passages on mankind as the image of God are Genesis 1:26–27 (the creation account); 5:1, 3 (the transmission of the image from Adam to his posterity); 9:6 (the doctrine of the image relative to homicide); 1 Corinthians 11:7 (discussion of headship in the family); Colossians 3:10 (exhortations to the believer to put on the new man); and James 3:9 (treatment of the proper use of the tongue). Psalm 8 does not contain the words "image of God," but the passage deals in poetic form with the creation of man and the area of his dominion[9] (Heb. 2:6–8). The only method for arriving at a correct solution of the problems related to the image of God is to carry through a careful and accurate exegesis of the Scripture passages involved.

Exegesis is possible only by beginning at the lexical gate of the words used. Genesis 1:26–27 employs the Hebrew words צֶלֶם ("image") and דְּמֻּח ("likeness"). The New Testament equivalents are εἰκών and ὁμοίωσις. Words in addition to these are ἀπαύγασμα and χαρακτήρ (both in Heb. 1:3). The words of Genesis 1:26 appear in the Vulgate as *imago* and *similitudo*. The use of two words in the original passage has occasioned a strange spate of interpretations in the history of theology. The employment of two nouns has been seen as teaching two aspects of the image of God. One is said to denote man's essence, which is unchangeable, whereas the other is held to teach the changing part of man. Thus the first use of image relates to the very essence of man, while the likeness is what may be lost. This distinction came to be a continuous element in theological anthropology.[10] A careful study of Genesis 1:26–27; 5:1, 3; and 9:6 shows beyond question that it is impossible to avoid the conclusion that the two Hebrew terms are not referring to two different entities. In short, use reveals the words are used interchangeably. The Greek and Latin Fathers distinguished between צֶלֶם and דְּמֻּח, the first referring to the physical and the latter to the ethical part of the divine image. The words, however, are used synonymously, the second emphasizing the first. Irenaeus (A.D. 130–ca. 200) made a distinction between "image" and "likeness." He said the first refers to man's freedom and reason and the last to the gift of supernatural communion with God (still the official view of the Roman Church). Genesis 5:1 and 9:7 do not support such a difference in meaning."[11]

What is the reason for the wide differences on the subject? Laidlaw's explanation is correct: "Although thus definite and significant, however, the phrase [image of God] is not explicit. . . . This is why the doctrine of the Divine Image in man has been a topic so fruitful of differences in theology."[12] Many have expressed their desire that the Scriptures had given a clear definition of the image and what it denotes. After all, what is the image of God? The biblical data furnish no systematic theory of the subject, no clue as to what is implied.[13]

Much light may be shed on the doctrine of the image of God if attention is directed to the unique setting of the creation of man in the Genesis account. All exegetes are agreed that the climax of creation is reached in Genesis 1:26. Even evolutionary theories must agree with the truth of Scripture that man is the apex of all creation. Man's creation by God comes as the last and highest phase of God's creative activity. To highlight this event the wording is entirely altered. To this point the simple, forceful statement was "God said, Let there be. . . ." Now there is counsel or deliberation in the Godhead. No others can be included here, such as angels, for none has been even intimated thus far in the narrative. Thus the creation of man took place, not by a word alone, but as the result of a divine decree.

Another distinguishing feature in the creation of man is his special nature. Although man is related on the physical side of his existence with material nature, so that physiologically he shares with lower organisms, yet he is far superior to all natural creatures, combining in himself certain immaterial elements never duplicated in the lower creation. Orr states it succinctly:

> The true uniqueness in man's formation, however, is expressed by the act of the divine inbreathing, answering somewhat to the *bara* of the previous account. This is an act peculiar to the creation of man; no similar statement is made about the animals. The breath of Jehovah imparts to man the life which is his own, and awakens him to conscious possession of it.[14]

A third distinctive factor in man's creation is his special dominion. None of the lower animals had power or dominion delegated to it. Man on earth was meant in a measure to reflect the dominion of his Creator over lower creatures. Concerning this dominion more will be said later. In sum, the creation of man is clearly separated and delineated by a special counsel and decision in the Godhead, marked off by a special nature (in the likeness and image of God), and characterized by a special dominion and sovereignty.

Coming to the heart of the matter, one is still faced with the perplexing questions: In what does the image consist? What is included? What is excluded? What factors may have a detrimental or beneficial influence on the image? How is Christ Himself related to this whole question, since the New Testament designates Him as the image of God also? Is any viable option possible in a field so thoroughly traversed and so warmly debated for centuries by both Jews and Christians, theologians and naturalists, humanists and believers? The mind of the reader must, first of all, be disabused of the illusion that there has been unanimity in any camp, or that there has been an unbroken continuum of view in any school. Actually, Jewish authorities have differed widely on the subject; the rabbis of the Talmud, the medieval philosophers in Judaism, the later Jewish mystics, and modern liberal Jewish opinion span a wide spectrum of views. Christian interpreters have been no less diverse in their positions. Scientists, humanists, sociologists, psychologists, and psychiatrists of all shades of belief and unbelief have espoused varying viewpoints according to their reasoning and predilection.[15]

Many have seen the meaning of the image in man's dominion over nature with the corollary concepts of endowment with reason and upright stature. They point out that Genesis 1:26 unmistakably affirms man's dominion in the immediate context where image is found. Thus it is reasoned, the image consists in man's lordship over lower creation about him, which is meant by God to be subject to man. It is more correct to declare that the image is the basis or foundation for the dominion. Psalm 8:6–7 does not substantiate the view that image equals dominion. Man as a free being, regardless of how he uses this freedom, is said to reflect the sovereignty residing in God.[16]

Could the image consist in man's immortality? Jamieson answers in the negative:

> And in what did this image of God consist? Not in the erect form or features of man; not in his intellect—for the devil and his angels are in this respect far superior; not in his immortality—for he has not, like God, a past as well as a future eternity of being; but in the moral dispositions of his soul, commonly called *original righteousness*. . . .[17]

Some have espoused the view that the image of God in man consists in his corporeality. It would seem that this position is not difficult to repute, for God is Spirit and has no human form and man's form has no divine likeness.[18] Smith, on the other hand, feels man's body is after God's image insofar as it is the means whereby man exercises his dominion, and surely dominion is an attribute of God, seeing He is the absolute and final Lord. For this reason man's body is erect, being endowed as well with speech in order to issue words of command.[19]

If corporeality has had its advocates as an explanation of the meaning of the image of God, noncorporeality has an even greater number of protagonists. Clark shows how the image and likeness cannot be man's body, for (a) God is spirit and has no body, and (b) animals have bodies but are not in the image of God.[20] Clarke, noted Methodist commentator, held that the image must be the intellect and the mind, not a corporeal image. The mind and soul were certainly, according to Clarke's reasoning, created after the perfections of God. His emphasis is: "God was now producing a spirit, and a spirit, too, formed after the perfections of his [that is, God's] nature."[21] Keil and Delitzsch find the image of God in the spiritual or self-conscious personality of man. Therein exists a creature copy of the holiness of the life of God.[22] Since God is incorporeal, reasons Chafer, the likeness of man to God must be limited to the immaterial part of man. Man's personality and self-consciousness, then, are the vantage point from which the personality of God is to be studied.[23] Calvin forthrightly affirms that "there is no doubt that the proper seat of his image is in the soul." The image of God is explicable only on the basis of the spiritual. The view that man is the image corporeally is "repugnant to reason," because it would have Christ speaking in Genesis 1:26 of Himself as the image of Himself.[24]

At this point it may be well to ascertain how the image concept fared through successive centuries and among Jews and Christians to the present time. The rabbis manifested a reluctance to define precisely the phrase "image of God." This is unmistakable in the Aramaic translations of the Pentateuch. Radical anti-anthropomorphism is seen in numerous ways.[25] The rabbis of the Mishnah embraced the image of God concept in the Philonic and Platonic sense, and utilized the idea for rabbinical enactments. For instance, the image was to remind people of the dignity of each person; it argued against celibacy; it underscored man's beauty and original androgynous nature; and it led to much speculation concerning the *Adam Qadmon* (The Primordial Man or *Urmensch*).[26] The rabbis made much of man's ability to think, create, and be aware of God. He is capable, not only of communing with God, but in later rabbinic literature he is designated as a "partner" of God the Creator.[27]

Medieval Jewish theologians generally followed Philo's view, replacing his Logos with Plotinus' Intellect (*Nous*) or Aristotle's Active Intellect. Man's superiority over lower creation resided in his rational soul or intellect. The *summum bonum* for man was to achieve through the exercise of reason a union of his intellect with God or with Active Intellect. Maimonides subscribed to this interpretation of the biblical terms, and it became standard for Jewish exegesis and philosophy.[28]

Early in Christian interpretation the Pauline concept of Christ as the image of God (Col. 1:15; see also Phil. 2:6 for the form of God) was made determinative for an understanding of the full import of man in the image of God. The appellation of Jesus Christ as the image of God related to a number of concepts, namely, the eschatological idea of "Son of man," the Pauline phrase, "last Adam" (1 Cor. 15:45), and the exhortation to put on the "new man" (Col. 3:9–10).[29] Before entering into a fuller consideration of Christ as the image of God, it may be helpful to continue the historical observations on the doctrine of the image through the Reformation era. Luther attacked Augustine's view that the image consists of memory, understanding, and will. In this case even Satan could be said to exhibit the image of God. Luther understood the image as essentially man's response to God by loving and glorifying Him.[30] Calvin claimed man could be like or resemble God only in the area of spiritual and rational attributes.[31] Reformed theologians subscribed to the position that image was knowledge, righteousness, and holiness.[32]

When one views the theological scene in the early 20th century, he is aware that religious liberalism was in its heyday. How have liberals dealt with the problem under discussion? Enamored with the Wellhausen approach to the religion of Israel, they saw the entire concept of the image of God as probably dependent on Babylonian mythology. It was the intention of God, according to this view, to make a man who looked like Him and the divine beings in His retinue. Included were spiritual powers like power of thought, communication, and self-transcendence, couched in concrete, rather than abstract terms.[33] Because this school was reluctant to take the Genesis narrative in the literal sense, it felt itself comfortable in the relational view, that is, the image consisted in man's relation to God.[34] This shifts the emphasis in the consideration from the creation account to the redemption account of the New Testament.

Emil Brunner saw a double aspect of the image, the formal phase which is unchangeable and cannot be affected by sin, and the material image which was lost through the Fall.[35] Karl Barth stressed the "I-thou" or "face-to-face" relation as in the divine life. He originally denied that God had created man in His own image, since He was "totally Other," but in later writings he admitted a divine image in man.[36] However, the central thrust of the image of God for Barth is relationship. Man is God's partner in the covenant of grace and a counterpart to God in creation.[37] Carrying the concept of the image to its eschatological conclusion, Barth places it in the body of the resurrection. It is the oft-quoted dictum of Irenaeus: "His becoming what we are enables us to become what He is." Thus the *imago* resides in the present hope of the resurrection of the body through Christ.[38]

The discussion must now turn to the consideration of Christ as the image of God. Prominent passages are 2 Corinthians 4:4; Colossians 1:15–17; and Hebrews 1:2–3. When these verses are scrutinized, it will be seen from the context in each case that the verses are dealing with Christ not so much as the incarnate Savior but as the eternal Son. Reference is made to the specific teaching of Christ's essential deity.[39] A word of caution is in order here: When the Scriptures represent man in the image of God, it is of the Godhead, not of Christ exclusively. Because man, even when redeemed and glorified, cannot be equated with God, his image of God must necessarily be imperfect. Chereso says, "This is because man can never achieve equality or identity of nature with God. Only the Son is so perfect an image of His Father as to be equal to, and identical in nature with, Him. Hence it is that the Word is called *the* image of God, while man is said to be created *to* that image."[40]

That the New Testament clearly designates Jesus Christ to be the image of God par excellence has been the point of greatest tension between the Jewish and Christian viewpoints on the image of God. Altmann meets the issue squarely: "The difference between Jewish and Christian exegesis in the area of the *homo imago Dei* motif concerned not so much the philosophical concept of man's dignity as a rational creature—this remained, in fact, common ground throughout medieval Christian scholasticism—as the theological equation of Logos and Christ."[41]

What effect did the Fall have on the image of God in man? The discussion of the image of God should not and cannot be restricted to the original creation. What of man after the Fall? Can one still regard him as in the image of God? In what sense is this true? The matter of sin's effect on man was debated in controversies with Pelagians and semi-Pelagians, with synergists and Arminians. How can man, fallen and corrupt (Rom. 1:21, 23) and rebellious against God, still be viewed as the image of God? If he is a child of wrath (Eph. 2:3), does he still bear the image of his Creator? Man's deeds show that he is not essentially good. And if he is not *essentially* good, then how can he reasonably be expected to mirror the nature of God?[42] Has man lost the image partially or entirely?

Lutheran theologians have held that man through the Fall lost the image of God completely.

> Lutheran thinking assumes that this "image of God" as well as the "righteousness given with creation" were *lost* through the Fall. It is not considered to be part of man's creaturely structure which indestructibly survives also in the sinner. This interpretation sees man, at one and the same moment, as creature and sinner, but as the bearer of the image of God only in the state of original integrity and again after the resurrection from the dead.[43]

Reformed theologians held that the image included man's rational faculties and his moral conformity to God. They spoke of the essential image of God (the very nature of the soul) and the accidental image (what could be lost without the loss of humanity itself).

Nowhere does the Old Testament indicate that the divine image and likeness are lost. For this reason some theologians who held first that the image was lost, have reversed themselves and have spoken of "remnants" of the image in fallen man. When one contemplates Genesis 9:6; James 3:9; and 1 Corinthians 11:7, it can be seen that it is incorrect to say unqualifiedly that the image of God was lost through sin. There are references where man's nature after the fall "is still the 'work and creature of God' (see Deut. 32:6; Isa. 45:11; 54:5; 64:8; Acts 17:25; Rev. 4:11; Job 10:8–12; Ps. 139:14–16)."[44] The insurmountable obstacle to the position that the image of God is entirely lost through the Fall is the fact that even fallen man is not shorn of his humanity. In short, if the divine image speaks of an inalienable part of his constitution, such as reason, freedom, will, and the like, it remains. But it is in a marred, corrupted, and impaired state. When moral likeness to God is in question, then this must be seen as largely defaced in man, who cannot naturally claim holiness with love and fear of God.[45] However, that which relates to rationality, conscience, and self-consciousness cannot be less, for then man would cease to be man. In spite of the Fall man did not become a beast or a demon, but retained his humanity. He did lose, however, his communion with God, his righteousness, his conformity to the will of God. And he became mortal.

When the New Testament refers to the new creation, it is speaking of the restoration of the image (cf. 1 Cor. 15:49). Christ is the pattern of the redeemed humanity. The principle emphasis in Pauline anthropology is the restoration of the image (cf. 2 Cor. 3:18). See Romans 8:29; Ephesians 4:24; and Colossians 3:10. A caution is here in order. To project back from the renewed image to the original image can lead to confusion, because here there would be an evaluation of the original image in terms of Christ (2 Cor. 4:4; Col. 1:15). Regeneration and sanctification serve to renew the believer after the image of his Creator. In redemption the divine image is restored and perfected in man. God has predestinated us to be conformed to the image of His Son.

Certain concluding observations are in order here. The image of God constitutes all that differentiates man from the lower creation. It does not refer to corporeality or immortality. It has in mind the will, freedom of choice, self-consciousness, self-transcendence, self-determination, rationality, morality, and spirituality of man.[46] The ability to know and love God must stand forth prominently in any attempt to ascertain precisely what the image of God is.

Thus the treatment of the image of God in man is eminently vital for proper views of creation, sin, redemption, Christology, and the future life. Only in theology—not in the natural or social sciences—can the true meaning of man's existence and destiny be correctly discerned.

CHAPTER 7

The Doctrine of the Conscience

Roy B. Zuck

A study of the conscience is perhaps one of the most neglected aspects of biblical anthropology and psychology. Comparatively few systematic theologies even mention it. And how many sermons on the subject of the conscience can the reader recall having heard?

The conscience is an important part of the immaterial nature of man and therefore deserves attention. Sanders stresses the need for knowing what the Bible teaches about the conscience.

> Ignorance of the function of conscience and of the divine provision for its healthy exercise leads to serious spiritual disorders. Many sensitive Christians have limped through life because of a morbid and weak conscience whose condemning voice allowed them no respite. Their very sincerity and desire to do the will of God only accentuated the problem and caused them to live in a state of perpetual self-accusation. Deliverance from this unhappy state is possible through the apprehension and appropriation of the teaching of Scripture on the subject.[1]

The Meaning of the Conscience

The English word "conscience" is from the Latin *conscientia*, a compound of *con* ("together" or "with") and *scio* ("to know"). This in turn is a translation of the Greek συνείδησις, literally, "knowledge with." This noun is used in the New Testament 30 times (19 times in Pauline writings, five times in Hebrews, three times in 1 Peter, twice in Acts, and once in John).[2]

The verb συεῖδον, related to the noun συνείδησις, is used only four times in the New Testament (three times in Acts, and once in 1 Corinthians). In Acts 12:12 and 14:6 συνει"δον clearly means "to see in one's mind, to understand or perceive" and therefore "to know with one's self." The perfect tense may also carry this same meaning in Acts 5:2. In 1 Corinthians 4:4 the perfect tense σύνοιδα is used with the reflexive dative pronoun ἐμαυτῷ.[3] The inept rendering of 1 Corinthians 4:4 in the King James Version, "For I know nothing by myself," is more accurately translated by the

New American Standard Bible, "I am conscience of nothing against myself," or by the Phillips paraphrase, "For I might be quite ignorant of any fault in myself."

Pierce suggests that this use of the verb ουνεῖδον with the dative of the reflexive pronoun is the verbal equivalent of the noun συνείδησις, "conscience."[4] For this reason, apparently two other translations[5] render the clause in 1 Corinthians 4:4 with the words, "My conscience is clear."

From this study of the verbal form, it appears that the nominal form—the conscience—is an inner awareness, a knowledge within one's self. However, many writers suggest that συνείδησις means "knowledge with *someone* or *something*." Hallesby, for example, suggests that it is an individual's knowledge of his conformity to the will of God.[6] Others suggest that the conscience means man's coknowledge with God Himself regarding man's morals.[7] However, σύν, as a verbal prefix, occasionally has a reflexive meaning ("with oneself" or "in one's mind or soul").[8] Delitzsch explains this as follows: "The σύν is not that of fellowship or intercommunion, but συνείδησις imports . . . the knowledge dwelling in the person of man. . . ."[9] He also observes that the conscience bears witness within man, not with God.[10]

But what does this inner knowledge or consciousness pertain to? The occurrences of "conscience" in the New Testament suggest that it pertains, broadly speaking, to one's ethics or morals, that is, the conscience is a moral consciousness. Therefore based on etymology and New Testament usage, the conscience can be defined as "the inner knowledge or awareness of, and sensitivity to, some moral standard."[11] That standard may differ with each individual, as will be discussed later, but even so the conscience is the faculty of a person by which he or she has an awareness of some standard of conduct.

However, this biblical view of the conscience has not always been accepted by others. For example Herbert Spencer, an English philosopher of the 19th century, thought, along with many others, that the conscience is not innate at birth, but is acquired in life as a result of education, child training, and other forms of environmental influence.[12] According to this view, a sense of oughtness varies from person to person because of one's training and social environment. The conscience, then, as Hegel taught, is acquired and is measured by social ethics.[13]

The Scriptures seem to suggest that the conscience is inherent in all persons rather than an acquired trait. Second Corinthians 4:2 refers to "every man's conscience," and in 1 Corinthians 10:29 Paul, in speaking of his own conscience and the conscience of another, apparently was presuming that the conscience is universal and innate.

Others have held that the conscience is the voice of God in man, the personal presence and influence of God Himself. Wordsworth held that the conscience is "God's most intimate presence in the soul and His most perfect image in the world."[14] But if that were true, the conscience could hardly be called evil (Heb. 10:22), weak (1 Cor. 8:7), defiled (Titus 1:15), or seared (1 Tim. 4:2).

A third and perhaps more popular view of the conscience is that it is a personal guide to one's moral actions. "Let your conscience be your guide" is the slogan of this viewpoint. The so-called "new morality" stresses the notion that each person is free to determine for himself his own moral standards. Following "the dictates of one's conscience" justifies whatever conduct one may desire, for if a person is persuaded that a thing is right, then, it is argued, for him it cannot be wrong. Pierce points out that when a person says "my conscience bids me do this," he is really saying he wants to or feels like doing it, or that he is conditioned by habit to do it.[15] But to justify morally wrong actions by hiding behind the cloak of personal opinions, inclinations, or desires distorts the New Testament meaning of the conscience.

The Function of the Conscience

A number of authors suggest a threefold function of the conscience, similar to those given by Rehwinkel: (1) it distinguishes the morally right and wrong, (2) it urges individuals to do what they recognize as right, and (3) it passes judgment on their acts and executes that judgment within their soul.[16] The *Encyclopaedia Britannica* refers to these same three functions: (1) discerning between right and wrong, (2) predisposing to moral action, and (3) bringing remorse to the person who recognizes he or she has broken a law.[17]

These three functions may be pictured by a courtroom scene, in which the conscience functions in a twofold way as both a witness and a judge. As a witness, the conscience tells the individual whether he is doing right or wrong (according to the moral standards he has accepted for himself). And as a judge the conscience (a) causes the individual to feel condemned (and remorseful) or not condemned (and not remorseful) regarding his actions, and (b) urges him, when he has done wrong, to follow his standards more faithfully in subsequent actions. Rehwinkel calls this prompting action the "obligatory" aspect of the conscience,[18] and Strong calls it the claim of duty, the obligation to do the right.[19] Romans 13:5 may suggest this judiciary action of prompting toward correct action. Believers should be submissive to "higher powers" not only to avoid punishment (διὰ τὴν ὀργήν) for wrongdoing, but also because their conscience urges them to do so (διὰ τὴν συνείδησιν).[20]

Three times Paul referred to the conscience as a witness (Rom. 2:15; 9:1; 2 Cor. 1:12). In Romans 2:14–15 three factors are said to demonstrate that the Gentiles have "the work of the Law written in their hearts" (2:15)—their actions, their consciences, and their thoughts (or reasonings).[21] Their actions show others that they are aware of an inward moral law; their consciences show themselves that they are aware of and sensitive to such a law; and their thoughts or reasonings that condemn or approve one another's conduct show that they possess and follow an inward law or moral standard of some sort.

Paul stated that his conscience witnessed to his honesty (Rom. 9:1). Here his conscience indicated internally to Paul himself that his statement about his felt grief for Israel was in accord with his actual feelings. If Paul had been speaking falsely when he expressed his deep concern for Israel, his conscience, like a witness in a court trial, would have called his attention to his falsehood.

Paul's third references to the function of the conscience as a witness is in 2 Corinthians 1:12. Here he stated that he rejoiced because of the testimony or witness of his conscience that he had lived "with devout motives and godly sincerity" (Berkeley Version). How wonderful if every Christian could state the same thing—that his conscience witnesses to devout motives and godly sincerity.

The second function of the conscience is that of a judge. As such, it adjudicates regarding the moral quality of one's actions. Strong calls the conscience "the moral judiciary of the soul, not the law, nor a sheriff, but a judge."[22] If the action is in accord with the person's standard of conduct, the conscience gives a "not guilty" verdict. But if the action is not in accord with his standard of conduct, the conscience pronounces a verdict of "guilty."

Because of this continual adjudicating, the conscience is called by Chafer "a monitor over human actions."[23] Calvin commented that the conscience "is appointed, as it were, to watch over man, to observe and examine all his secrets."[24] Hodge stated that this function of the conscience as a judge "is accompanied with vivid emotions, pleasurable in view of that which is right, and painful in view of that which is wrong."[25]

Feeling inward remorse or moral pain over a wrong action indicates that one's conscience as a judge has pronounced him guilty. Many Greek authors wrote of this aspect of the conscience. Plutarch called the condemning conscience a painful disease. Demosthenes described it as paralyzing in its effect and "as full of fear and trembling as the expectation of blows." Philo wrote that it is a chastisement from which there is no escape and which injects fear into the soul.[26] Also modern-day literary artists have made much of the fear and remorse of a guilt-ridden conscience in the lives of their leading characters. In Hamlet (Act III, Section I) Shakespeare wrote, "Thus conscience does make cowards of us all." And Byron wrote, "No ear can hear nor tongue can tell the tortures of that inward hell."[27]

Because the conscience is frequently associated with this moral remorse, Pierce seeks to build a case for his view that συνείδησις in the New Testament is always used in a bad sense—bad acts, conditions, or character.[28] In fact he limits his definition of the conscience to "the painful consciousness that a man has of his own sins, past, or if present, begun in the past."[29] "It is the pain a man suffers when he does wrong."[30]

There are several problems with this view. First, Pierce wrongly equates the pain itself with the agent that inflicts the pain. Rather than saying the conscience is the moral pain suffered when a person violates his standards of conduct, it would be better to say the conscience inflicts moral pain. Second, Pierce's view forces him toward a strained interpretation of the good, pure, cleansed, and void-of-offense conscience. A good conscience, according to Pierce, is an absent conscience![31] Accordingly his explanations of Romans 9:1 and 2 Corinthians 1:12, in which the conscience is referred to as a witness, appear exegetically weak.[32]

The Fallibility of the Conscience

Why do some people say they can follow a certain course of action without their conscience bothering them, whereas the same course of action greatly disturbs (brings moral pain and remorse to) other people? Why is it that, as Sanders observes, "in former times the conscience of a Hindu would protest loudly against the killing of a cow but would remain quiescent while he sacrificed his child"?[33]

The answer is that standards of moral conduct vary from person to person. "That standard may be imperfect or flagrantly wrong, but such as it is, conscience will adjudicate according to it."[34] Whether a person's conscience accuses and disturbs him regarding a certain action depends on whether that action is in keeping with his standard of conduct or violates it.

Using a speed monitor in an automobile, a driver may set the controller at a given speed. Then if his actual driving speed exceeds the speed set on the monitor, a buzzer is automatically triggered. This buzzer calls the driver's attention to the fact that he or she has exceeded the set speed and thus prompts the driver to reduce the speed. Of course if the driver does not exceed the speed set on the controller, the buzzer is not sounded.

The conscience is much like the speed monitor. When a person violates his moral standard, his conscience informs him that that act was wrong.

Suppose the driver sees a road sign that indicates he is in a 30-mile-an-hour zone, but deliberately sets the speed monitor at 40 miles per hour. Obviously he will not hear the buzzer when driving between 30 and 40 miles an hour, even though he is violating the speed law. Likewise a person may willingly choose to ignore God's standard and therefore is not bothered by an accusing conscience when violating that law. Sometimes a driver may ignorantly (rather than deliberately) set the monitor above the speed limit. But this ignorance does not excuse his wrongdoing. To have one's speed in accord with the law, the monitor must be aligned with the law. Similarly for a person's moral actions to be pleasing to the Lord, they must be aligned with His moral laws, as revealed in Scripture.

However, the Fall has affected the conscience, making it fallible and unreliable. Like a speed monitor set at the wrong speed, the conscience is not properly aligned with God's standards. Only spiritual regeneration and a Spirit-filled life lived in full obedience to God's Word can bring one's conscience in conformity to God's standards.[35]

The Kinds of Conscience

A COMMENDING CONSCIENCE

When the conscience acts as a judge or monitor over one's conduct, it either commends or condemns each action. If one's conscience commends or approves his actions and if those actions are aligned with God's standards, then his conscience is a "good" or "commending" conscience. But if his conscience condemns his actions and if those actions are aligned with God's standards, then his conscience is a "bad" or "condemning" conscience.

It is noteworthy that almost every time a pure (καθαρος) conscience is referred to in the New Testament, it is related to spiritual service (λατρεύω). The blood of bulls and goats cannot perfect (τελειόω) the conscience (Heb. 9:9). Only the blood of Christ can purify (καθαρέω) the sinner's conscience from dead or useless works and enable him to serve (λατρεύω) the living God (Heb. 9:14). In other words only salvation through faith in Christ can remove the condemnation of a guilty conscience before God and qualify the believer for spiritual service.

If those animal sacrifices had purified (καθαρίζω) those who served (λατρεύω) in the tabernacle, they would have had no more conscience of sins (Heb. 10:2). That is, they would not have had a condemning conscience filled with remorse because of failure to live up to God's standards.

Only those whose hearts have been sprinkled from an evil conscience (made clean from a guilty conscience) can draw near to God (Heb. 10:22) in spiritual worship and service.

Paul stated that deacons (spiritual servants) are to have a pure (καθαρός) conscience (1 Tim. 3:9). He also stated that he himself served (λατρεύω) God with a pure (καθαρος) conscience (2 Tim. 1:3).

A good conscience is one that is free from guilt because of a life lived according to God's standards. Salvation gives the believer "the ability to face God with a clear [good, ἀγαθός] conscience" (1 Peter 3:21, Phillips). According to this, salvation is pictured by water baptism, which in turn was prefigured by the water of the Flood.

Paul affirmed that he had "lived with a perfectly good (ἀγαθος) conscience before God" (Acts 23:1), and the writer to the Hebrews said he had a good or noble (καλός) conscience (Heb. 13:18). A good conscience enables the believer (a) to love the Lord and others ("love from a pure heart and a good conscience and a sincere faith," 1 Tim. 1:5), (b) to be a strong soldier for Christ ("faith and a good conscience," 1 Tim. 1:19), and (c) to bring shame to those who falsely accuse him (1 Peter 3:16).

A good and pure conscience is one that is void of offense (ἀπρόσκοπος) toward God and men (Acts 24:16). Paul wrote that he "exercises" (ἀσκέω) himself to have that kind of conscience free from known sin. Though a conscience free from accusations and inward remorse requires labor and effort, it "imparts a new worthwhileness to a person's whole life, gives it a new wealth and fullness and a quiet, peaceful joy which transcends all other joys."[36]

A CONDEMNING CONSCIENCE

A less-than-desirable conscience is said to be weak (1 Cor. 8:7; 10:12), defiled (1 Cor. 8:7; Titus 1:15), evil (Heb. 10:22), or seared (1 Tim. 4:2).

The conscience is also referred to five times in 1 Corinthians 10 (vv. 25, 27–28, and twice in v. 29). Though these verses do not call the conscience "weak," the context does suggest that a weak conscience is being discussed. The situation in 1 Corinthians 10 is similar to that of the weak conscience discussed in chapter 8.

What is a weak conscience? According to 1 Corinthians 8, a weak conscience is one that is overscrupulous or oversensitive.

In seeking to answer the Corinthians' question about the morality of eating food that had been offered to idols, Paul stated that idols do not really exist (8:4). But, he added, not everyone is knowledgeable of that fact because they have become "so accustomed to think in terms of idols" (8:7, Berkeley). Therefore the weak (oversensitive) conscience of a person who eats such food becomes defiled (μολύνω, "contaminated, soiled," 8:7). If a Christian with an oversensitive conscience sees another Christian eating offered-to-idols food in a pagan temple, that weak-conscience Christian may be encouraged to do the same, thus going against his standards. Eating food in a pagan temple, though not wrong in itself, Paul argued, should therefore be avoided in order not to damage another's testimony and thus sin against Christ.

This passage demonstrates that one's conscience is weak because of a deficient knowledge of spiritual truth (1 Cor. 8:7a). The answer to a weak conscience, then, is a greater knowledge of God's Word. The inability "to distinguish clearly between things lawful for a Christian and things unlawful"[37] can be overcome as one becomes more knowledgeable of God's ways.

The situation discussed in 1 Corinthians 10 also pertains to the question of eating meat that has been offered to idols. If a Christian is invited to have dinner with an unbeliever, the Christian should ask no questions about what is served. But if someone (apparently someone with a conscience oversensitive about such matters) explains to the Christian that it has been offered to idols, the Christian should refrain from eating it out of consideration for the person with the weak conscience (10:28–29). Though it may seem strange to have one's actions determined by the conscience of another (10:29), this is desirable because such action, borne out of concern for the other person, brings glory to God.

The principles given in 1 Corinthians 8 and 10 could be summarized as follows: (1) Do not have an overscrupulous conscience. (2) But on the other hand, be careful not to offend someone whose conscience is overscrupulous. To refer to the speed monitor again, an automobile driver need not set the monitor below the lawful speed limit. But if some driver does set it below the limit (at say, 20, in a 30-mile speed zone), his companions in the car should not insist that he drive 30, because that would force him to go beyond his set limit and thus would disturb his conscience.

A weak conscience may easily degenerate into one that is defiled (1 Cor. 8:7). "If we persist in some action against which conscience has witnessed, we thereby defile it and thus prevent its faithful functioning. When a watch stops, it is not the fault of the watch but of the dust which has clogged its delicate mechanism. So with conscience, especially in the realm of purity."[38] According to Titus 1:15 morally defiled unbelievers have minds and consciences that are defiled (μιαίνω). In other words they are so involved in sin that their consciences are unreliable. The more one sins, the more he becomes comfortable in his sins (cf. Ps. 1:1). By lowering standards, he is less sensitive to and feels less remorse about previously accepted standards. As a poor judge, his conscience renders unreliable judgments and does not adequately prompt him toward morally correct actions. Such a person possesses an evil (πονηρά) conscience (Heb. 10:22), in need of the spiritual cleansing of regeneration.

It is possible for a person to defy the voice of his conscience habitually until it is reduced to insensibility. Paul described this condition as "seared . . . as with a branding iron" (καυτηριάζω, 1 Tim. 4:2), that is, made insensitive like the skin of an animal cauterized by a branding iron. An automobile driver may refuse to listen to his speed monitor even when it is buzzing. It is possible for one's ears to become so accustomed to a continuous sound that he no longer consciously hears it. A person who continually refuses to heed the warnings sounded by his conscience will find that it becomes dulled and insensitive to his previously accepted standards.[39]

The Exercise of the Conscience

To have a clean conscience with no offense to God or man (Acts 24:16), a Christian should do five things. (1) Make a deliberate effort to avoid sinning. Paul stated that he exercised himself to have a clear conscience (Acts 24:16). Disciplining himself he strived deliberately and continually to avoid known sin. (2) Know God's standards. As the Word of Christ dwells in a believer richly in all wisdom (Col. 3:16), his oversensitive conscience becomes more fully aligned with God's standards and is thereby strengthened.[40] (3) Let one's conscience be ruled by the Holy Spirit and not by human self-will. If a Christian desires to please the Lord and thus have a good conscience, he will seek to be led by the Holy Spirit and not his own desires.[41] (4) Avoid offending an overscrupulous believer in the name of spiritual liberty. (5) Confess sin. This is essential for spiritual joy and fellowship with the Lord, and therefore it is essential for a removal of remorse caused by the sin.

Only by following these five steps can a Christian testify, "I have lived in all good conscience before God" (Acts 23:1).

CHAPTER 8

Untold Billions:
Are They Really Lost?

J. Ronald Blue

Planet earth now strains under the weight of more than five billion people. Like some dusty tennis ball, the globe wobbles its way through space in an erratic but carefully designed course around God's unrivaled source of energy, the sun. With each spin some of earth's people die and others are born. The net increase each day is about 200,000. Every morning there are 200,000 more mouths to feed![1]

In the year 2000 the world must make room for an additional two billion people and, within the lifetime of many reading this article, the globe will be packed with what demographers are now calling the world's *projected ultimate population size*—close to 10 billion people![2]

It is hard to grasp the magnitude of the word "billion." Government budgets and world bank transfers have made billions seem like so many buttons lined up behind a lone needle. It is easy for a meticulous accountant to record the figures "1,000,000,000" in the neat columns of some ledger. Easier yet is it for a congressman to add a few billion to an already fat "pork barrel" project.

A billion takes on more realistic value when it is divorced from the shifting value of dollars and is applied to the more constant measure of time. One billion days ago the earth may not yet have been created. One billion hours ago Genesis had not yet been written. One billion minutes ago Christ was still on earth. One billion seconds ago the first atomic bomb had not yet exploded. Yet, one billion dollars ago, in terms of governmental spending, was yesterday!

Neither dollars nor days can adequately measure the significance of the growing billions of people who comprise the global village. It is imperative that Christians visualize the multiplied billions as

71

individual people. It is not a matter of billions but of beings. The calculations and statistics must be interpreted with a concern for souls. Every life is of eternal worth. The billions must be portrayed in terms of individual spiritual needs on a stage as broad as the earth and in a time span as long as eternity.

A Challenge

Of the more than five billion beings presently residing on planet earth, about one-third are nominally Christian, one-third are unresponsive to Christ, and the remaining third have not even heard the name of Christ.[3]

The one-third "nominally Christian" are of course Christian in name only. The number of true Christians in the New Testament sense is probably a minimal part of that total.[4] The Lord alone maintains access to the exclusive record of true Christian: the Lamb's book of life. The estimates of genuine born-again believers may be more accurately portrayed in the unique guide to intercession entitled *Operation World*. Johnstone indicates that the ratio of true Christians to the total population of the middle East stands at 1 in 3,600, Communist Asia at 1 in 1,000, and Roman Catholic Europe at 1 in 900.[5] Much of God's earthly real estate is all too sparsely populated with those who can be rightfully called Christians.

Of an even greater challenge, however, is the vast expanse where there is *no* viable Christian witness. Attention must be given to that one-third of the world's population who have not heard of Christ. McGavran numbers these unevangelized at two billion.[6] Winter indicates that they include as many as two and one-half billion.[7] Whatever their number, these people are not only unreached but are living where there is no Christian contact. They are sometimes called "hidden places."[8] Just as one side of the globe is always turned from the sun's rays, so one half of the world's peoples remains in spiritual darkness. Masses are hidden from God's light of the gospel.

The challenge to the church is immense. The chorus still sung in some missions conferences, "untold millions are still untold," is out of date. There are now untold *billions*, with thousands added every day, who will never hear of Jesus Christ unless someone crosses the cultural and linguistic barriers and penetrates that dark half of the globe with the good news. It is estimated that there are between 25,000 and 30,000 "people groups" in the world[9] of which about 3,000 "unreached peoples" are identified and cataloged.[10] Some 10,000 languages and dialects are said to exist in the world[11] of which only 1,500 have even a part of the Word of God.[12]

As impressive as it may seem, the present number of missionaries is not adequate. Winter states that only five percent of the total missionary force is involved in cross-cultural evangelistic activity in the three major blocs of unreached peoples—the Chinese, Hindus, and Muslims. Ninety-five percent of all missionaries work among peoples who have already heard the gospel.[13] Unless present missionaries are redeployed and new missionaries are directed to the unreached, the dark side of the globe will not only continue in darkness but will continue to multiply in that darkness.

Interestingly enough, one of the reasons for the rather restrained response to the overwhelming need to evangelize to these neglected masses lies in a basic theological issue: Are these people who have not heard of Christ really lost?

A Controversy

In the midst of the challenge for world evangelization, the church is faced with an unending controversy over the spiritual state of those billions who have never heard of Christ.

It is not only the university intellectual who asks the burning question, Are the heathen lost? Well-meaning Christians face the question with sincere interest. This is as it should be. Those who have received new life in Christ are the ones who should care most about the state of the unevangelized.

Are the unevangelized billions really on their way to a place so fearfully described in the Bible as *hell*? It is awesome enough to ask the question; to answer affirmatively is considered by some people as an affront to the loving nature of God.

There is disagreement on the state of the unevangelized even among those who appear vitally interested in missions. At one of the Urbana conferences, out of 5,000 replies to over 8,000 questionnaires distributed, only 37 percent believed that "a person who doesn't hear the gospel is eternally lost." Only 42 percent believed that "unbelievers will be punished in a literal hell of fire," and 25 percent believed that "man will be saved or lost on the basis of how well he followed what he *did* know."[14]

A Complexity

Though it may appear to be a rather peripheral question designed for heated debates among theologians or stimulating discussions in college dorm rooms, the fate of the unevangelized is of utmost importance. Inherent in the seemingly simple question, "Are the heathen lost?" are several basic and exceedingly critical questions:

The character of God is questioned: "Is God just?" This is a challenge to theology proper.

The sufficiency of Christ is questioned: "Is Christ the only way?" This is a challenge to Christology.

The necessity of the Cross is questioned: "Did Christ have to die?" This is a challenge to soteriology.

The depravity of man is questioned: "Is man inherently sinful?" This is a challenge to biblical anthropology.

The judgment of sin is questioned: "Is not evil relative?" This is a challenge to hamartiology.

The role of the church is questioned: "Is the church God's unique witness?" This is a challenge to ecclesiology.

The culmination of history is questioned: "Is there a future reckoning?" This is a challenge to eschatology.

The seemingly innocent question strikes at the very foundations of theology.

A Confusion

Are the heathen lost? The diverse reactions to this question are an indication of its importance. Some react strongly to the mere suggestion that those who have never heard might be eternally lost. They contend that all religions are basically the same. One theologian argues that "Christ came not to destroy but to fulfill the strivings of mankind everywhere throughout the ages. . . ." He concludes, "To discover the reality of Christ in all the religions of the world is the essence of the ecumenical approach."[15] Christianity becomes simply another ingredient in a universal religious succotash. "God does not condemn anybody," writes Pannikan, "God is at work in the 'pagan' religions. . . ."[16]

While it is true that the religions of the world may embody man's thoughts about God, Christianity is founded on God's revelation to man. Reason must give way to revelation; religious ritual to a righteous relationship. Biblical Christianity is centered on the God who in times past spoke "by the prophets" and in these last days has spoken "by his Son" (Heb. 1:1–2, KJV). To consider Christianity as but one more commodity on the world-religion market is to deny biblical authority and God's clear revelation.

Certain scholars attempt a more orthodox position with appeals to Scripture to avoid the fate of the unevangelized billions. They suggest some kind of second chance after death citing 1 Peter 3:19–20, Christ's "proclamation to the spirits . . . who were once disobedient." Pinnock contends that this "second chance" is more accurately a first chance at death. He sees the exegetical possibility of Christ's proclamation to the spirits now in prison as "the occasion when the unevangelized have an opportunity to make a decision about Jesus Christ."[17] However, this "exegetical possibility" is both inconsistent with the whole tenor of Scripture and with the immediate context. First Peter 3:19 simply states that Christ, by the Spirit, spoke through the prophet Noah to the ungodly prior to the Flood, whose spirits are now locked in the prison of eternal separation from God. (Compare 1 Peter 3:20 with 1 Peter 1:11 and Genesis 6:3). There is no hint of a chance for salvation after death. "It is appointed for men to die once and after this comes" not a chance for salvation, but "judgment" (Heb. 9:27).

A third position taken to skirt the reality of the finality of death for the unevangelized of the world is centered in the apparent sincerity of the so-called heathen. "They will be judged according to the light which they have received," they say. Espousing this view, Salmond states, "We need nothing beyond Paul's broad statement that those who have the law shall be judged by law, and that those who are without law shall be judged without law."[18] However, the verse Salmond quotes, Romans 2:12, actually teaches that those who have sinned without the law will *perish* just as surely as those who have sinned with the law. The verb ἀπόλλυμι is not "be judged" but "perish," "be destroyed," or "be lost." The argument of the passage is not to excuse men but to show that they have no excuse. They will all perish before God's righteous and impartial judgment. The focus is on the verdict of destruction regardless of the revelation given.

Although Kane takes the position that the heathen are indeed lost, he hints at some benevolent conclusions. "The heathen on the other hand will have a much easier time. But he will not go scot-free. He had the light of creation, providence, and conscience and will be judged by that light. If he is finally condemned it will . . . be . . . because he failed to live up to the light he had."[19]

Pinnock combines his erroneous arguments from Romans 2 and 1 Peter 3 discussed above to conclude, "Of one thing we can be certain: God will not abandon in hell those who have not known and therefore have not declined His offer of grace. Though He has not told us the nature of His arrangements, we cannot doubt the existence and goodness of them."[20]

As comfortable as Pinnock's conclusion may appear, it is dead wrong on two counts. First, Scripture confirms that God indeed *does* abandon or give up those who, not knowing of Christ's redemption, have suppressed divine truth; and second, God *has* revealed the nature of His arrangements in Scripture.

A Resolution

The only valid resolution to the seeming dilemma over the state of the unevangelized is to be found in God's Word. All other solutions are mere conjecture. Man's attempt to bridge the gap between a holy God and a depraved human race is a part of that continuing conjecture. The average unbeliever makes God a little less "hard and judgmental" and thereby a little less righteous than He really is. These futile attempts to bring God down or to lift man up are shattered by Scripture.

Paul made it clear in the opening section of his letter to the Romans that all men are by nature sinners and *all* stand under God's just retribution. Already under condemnation, no one has any rights before an almighty God. This is not some new truth. Paul quoted the Old Testament to show that "there is none righteous, not even one . . . there is none who seeks for God" (Rom. 3:10–11). From Adam condemnation has come on all men (5:18). The question of the lostness of mankind is not so much a question of God's sovereign justice as it is man's sinful nature.

Nonetheless the just judgment of God on the unevangelized is not irrational. God can be shown fair, even by the standards of reason. To say that God sends people to hell because they have not trusted a Person of whom they have never heard seems unjust. Regardless of the divine standard, by human standards such action would be declared unfair. In developing his argument in his letter to the Romans Paul made it clear that God neither sends people to hell, nor does He judge them on the basis of their response to Christ of whom they have not heard.

JUDGMENT BASED ON GOD'S REVELATION

The judgment of God in relation to the untold billions of the world is based not on their response to unrevealed truth but to revelation they *have* received. Though the righteousness of God is only revealed to those who believe in the gospel of Jesus Christ (Rom. 1:16–17), God's wrath is revealed against all unrighteousness of those who suppress the truth they have both received and understood. In other words, if a person in this present age has not been drawn by God's grace and mercy to salvation through faith in Christ's atonement, he faces God's wrath. That might seem harsh and unfair were it not for Paul's clear explanation.

Man is not said to face God's wrath because he has failed to accept a gospel he never heard, or because he failed to put his faith in a Savior he has not known. God's wrath is on "all ungodliness and unrighteousness" (Rom. 1:18). Some confusion has existed because of the faulty translation of this verse in the King James Version. The verb κατέχω is not merely "to hold" the truth but "to hold down" the truth, or as Lenski puts it, "to suppress the truth, to prevent the truth from exerting its power in the heart and the life."[21] Calvin writes, "to hold down the truth is to suppress or obscure it."[22] Chalmers identifies those who face God's wrath as individuals "who stifle the truth."[23]

Paul continued his argument by giving just cause for God's wrath. He showed that God's revelation has been both penetrating and persistent. He explained that the truth of God has been revealed to everyone in two ways.

First, the truth or "reality" (ἀλήθεια) of God is an integral part of every person's *conscience* (Rom. 1:19). Those who have never heard of Christ nonetheless know of God. That knowledge, by the way, is not as superficial as some would make it. Paul used the second aorist active participle of γινώσκω, "to know by personal experience."

Not only do they know of God, but also they instinctively know of His law. God's law is written in their hearts, "their conscience bearing witness, and their thoughts alternately accusing or else defending them" (Rom. 2:15). DeHaan writes, "Even though the light of conscience has been dimmed because of deliberate wickedness, it still exists everywhere."[24]

Second, the truth of God's eternal power and divine nature has been clearly seen and has been understood through *creation*. One Greek article combines δύναμις with θειότης (Rom. 1:20). There is no eternal power apart from divinity and no divine nature apart from supernatural power. God's nature and power are together clearly revealed in nature. The Maker is known through what has been made. Barnhouse explains, "No man can truly ask, 'Who is God?' 'What is God?' 'Where is God?' 'What does God want?' The creation 'round about us is witness that there is a supreme Being."[25]

Paul concluded that everyone is without excuse. The truth of God is revealed to all through conscience and creation. In unrighteousness people everywhere suppress that revealed truth. Consequently they are held inexcusable (Rom. 1:20). The Greek εἰς τό with the infinitive, an expression of purpose, came to signify *result*. Here it is not "that they *may be* without excuse" but "so that they *are* without excuse." As Archer explains, "There is sufficient knowledge for each person after the fall to be criminally liable for sin."[26]

The issue therefore is not that the unevangelized have not put their trust in a Person of whom they have never heard, but that they have suppressed the truth they have both received and understood.

Paul then continued with an explanation of what the unsaved person does with God's revelation. In fact the apostle did more than merely explain. He gave the reason for God's wrath and man's inexcusable state. In Romans 1:21 Paul did not use γαρ ("for"), but διότι ("because"). The cause is clear. Even though people knew God (γνόντες τόν θεὸν, a concessive aorist participle), they did not honor Him as God or give thanks.

Individuals start their descent down a sin-slick staircase to destruction. The first two of the seven steps downward are convicting. They might be labeled "no praise" and "no thanks." To move down those two steps requires little effort. In fact it requires *no* effort. The person who does nothing is not standing still; he is sliding from God. Even the Christian needs to be reminded that the day he fails to honor God and fails to thank God, he may well be in a tailspin.

Failure to honor or thank God brings futile, empty speculations and foolish, darkened sensitivities. The mind puffs up while the heart shrinks (Rom. 1:21).

Professing to be wise, they become fools (Rom. 1:22). Pride

becomes the precipice from which the sinner falls into perdition. Fully confident of his own capabilities, like some puffed-up toad, the individual jumps to his destruction. The basement of the sordid seven-step descent is where the sinner performs his most rebellious act. He exchanges the glory of an incorruptible God for an image shaped after his own corruptible frame, some flitting bird, a four-footed beast, or some creepy crawler. The sovereign wonder of God is depicted as some slimy worm (Rom. 1:23). The lowest form of idolatry is depicted. Not only creature worship (ὁμοιώμα   εἰκών) but image worship (ὁμοιώματι εἰκόνος) is employed.

Interestingly some point to the idolatrous condition of the heathen as evidence of their search for a way to God. Idolatry is viewed as piety and reverence yet to be perfected. Nothing could be further from the truth. These are not gropings for God. They are evidence of rebellion against God. "The idolatrous systems of the world," says Watts, "are actually states of man's departure from God and expression of his desire for other gods rather than the true, living God."[27]

To understand better the severity with which God views idolatrous worship, one need only review the Old Testament denunciations of the evil practice. Idolatry is hardly a search for God. Forsaking God who made him, the idolater sacrifices to demons, not God (Deut. 32:17). Israel's adoption of idolatrous Canaanite practices is considered a snare and a pollution, and is roundly condemned by God (Ps. 106:26–39).

Paul's point is clear. The apparently innocent heathen are far from innocent. They have received a clear revelation from God through conscience and creation. The revelation inwardly experienced, outwardly witnessed, and clearly understood has been repressed. That repression is evidenced in the degradation of the sinner's thoughts, emotions, and actions. No matter how isolated a person may be from the revelation of God's righteousness in the gospel of Jesus Christ, that one is entirely without excuse. The wrath of God is on him because of his ungodliness and unrighteousness, not because of his lack of faith in Christ.

DESTRUCTION RESULTING FROM MAN'S REBELLION

God might be charged with injustice were He to send people to hell on the basis of their failure to respond to revelation they have never received. It has been shown that the basis of His judgment is not on unrevealed truth but on the clear revelation received and rejected by those who are condemned. McQuilkin expressed it well: "They are not condemned for rejecting a Savior of whom they have never heard. They are condemned for sinning against the light they have."[28]

Paul's argument in Romans not only outlines the basis of God's judgment but also shows that God does not *send* people to destruction. He simply *lets them go* on that self-designated course.

Like some terrible refrain, the desperate sentence is thrice repeated. "God gave them over" (παρέδωκεν αὐτοὺς ὁ θεος). There is a stress on the constative aorist verb, God *did* give them up. God's action is judicial. Since these who have suppressed the truth are determined on self-destruction, justice decrees that it be so. It is as if God responded, "Let them go!"

It is probably best not to view three stages in the giving over or abandonment by God. Robertson is undoubtedly correct in seeing "a repetition of the same withdrawal."[29] These are not three phases but three aspects of God's release of the ungodly to their own devastating destiny.

It is not within the scope of this article to deal with the details recorded in man's self-designed destruction. However, it is important to note the extent of God's threefold release. God gave them over to sexual impurity (Rom. 1:24–25), to degrading passions (vv. 26–27), and to a depraved mind (vv. 28–32). The destruction is all-inclusive. In direct contrast to God's great commandment, "You shall love the Lord your God with all your *heart*, and with all your *soul*, and with all your *mind*" (Matt. 22:37), mankind is left with a darkened *heart*, degraded *soul*, and depraved *mind*.

One of the most sordid lists in all Scripture follows like a whole lineup of devastating character witnesses against the accused (Rom. 1:29–31). Paul concluded this section of his argument by reminding the reader that though they know the ordinance of God, these who are abandoned to destruction and a death well deserved not only participate in all the ungodly atrocities listed, but also give hearty approval to that sordid behavior (Rom. 1:32). These are not innocent acts of the misinformed. Their action is willful. God's judgment is certainly as warranted as it is sure. He does not send people to hell; He lets them go. The judgment of course is for God to make, not other people, no matter how righteous they may seem (Rom. 2:1–3).

Nonetheless it is abundantly evident that God *has* judged the unevangelized billions of the world. His judgment is just. It is based on revelation clearly received and willfully refused by the defendant. His sentence is fair. It is a release by God for man to pursue his own destruction and eternal death. The world's untold billions are lost!

Contrary to the restricted views that Paul was simply describing "the moral condition of the pagan world when he wrote" the letter to the Romans,[30] or that "Paul presents in Romans 1:18–32 a theological interpretation of the religious history of the nations as it took place after the dispersion of the people from Babylon as recorded in Genesis 11:1–9,"[31] the extent of Paul's arguments are clearly of a broader scope. He is speaking of mankind universally. The word "Gentiles" or "nations" (ἔθνοι) does not occur. The force of Paul's presentation is that "all the world may become accountable to God" (Rom. 3:19). Furthermore his remarks are not limited to a historical account. The truth of Romans spans the entire age. The stark contrast between man's sin and God's salvation are as pertinent today as the day the letter was penned.

The conclusion is clear. The untold billions are lost. They are desperately lost! There is no way for well-meaning Christians or conscientious unbelievers to bridge the gap between a righteous God and a reprobate mankind. Only the God-Man, Jesus Christ, can reach across the gulf between a perfect God and a perverse human race. If the unevangelized billions are truly lost, one burning question remains. How will they hear the unique message of hope? Human agents must be mobilized by the Lord to cross the frontiers that stand as barriers to gospel penetration. God has so willed it. As Kane points out, "There is not a single line in the Book of Acts to suggest that God can save a human being without employing a human agent. On the contrary there are several examples of God's going to great lengths to secure the active cooperation of one or another of His servants."[32]

Even when an unevangelized heathen shows an initial response in line with the revelation afforded him, as in the case of Cornelius in Acts 10, the Lord employed one of His servants to bring the fuller revelation of Jesus Christ necessary for salvation. Packer summed it up well: "We must never forget that it is God who saves. It is God who brings men and women under the sound of the gospel, and it is God who brings them to faith in Christ. . . ."[33] It may also be stressed that it is God who imparts His vision to His servants of a desperate, dying world and in His grace involves those servants in the exciting enterprise of carrying the message of eternal life in Christ to that world.

Will the untold billions remain untold? A world in crisis needs the Word of Christ. Responsive and responsible agents are needed to serve as ambassadors of the King in that exciting enterprise called world missions—an enterprise dedicated to the untold billions!

CHAPTER 9

The Impeccability of Jesus Christ

Joseph G. Sahl

C ould Jesus Christ sin? Was it possible that He could have succumbed to the temptations He faced in the world and at the instigation of Satan? All evangelical scholars affirm that Christ did not sin. But the question is whether He *could* have sinned. The problem centers on the question of Christ's susceptibility to sin. Theologically the question is whether the Savior is *posse non peccare* (able not to sin) or *non posse peccare* (not able to sin). In other words, is it only that the Lord Jesus was able to overcome sin and temptation or rather that He *could* not be overcome by them? Peccability refers to Christ's being liable to or prone to sin, and impeccability speaks of His not being liable to sin and being incapable of sinning.

The Significance of the Problem

Is such a discussion purely an academic exercise with no genuine significance? After all, the Lord Jesus Christ did not sin and in fact He remained sinless, so what is the difference whether He was *posse non peccare* or *non posse peccare*? Actually the problem makes a big difference. Besides a proper understanding of the person of Christ and the character of God Himself, several other doctrines are involved.

First, since the Lord Jesus Christ is the same yesterday, today, and forever (Heb. 13:8), whatever attributes were true of Him during His earthly existence also must be true in His preincarnate state, as well as in His present state of glory. Therefore any possibility that He could sin has ramifications for the eternal character of God.

Second, the virgin birth, the Incarnation, and the hypostatic union, are all influenced by one's understanding of the question concerning the impeccability of Jesus Christ. Christ, the God-Man, had a divine nature and human nature that were inseparably linked without confusion. This union demonstrated the humanity of the God-Man prepared by the Holy Spirit (Luke 1:35; Heb. 10:5). If Christ could sin, then Deity was capable of sinning.

Third, this doctrine has ramifications for angelology. The Scriptures affirm the existence of a personal being known as Satan, who is the primary instigator and sole originator of evil within the universe. Yet, if the Lord Jesus Christ is not impeccable, one can begin to question the temptation accounts of the Lord in the wilderness. If it is possible that He could sin or be overcome by temptation, what assurance does one have that these temptations were not just self-induced lustful thoughts within His human intellect and were not attacks by Satan?

Fourth, the question of the impeccability of Jesus Christ also has implications for biblical inerrancy and integrity. Without a doubt, at times within His earthly life the Lord Jesus spoke from within the limits of His unfallen humanity. For example, He declared His thirst (John 19:28) or His lack of information on the exact time of His return (Matt. 24:36). If it is possible that the Lord Jesus Christ could succumb to or be deceived by sin, then one must also conclude that it is possible for Him to have given inaccurate information about eternal things when He was growing in wisdom and stature and favor with God and man (Luke 2:52). Yet in actuality the Scriptures paint a much loftier concept of the only begotten Son of God. As the God-Man, He is said to be incapable of sinning even though He faced the extremes of temptation during His earthly life. Therefore this present discussion will seek to set forth the biblical position of the Lord's *non posse peccare* while at the same time seeking to refute the *posse non peccare* position.

Arguments for Christ's Peccability

Three arguments are given in support of the peccability of Jesus Christ. (1) Since Christ's temptations were genuine, He had to be peccable. (2) Since Christ was truly human, He had to be peccable. (3) Since Christ as the second Adam corresponds to the first Adam, He had to be peccable.

THE TEMPTATION OF CHRIST

The Scriptures make it clear the Savior was indeed tempted. "Then Jesus was led up by the Spirit into the wilderness to be tempted by the devil" (Matt. 4:1). "For we do not have a high priest who cannot sympathize with our weaknesses, but one who has been tempted in all things as we are, yet was without sin" (Heb. 4:15). Therefore since the Scriptures affirm the reality of His temptations, some conclude that for the temptations to be genuine He must have been capable of sinning. If a person has no susceptibility to sin or if sin has no appeal for him, the temptation is a farce.

Several answers may be given to this argument. First, the Greek word "to tempt" does not mean to induce to evil. The word πειράζω means "to try, make a trial of, put to the test."[1] According to Homer, the basic idea is "to make proof of."[2] Thus the word came "to signify the trying intentionally . . . with the purpose of discovering what of good or evil, of power or weakness, was in a person or thing (Matt. 16:1; 19:3; 22:18; 1 Kings 10:1); or, where this was already known to the trier, revealing the same to the tried themselves. . . ."[3] Temptation, rather than inducement to evil, is a problematic experience God uses to manifest a person's true condition and character. That is why Job could declare in the midst of his temptation, "But He knows the way I take; when He has tried me, I shall come forth as gold" (Job 23:10). Surely the Savior was "proven, assayed, tested" in all the circumstances and ways in which man is tested, and He was shown to be impeccable.

Second, temptation to sin does not necessitate susceptibility to sin. As Walvoord stated,

> It is possible for a rowboat to attack a battleship, even though it is conceivably impossible for the row-boat to conquer the battleship. The idea that temptability implies susceptibility is unsound. While the temptation may be real, there may be infinite power to resist that temptation; and if that power is infinite, the person is impeccable.[4]

Certainly the temptations of Jesus Christ were real and strenuous. While His temptations were similar to those of ordinary human beings, they were infinitely greater in magnitude. When an object is tested to determine its strength or character, the testing ends once the point of breaking is reached. Jesus would have endured testing beyond what frail, weak men and women can even comprehend.

Third, temptability does not rule out one's ability to sympathize with others. Could Jesus associate with man's weaknesses if He had no possibility of succumbing to His temptations? Hodge, believing that Christ could sin, says no. "If from the constitution of His Person it was impossible for Christ to sin, then His temptation was unreal and without effect, and He cannot sympathize with His people."[5] However, the ability to sympathize is unrelated to susceptibility to sin. A person not involved in some sin can give help and compassion to another person in that sin. In fact he can do so more capably than someone who has been enticed by it. If one is drawn into sin, he is less able than others to comfort and help. Thus Christ is the only One who can most adequately and completely aid and console believers when they face attacks by Satan.

Must Christ, in order to sympathize with mankind, be inwardly polluted by sin? Certainly not, because the Scriptures affirm both His sympathizing ability (Heb. 4:15), and His total absence of any taint of sin. Though He was a man, He was not a sinner (Rom. 8:3). He was "without sin" (Heb. 4:15), He "knew no sin" (2 Cor. 5:21), and "in Him there is no darkness" (1 John 1:5). Man "is tempted when he is carried away and enticed by his own lust" (James 1:14), but such was not true of Christ. To suggest that Christ had to have an inward struggle with the lustful desires that reside within sinful humanity is totally foreign to the Scriptures.

THE HUMANITY OF CHRIST

Those who believe Christ was capable of sinning seek to support their view from His humanity. Hodge states, "This sinlessness of our Lord, however, does not amount to absolute impeccability. It was not a *non potest peccare*. If He was a true man He must have been capable of sinning."[6] In responding to this argument, one must first be careful to establish and maintain the biblical teaching concerning the humanity of Jesus Christ. The Scriptures do provide abundant testimony that He was genuinely human and was thereby subject to the sinless limitations that are associated with true humanity. He grew (Luke 2:52), hungered (Matt. 4:2), slept (Matt. 8:24–25), was tired (John 4:6), thirsted (John 19:28), had flesh and bones (Luke 24:39), and died (1 Cor. 15:20).

However, one must remember that the Scriptures also affirm His deity. In the Incarnation the eternal Son of God was inseparably united to an unfallen human nature. Thus He is unique from all other men not only in that He was kept from the consequences of Adam's sin in His perfect humanity but also in that He was the God-Man. In this way one Person, the Lord Jesus Christ, possessed a divine nature as well as a human nature. Though the divine nature of Christ had eternal existence apart from the humanity of Jesus Christ (Heb. 10:5), that was not true of His human nature. His humanity exists only in union with His deity. Thus the personality expressed in the humanity of Jesus Christ was nothing less than that personality of God the Son, the Eternal Word who became flesh. As Dabney states, "It is the unanimous testimony of the Apostles, as it is the creed of the church, that the human nature never had its separate personality. It never existed, and never will exist for an instant, save in personal union with the Word."[7] When Philip asked to see God the Father, Christ replied, "Have I been so long with you, and yet you have not come to know Me, Philip? He who has seen Me has seen the Father; how do you say, 'Show us the Father'?" (John 14:9). Christ thereby affirmed that the divine personality of the Eternal Son which was flowing through His perfect humanity was beheld by the disciples.

The foundation of Christ's person was His divine nature, not His human nature. He was the God-Man and not the Man-God.

> It is the divine nature, and not the human which is the basis of Christ's person. The second trinitarian person is the root and stock into which the human nature is grafted. The wild olive is grafted into the good olive, and partakes of its root and fullness. The Eternal Son, or the Word, is personal per se. He is from everlasting to everlasting conscious of Himself as distinct from the Father and from the Holy Spirit. He did not acquire personality by union with a human nature. The Incarnation was not necessary in order that the trinitarian Son of God might be self-conscious. On the contrary, the human nature which He assumed to Himself acquired personality by its union with Him. By becoming a constituent factor in the one theanthropic person of Christ, the previously impersonal human nature, "the seed of the woman" was personalized. If the Logos had obtained personality by uniting with a human nature, He must have previously been impersonal. The Incarnation would then have made an essential change in the Logos, and thereby in the Trinity God-head, even by so remarkable an act as the incarnation.[8]

Though Christ was of both human and divine desires, He had only one determinative will. That determinative will is in the eternal Logos and continuously follows the will of the Father. Therefore statements one may make about what the humanity of Christ could or could not do must always be tempered by this understanding of the theanthropic Person.

This understanding of the person of Jesus Christ is essential to evaluate adequately the argument that since Jesus Christ was human He had to be peccable. Succumbing to sin or susceptibility to sin is a reality for a person, but not for a nature. Dabney states, "Since the humanity never was, in fact, alone, the question whether, if alone, it would not have been peccable, like Adam, is idle. . . . It is impossible that the person constituted in union with the eternal and immutable Word can sin; for this is an absolute shield to the lower nature, against error."[9]

It is the person, the rational being, who sins against God. Man is a sinner, and therefore sins. The person, not just a nature within the person, is held accountable for sin. Thus one is wrong in suggesting that Christ could sin because He possessed a human nature. Instead one must ask what the Person of Jesus Christ can do. He possessed a genuine sinless human nature, and as a Person He was impeccable. To state anything else is to impugn the character of God. As Chafer stated, "Since this bond of union which unites Christ's two natures—for He is one Person—is so complete, the humanity of Christ could not sin. Should His humanity sin, God would sin."[10]

THE HEADSHIP OF CHRIST

A third argument used to support the peccability of Jesus Christ is His correspondence with Adam. Some argue that since Christ the second Adam corresponds to the first Adam, He had to be peccable.

The Scriptures do state that Jesus Christ has a correspondence to the first Adam. Yet that correspondence does not imply nor demand peccability. Adam was the head over all humanity, and Christ is the Head over redeemed humanity. Adam was created in holiness without the inward compulsion toward sin that now characterizes his progeny, and so Jesus Christ came in holiness without any taint of sin. Adam was given every natural faculty which constituted him human, as one reflecting the image of the true God; also Christ possessed every natural faculty of true humanity as one perfectly manifesting God Himself.

But those promoting Christ's peccability add that for Jesus Christ to be a true representative for mankind, He also had to be free to choose between good and evil. They say if He were impeccable, He would have no real choice and He would thereby no longer be a proper Substitute for men. Thus from this theological perspective it is implied that only through a mutable will is one able to be free in his choice or actions. Therefore, it is argued, Jesus Christ had to be peccable.

The error in such an argument involves more than an evaluation of Christ's impeccability. It also reveals a misunderstanding of true moral freedom and the operation of the human will.

Moral freedom is not based on opportunities to choose between good and evil or right and wrong. Rather, it is found in the ability to determine what is good and right without any coercion toward evil. In an ultimate sense, then, God alone is free. He alone has neither taint of sin within nor inward compulsion urging Him away from what is good. Obviously that is not so with the fallen human race. They are carried away by their own lusts (James 1:14), and because of sin within, they are unable to do the good they know they should perform (Rom. 7:18–20). If the Son sets a person free, he is free indeed (John 8:32). Thus moral freedom for the Savior does not necessitate peccability.

Those believing in Christ's peccability reason that if He were impeccable, He could not be a moral agent in the same sense as man, since His will was infallibly inclined to holiness. Yet is such an evaluation valid? Is it not also true that the freedom of man's volition is seen only in relationship to external pressures? The will cannot be free from an individual's basic constitution. All individuals exercise their wills in accord with their moral nature. Thus though their choices are free, they are still determined with certainty, based on their character. In the same way God Himself, while immutable, is a moral agent. It is the same with the Lord Jesus Christ. His moral actions were based on the uncoerced decisions of His will acting within the confines of His impeccable nature. This is also Dabney's conclusion.

> . . . a holy will may be perfectly free, and yet determined with absolute certainty to the right. Such is God's will, He cannot lie. Yet, He speaks truth freely. The sinner represents the counterpart case when his eyes are full of adultery, and he cannot cease from sin. Yet, is this sinner free in continuing his course of sin and rejecting the monitions of duty? This case sufficiently explains, by contrast, the impeccability of Jesus. He has every natural faculty which, in Adam's case, was abused to the perpetration of his first sin. But they were infallibly regulated by what Adam had not, a certain, yet most free, determination of His disposition to holiness alone.[11]

As God, Christ is certain to do only good, and yet He is a moral agent making uncoerced choices. He need not have the capacity to sin.

Arguments for Christ's Impeccability

HIS DEITY

The Scriptures, by affirming Christ's deity, also affirm His impeccability. As God Himself, it is not possible for Him to sin.

He cannot be tempted with evil (James 1:13). In fact sin itself is abhorrent to Him; He finds only holiness and righteousness His chief delight (Ps. 45:6–7; Heb. 1:1–3).

HIS UNIQUE PERSON

The uniqueness of the Person of Jesus Christ establishes His impeccability. He was the eternal Son who took to Himself a perfect human nature (Isa. 9:6; John 1:1–14; Heb. 1:1–6; 10:5; 1 John 1:1–3). This hypostatic union of the divine nature and the human nature welded them together in an inseparable bond within His one person without altering His essential essence. Thus the God-Man always expressed the determinative will of the eternal Word and thereby was impeccable.

HIS OMNIPOTENT DESIRE

The chief desire of the Lord Jesus Christ, with His omnipotent capability to perform that desire, assures His impeccability. His chief desire was to do the will of the Father. "Then I said, 'Behold, I have come (in the roll of the book it is written of Me) to do Thy will, O God'" (Heb. 10:7). The psalm, from which this quotation was taken, emphasizes that the Savior not only was determined to do the Father's will but also delighted to do it. "I delight to do Thy will, O my God; Thy Law is within my heart" (Ps. 40:8).

Thus Jesus declared that He always does the Father's will. For example, "My food is to do the will of Him who sent Me, and to accomplish His work" (John 4:34). The desires, delights, and motivations of the Lord Jesus Christ would also have a determinative power over His will, as is true with any moral creature. In His case, since His motivation and delight were eternal, He would be impeccable. He had no inner desire for or compulsion toward sin.

HIS SUBMISSION TO THE DIVINE WILL

God's eternal plan assures the impeccability of the Savior. The Father's will for the Son was His sacrificial death to secure the eternal salvation of His elect. He experienced sorrow and suffering but not sin (Isa. 53:2–3). As Shedd states, "The Logos could consent to suffering in a human nature, but not to sin in a human nature. The God-Man was commissioned to suffer (John 10:18) but was not commissioned to sin."[12] In contrast to sinful and helpless humanity, the Savior must be sinless and mighty to save in order to keep His people from stumbling and to present them before the throne of His glory without any spot or taint of sin (Jude 24). Thus the eternal plan of God assures that Christ must be impeccable.

HIS PERSONAL DECLARATION

Christ Himself declared that He was unable to sin. When He healed the paralyzed man, He demonstrated His ability to do what only God can do, namely, forgive sins (Mark 2:1–12). While addressing the nation at the Feast of Tabernacles, He asserted His righteousness: "He who speaks from himself seeks his own glory; but He who is seeking the glory of the one who sent Him, He is true, and there is no unrighteousness in Him" (John 7:18). As He was debating with the religious leaders, He affirmed His righteous character and also His distinction from sinful man. He said, "He who sent Me is with Me; He has not left Me alone, for I always do the things that are pleasing to Him" (John 8:29). "If I say that I do not know Him, I shall be a liar like you, but I do know Him, and keep His word" (John 8:55). Then, when speaking to Thomas concerning eternal life, He said, "I am the way, and the truth, and the life; no one comes to the Father, but through Me" (John 14:6). He was a witness to truth, and also Truth itself. Yes, He is none other than the infallible, inerrant, invincible Truth of God, which cannot be broken nor rendered void. He is the impeccable Savior who saves His people from their sins.

Conclusion

Could Jesus Christ have sinned? When a child of God is asked that question, he can take comfort in the fact that the Scriptures declare that the God-Man is the impeccable Savior. Because He as God was incapable of sinning, He is able to save completely all who come to God through Him (Heb. 7:25). When on earth, He was the same as He was in eternity past—the sinless, eternal Son of God. Therefore He is able to keep those who trust Him. As the Lamb of God, He is worthy to receive all praise, honor, glory, and power (Rev. 5:13)!

CHAPTER 10

For Whom Did Christ Die?

Lewis Sperry Chafer

For many centuries the question, For whom did Christ die? has divided and still divides some of the most orthodox and scholarly theologians. On the one hand those who according to theological usage are known as "limited redemptionists" contend that Christ died only for that elect company who were predetermined of God to be saved; and on the other hand those who are known as "unlimited redemptionists" contend that Christ died for all men. The issue is well defined, and men of sincere loyalty to the Word of God and who possess true scholarship are found on both sides of the controversy.

It is true that the doctrine of a limited redemption is one of the five points of Calvinism, but not all who are rightfully classified as Calvinists accept this one feature of that system. It is equally true that all Arminians are unlimited redemptionists, but to hold the doctrine of unlimited redemption does not necessarily make one an Arminian. There is nothing incongruous in the fact that many unlimited redemptionists believe, in harmony with all Calvinists, in the unalterable and eternal decree of God whereby all things were determined after His own will, and in the sovereign election of some to be saved (but not all), and in the divine predestination of those who are saved to the heavenly glory prepared for them. Without the slightest inconsistency the unlimited redemptionists may believe in an election according to sovereign grace that none but the elect will be saved, that *all* the elect will be saved, and that the elect are by divine enablement alone called out of the state of spiritual death from which they are impotent to take even one step in the direction of their own salvation. The text, "No man can come to me, except the Father which hath sent me draw him" (John 6:44), is as much a part of the one system of doctrine as it is of the other.

It is not easy to disagree with good and great men. However, as they appear on each side of this question, it is impossible to entertain a conviction and not oppose those who are of a contrary mind. The disagreement now under discussion is not between orthodox and heterodox men; it is within the fellowship of those who have most in common and who need the support and encouragement of each other's confidence. Few themes have drawn out more sincere and scholarly investigation.

Three Doctrinal Words

Though common to theological usage, the terms *limited redemption* and *unlimited redemption* are inadequate to express the whole of the problem which is under consideration. Three major aspects of truth are set forth in New Testament doctrine relative to the unmeasured benefits provided for the *unsaved* through the death of Christ, and redemption is but one of the three. Each of these aspects of truth is in turn expressed by one word, surrounded as each word is by a group of derivatives or synonyms of that word. These three words are ἀπολύτρωσις, translated "redemption," καταλλαγή, translated "reconciliation," and ἱλασμός, translated "propitiation." The riches of divine grace which these three words represent transcend all human thought or language: but these truths must be declared in human terms if declared at all. As it is necessary to have four Gospels, since it is impossible for one, two, or even three to present the full truth concerning the Lord Jesus Christ, so the Scriptures approach the great benefit of Christ's death for the unsaved from three angles, so that what may be lacking in one may be supplied in the others. There are at least four other great words—"forgiveness," "regeneration," "justification," and "sanctification"—which represent spiritual blessings secured by the death of Christ; but these are to be distinguished from the three already mentioned in that these four words refer to aspects of truth that belong only to those who are *saved*.

Over against these, the three words "re᾿emption," "reconciliation," and "propitiation," though incorporating in the scope of their meaning vital truths belonging to the state of the saved, refer in particular to what Christ wrought for the unsaved in His death on the cross. What is termed the finished work of Christ may be defined as the sum total of all that these three words connote when restricted to those aspects of their meaning that apply alone to the unsaved.

Redemption is within the sphere of relationship that exists between the sinner and his sins. This word, with its related terms, contemplates sin as a slavery, with the sinner as the slave. Freedom is secured only through the redemption, or ransom, available in Christ Jesus (John 8:32–36; Rom. 6:17–20; 8:21; Gal. 5:1; 2 Peter 2:19).

Reconciliation is within the sphere of relationship that exists between the sinner and God, and contemplates the sinner as at enmity with God, and Christ as the maker of peace between God and man (Rom. 5:10; 8:7; 2 Cor. 5:19; James 4:4).

Propitiation is also within the sphere of relationship that exists between God and the sinner, but propitiation contemplates the larger necessity of God being just when He justifies the sinner. It views Christ as an Offering, a Sacrifice, a Lamb slain, who, by meeting every demand of God's holiness against the offender, renders God righteously propitious toward that offender (Rom. 3:25; 1 John 2:2; 4:10). Thus it may be seen that redemption is the sinward aspect of the Cross, reconciliation is the manward aspect of the Cross, and propitiation is the Godward aspect of the Cross. These three great doctrines combine to declare one divine undertaking.

The question at issue between the limited redemptionists and the unlimited redemptionists is as much a question of limited or unlimited reconciliation, and limited or unlimited propitiation, as it is one of limited or unlimited redemption. Having made a careful study of these three words and the group of words that must be included with each, one can hardly deny that there is a twofold application of the truth represented by each.

REDEMPTION

There is the aspect of redemption that is represented by the word ἀγοράζω ("to buy, redeem") which means "to purchase in the market"; and, while it is used to express the general theme of redemption, its technical meaning implies only the purchase of the slave, but does not necessarily convey the thought of his release from slavery. The word ἐξαγοράζω ("to redeem") implies much more, in that ἐκ, meaning "out of," or "out from," is combined with ἀγοράζω and thus indicates that the slave is purchased out of the market. (The even stronger terms λυτρόω and ἀπολύτρωσις connote "to loose" and "to set free.") There is, then, a redemption that pays the price, but does not of necessity release the slave, and there is a redemption that is unto abiding freedom.

RECONCILIATION

According to 2 Corinthians 5:19 there is a reconciliation declared to be worldwide and wholly wrought of God; yet the following verse indicates that the individual sinner has the responsibility to be himself reconciled to God. What God has accomplished has so changed the world in its relation to Himself that He, agreeable to the demands of infinite righteousness, is satisfied with Christ's death as the solution to the sin question for each and every one. The *desideratum* is not reached, however, until the individual, already included in the world's reconciliation, is himself satisfied with that same work of Christ (which has satisfied God) as the solution to his own sin question. Thus there is a reconciliation which of itself saves no one, but which is a basis for the reconciliation of any and all who will believe. When they believe, they are reconciled *experientially* and *eternally*. At that moment they become the children of God through the riches of His grace.

PROPITIATION

In one brief verse, 1 John 2:2, God declares that there is a "propitiation for our [the Christian's] sins: and not for ours only, but also for the sins of the whole world." While due recognition will be given later on to the interpretation of this and similar passages as offered by the limited redemptionists, it is obvious that the same twofold aspect of truth—that applicable to the unsaved and that applicable to the saved—is indicated regarding propitiation as is indicated in the case of both redemption and reconciliation.

From this brief consideration of these three great doctrinal words it may be seen that the unlimited redemptionist believes as much in unlimited reconciliation and unlimited propitiation as he does in unlimited redemption. On the other hand the limited redemptionist seldom includes the doctrines of reconciliation and propitiation specifically in his discussion of the extent of Christ's death.

The Cross Is Not the Only Saving Instrumentality

One of the points limited redemptionists depend on is to claim that redemption, if wrought at all, necessitates the salvation of those thus favored. According to this view, if the redemption price is paid by Christ it must be the thought of as ἐξαγοράζω or ἀπολύτρωσις, rather than ἀγοράζω, in every instance. It is confidently held by all Calvinists that the elect will, in God's time and way, each and every one, be saved, and that the unregenerate believe only as they are enabled by the Spirit of God. But the question here is whether the sacrifice of Christ is the only divine instrumentality whereby God *actually* saves the elect, or whether that sacrifice is a divine work (finished, indeed, as to its scope and purpose) that renders all men *savable*, but is applied in sovereign grace by the Word of God and the Holy Spirit only when the individual *believes*.

Certainly Christ's death of itself forgives no sinner, nor does it render unnecessary the regenerating work of the Holy Spirit. Any one of the elect whose salvation is predetermined, and for whom Christ died, may live the major portion of his life in open rebellion against God and during that time manifest every feature of depravity and spiritual death. This alone should prove that individuals are not severally saved by the act of Christ in dying, but rather that they are saved by the divine *application* of that value when they *believe*. The blood of the Passover lambs became efficacious only when applied to the doorposts.

The fact that an elect person does live some portion of his life in enmity toward God, and in a state in which he is as much lost as any unregenerate person, indicates conclusively that Christ must not only die to provide a righteous basis for the salvation of that soul, but that that value must be applied to him at such a time in his life as God has decreed, which time, in the present generation, is almost two thousand years subsequent to the death of Christ. By so much it is proved that the priceless value in Christ's death does not save the elect, nor hinder them from rejecting the mercies of God in that period of their life that precedes their salvation.

The unlimited redemptionist claims that though the value of Christ's death is extended to all men, the elect alone come by divine grace (wrought out by an effectual call) into its fruition, while the nonelect are not called but are those passed by. They hold that God indicates who are the elect, not at the Cross, but by the effectual call and at the time of regeneration. The unlimited redemptionists also believe that it pleased God to place the whole world in a position of infinite obligation to Himself through the sacrifice of Christ. Though the mystery of personal condemnation for the sin of unbelief when one has not been moved to faith by the Spirit cannot be solved in this world, the unregenerate, both elect and nonelect, are definitely condemned for their unbelief so long as they abide in that condition (John 3:18). There is nothing more clarifying in connection with this age-long discussion than the recognition of the fact that while they are in their unregenerate state no vital distinction between the elect and the nonelect is recognized in the Scriptures (1 Cor. 1:24 and Heb. 1:14 might suggest this distinction along lines comparatively unimportant to this discussion). Certainly that form of doctrine that would make redemption equivalent to salvation is not traceable when people are contemplated in their unregenerate state, and a salvation, which is delayed for many years in the case of an elect person, might be delayed forever in the case of a nonelect person whose heart God never moves. Was the objective in Christ's death one of making the salvation of all men *possible*, or was it the making of the salvation of the elect *certain*? Some light is gained on this question when it is thus remembered that the consummating divine acts in the salvation of an individual are wrought when he believes on Christ, and not before he believes.

Universal Gospel Preaching

A very difficult situation arises for the limited redemptionist when he confronts the Great Commission which enjoins the preaching of the gospel to *every* creature. How, it may be urged, can a universal gospel be preached if there is no universal provision? To say on the one hand that Christ died only for the elect and on the other hand that His death is the ground on which salvation is offered to all men is perilously near contradiction. It would be mentally and spiritually impossible for a limited redemptionist, if true to his convictions, to urge with sincerity those who are known to be nonelect to accept Christ. Fortunately, God has disclosed nothing whereby the elect can be distinguished from the nonelect while both classes are in the unregenerate state. However the gospel preacher who doubts the basis for his message in the case of even one to whom he is appealing, if sincere, does face a problem in the discharge of his commission to preach the gospel to every creature. To believe that some are elect and some nonelect creates no problem for the soulwinner provided he is free in his convictions to declare that Christ died for each one to whom He speaks. He knows that the nonelect will not accept the message. He knows also that even an elect person may resist it to near the day of his death. But if the preacher believes that any portion of his audience is destitute of any basis of salvation, having no share in the values of Christ's death, it is no longer a question in his mind of whether they will accept or reject: it becomes rather a question of truthfulness in the declaration of the message. As Alexander points out:

> On this supposition [that of a limited atonement] the general invitations and promises of the gospel are without an adequate basis, and seem like a mere mockery, an offer, in short, of what has not been provided. It will not do to say, in reply to this, that as these invitations are actually given we are entitled, on the authority of God's Word, to urge them and justified in accepting them; for this is mere evasion.[1]

On the question of the beliefs of sincere gospel preachers, it would repay the reader to investigate how universally all great evangelists and missionaries have embraced the doctrine of unlimited redemption, and made it the very underlying structure of their convincing appeal.

Is God Defeated If Men Are Lost for Whom Christ Died?

One objection often raised by limited redemptionists is that if Christ died for those who are never saved, then He has experienced defeat. Of course it must be conceded that if the finished work is a *guarantee* of salvation then God is defeated if even one fails to be saved. But does Christ's redemptive work automatically guarantee salvation for all, or does Christ become the surety of salvation only when one *believes*? Christ's death is a finished transaction, the value of which God has never applied to any soul until that soul passes from death to life. It is *actual* as to its *availability*, but *potential* as to its *application*.

To state that the value of Christ's death is suspended until the hour of regeneration is not to intimate that its value is any less than it would be were it applied at any other time. There are reasons based on the Scriptures why God might provide a redemption for all when He merely purposed to save *some*. He is justified in placing the whole world in a particular relation to Himself so that the gospel might be preached with all sincerity to everyone, and so that on the human side men might be without excuse, being judged, as they are, for their rejection of what is offered to them. People of this dispensation are condemned for their unbelief. This is expressly declared in John 3:18 and implied in John 16:7–11, in which latter context the Spirit is seen in His work of convincing the world of but one sin, namely, "that they believe not on me." But to reject Christ and His redemption, as every unbeliever does, is to demand that the great transaction of Calvary be reversed and that his sin, which was laid on Christ, be retained by himself with all its condemning power. It is not asserted here that sin is thus ever retained by the sinner. It is stated, however, that since God does not apply the value of Christ's death to the sinner until that sinner is saved, God would be morally free to hold the sinner who rejects Christ accountable for his sins; and to this unmeasured burden would be added all the condemnation that justly follows the sin of unbelief. In this connection reference is made by the limited redemptionists to three passages which, it is argued, indicate that impenitent men die with their sins on them, and therefore, it is asserted, Christ could not have borne their sins.

JOHN 8:24

"If ye believe not that I am he, ye shall die in your sins." This is a clear statement that calls for little exposition. It is a case of believing on Christ or dying in the condemnation of sin. It is not alone the one sin of unbelief, but "your sins" to which Christ refers. There is occasion for some recognition of the fact that Christ spoke these words *before* His death, and also that He here required them to believe that He is the "I am," that is, Jehovah. These facts are of importance in any specific consideration of this text; but enough may be said if it be pointed out that the issue is as much a problem for one side of this discussion as for the other. Suppose the limited redemptionist were to claim that the reason these people to whom Christ spoke would die in their sins is that they were nonelect and therefore their sins were not borne by Christ. Two replies may be given to this argument. (a) The condition on which they may avoid dying in their sins is not based on the extent of His death but rather on the necessity of belief ("*If ye believe not* . . . ye shall die in your sins"). (b) If it were true that these people would die in their sins solely because of their position as nonelect for whom Christ did not die, then it would be equally true that those among them who were of the elect (cf. v. 30) and whose sins were laid on Christ, would have no need to be saved from a lost estate since their sins were already removed. Yet the context clearly stresses the necessity of belief for the removal of sin ("If ye believe not . . . ye shall die in your sins. . . . As *he spake* these words, *many believed* on him"). What this important passage actually teaches is that the value of Christ's death, as marvelous and complete as it is, is not applied to the unregenerate until they believe. It is the effectual calling of the Spirit which indicates God's elect and not some partial, unidentified, and supposed discrimination wrought out in the death of Christ.

EPHESIANS 5:6

"Because of these things cometh the wrath of God upon the children of disobedience." The designation "children of disobedience" does not refer to the personal disobedience of any individual in this class, but rather to the fact that all unregenerate people are disobedient in the federal headship of Adam. This includes the elect and nonelect in their unsaved state; besides it should be noted that those elect saved people to whom the apostle was writing were, until saved, not only children of disobedience but also under the energizing power of Satan they were also in a state of spiritual death (Eph. 2:1–2). Thus the value of Christ's death is applied to the elect, not at the Cross, but when they believe.

REVELATION 20:12

"And the dead were judged out of those things which were written in the books, according to their works." This scene is related to the great white throne judgment of the unregenerate of all ages. The sum total of sin in the present age is *unbelief* (John 16:9), as the sum total of human responsibility toward God in securing a right relation to God is *belief* (John 6:29). It is very possible that those of this vast company who were of this dispensation may be judged for the one inclusive sin of unbelief, while those of other ages may be judged for many and specific sins. But from the foregoing proofs it is evident that it is in no way unscriptural to recognize that the impenitent of this age are judged according to their own specific sins, since the value of Christ's death is not applied to or accepted for them until they believe, and these, it is evident, have never believed.

It is appropriate to consider the challenge which the limited redemptionists universally advance, namely, that if Christ bore the sins of the nonelect, they could not be lost, for it is claimed even the condemning sin of unbelief would thus be borne and therefore would have lost its condemning power. By this challenge the important question is raised whether Christ bore all the individual sins except *unbelief*.

To this it may be replied that the sin of unbelief assumes a specific quality in that it is man's answer to what Christ wrought and finished for him when bearing his sins on the Cross. Doubtless, divine freedom is secured by Christ's death whereby God may pardon the sin of unbelief since He freely forgives *all* trespasses (Col. 2:13), and "there is therefore now no condemnation to them which are in Christ Jesus" (Rom. 8:1). The sin of unbelief, being particular in character, is evidently treated as such in the Scriptures. Again, if Christ bore the sin of unbelief along with the other sins of the elect, then no elect sinner in his unregenerate state is subject to any condemnation, nor is he required to be forgiven or justified in the sight of God.

At this point some might question whether the general call of God (John 12:32) could be sincere in every instance since He does not intend to save the nonelect. In response it may be asserted that since the inability of the nonelect to receive the gospel is due to human sin, from His own standpoint God is justified in extending the invitation to them. In this connection there is an important distinction to be observed between the sovereign purpose of God and His desires. For specific and worthy reasons, God, as any other being, may purpose to do more or less than He desires. His desire is evidently toward the whole world (John 3:16; 1 Tim. 2:4), but His purpose is clearly revealed to be toward the elect.

The Nature of Substitution

The limited redemptionists sincerely believe that Christ's substitution for a lost soul *necessitates* the salvation of that soul. This is a fair issue and there is some light available through the careful consideration of the precise nature of substitution itself.

Man did not first discover the necessity of a substitute to die in his place; this necessity was in the heart of God from all eternity. Who can declare what sin actually is in the sight of infinite rectitude? Who will assume to measure the ransom price God must require of the sinner? Who can state what the just judgments of outraged holiness were which were required by the Father and rendered by the Son? Or who can declare the cost to God of the disposition of sin itself from His presence forever?

Two Greek prepositions are involved in the doctrine of substitution. Ὑπέρ (translated "for") is broad in its scope and may mean no more than that a thing accomplished becomes a benefit to others. In this respect it would be declared by this word that

Christ's death benefited those for whom He died. However, this word is invested at times with the most absolute substitutionary meaning (cf. Titus 2:14; Heb. 2:9; 1 Peter 2:21; 3:18). Ἀντί (also translated "for") conveys the thought of complete substitution of one thing or person in the place of another. Orthodox men, whether of one school or the other, will contend alike that Christ's death was *for* men in the most definite sense. However, substitution may be either absolute or conditional, and in the case of Christ's death for the sinner it was both absolute and conditional. Randles states this twofold aspect of truth.

> Substitution may be absolute in some respects, and conditional in others, e.g., a philanthropist may pay the ransom price of an enslaved family so that the children shall be unconditionally freed, and the parents only on condition of their suitably acknowledging the kindness. Similarly, the substitution of Christ was partly absolute, partly conditional in proportion to man's capacity of choice and responsibility. His death availed for the rescue of infants from race guilt; their justification, like their condemnation, being independent of their knowledge and will, and irrespective of any condition which might render the benefit contingent. But for the further benefit of saving men who have personally and voluntarily sinned, the death of Christ avails potentially, taking effect in their complete salvation if they accept Him with true faith.[2]

The debate between limited and unlimited redemption is not a question of the perfect character of Christ's substitution; His substitution is complete whether applied at one time or another, or if it is never applied. Likewise it is not a question of the ability or the inability of the sinner to believe apart from divine enablement. Rather it is a question of whether the full value of Christ's death might be *potentially* provided for the nonelect, even though they never benefit from it, but are only judged because of it. The elect are saved because it is *necessary* for them to be saved in view of the fact that Christ died for them. The unlimited redemptionists believe that the substitutionary death of Christ accomplished to infinite perfection all that divine holiness could ever require for each and every lost soul, that the elect are saved on the ground of Christ's death for them through the effective call and divine enablement of the Spirit, that the value of Christ's death is rejected even by the elect until the hour that they believe, and that that value is rejected by the nonelect forever, and for this rejection they are judged.

It has been objected at this point that the belief of the unlimited redemptionist results in the end in man being his own savior; that is, he is saved or lost according to his works. One passage of Scripture will suffice to clear this matter. In Romans 4:5 it is written, "But to him that worketh not, but believeth on him that justifieth the ungodly, his faith is counted for righteousness." Here the thought is not that the candidate for salvation performs no works *except* belief, but rather that by believing he turns from all works of his own, on which he might depend, and confides in Another to do that which no human works could ever do. By so much the determination rests with man, though it is recognized that no man possesses saving faith apart from a divine enablement to that end. The peculiar manner in which God enlightens the mind and moves the heart of the unsaved to the end that they gladly accept Christ as Savior is in no way a coercion of the will; rather the human volition is strengthened and its determination is the more emphatic. It is futile to attempt to dismiss the element of human responsibility from the great gospel texts of the New Testament.

It is both reasonable and scriptural to conclude that a perfect substitution avails for those who are saved, that in the case of the elect it is delayed in its application until they believe, and that in the case of the nonelect it is never applied at all.

The Testimony of the Scriptures

In the progress of the discussion between the limited redemptionists and the unlimited redemptionists, much Scripture is noted on each side and, naturally, some effort is made by each group to harmonize what might seem to be conflicting between these lines of proof. Some of the passages cited by the limited redemptionists are the following.

John 10:15. "I lay down my life for the sheep." This statement is clear. Christ gave His life for His elect people; however, it is to be observed that both Israel's election and that of the church are referred to in this text (v. 16).

John 15:13. Christ laid down His life for His friends.

John 17:2, 6, 9, 20, 24. In these important verses Christ declared that He gives eternal life to as many as are given to Him, that an elect company has been given to Him, that He prays now only for this elect company, and that He desires that this elect company may be with Him in glory.

Romans 4:25. Christ is here said to have been delivered for the sins of the elect and raised again for the justification of the elect. This, too, is specific.

Ephesians 1:3–7. In this extended text the fact that Christ is the Redeemer of His elect people is declared with absolute certainty.
Ephesians 5:25–27. In this passage Christ is revealed as both loving the church and giving Himself for it so that He might bring it with infinite purity and glory into His own possession and habitation.

In contemplating the Scriptures cited above and others of the same specific character, the unlimited redemptionists assert that it is the primary purpose of Christ to bring many sons into glory. He never lost sight of this purpose (that it actuated Him in all His sufferings and death is beyond question), and His heart is centered on those who are thus given to Him of the Father. However, not once do these passages *exclude* the truth, equally emphasized in the Scriptures, that He died for the whole world. There is a difference to be noted between the fact of His death and the motive of His death. He may easily have died for all men with a view to securing His elect. In such a case, Christ would have been motivated by two great purposes: to pay the forensic ransom price for the world, and to secure His elect body and bride. The former seems to be implied in such texts as Luke 19:10, "For the Son of man is come to seek and to save that which was lost," and John 3:17, "For God sent not his Son into the world to condemn the world: but that the world through him might be saved." The other purpose seems to be implied in such passages as John 10:15, "As the Father knoweth me, even so know I the Father: and I lay down my life for the sheep." The Scriptures do not always include all aspects of a truth in any one passage. If these texts are used in isolation to "prove" that Christ died only for the elect, then it could be argued with equal logic from other isolated passages that Christ died only for Israel (cf. John 11:51; Isa. 53:8) or that He died only for the Apostle Paul (for Paul declared of Christ, "Who loved me, and gave himself for me," Gal. 2:20). As well might one contend that Christ restricted His prayers to Peter because of the fact that He said to Peter, "But I have prayed for thee" (Luke 22:32).

The problem both groups face is the need to harmonize passages that refer to limited redemption with passages that refer to unlimited redemption. To the unlimited redemptionist the limited redemption passages present no real difficulty. He believes that they merely emphasize one aspect of a larger truth. Christ did die for the elect, but He also died for the sins of the whole world. However, the limited redemptionist is not able to deal with the unlimited redemption passages as easily. These passages may be grouped together in the following way:

1. Passages that declare Christ's death was for the whole world (John 1:29; 3:16; 2 Cor. 5:19; Heb. 2:9; 1 John 2:2).

The limited redemptionist states that the word "world" in these and similar passages is restricted to the world of the elect, basing the argument on the fact that the word "world" may at times be restricted in the extent of its scope and meaning. They claim that these universal passages, to be in harmony with the revelation that Christ died for an elect company, must be restricted to the elect. According to this interpretation, John 1:29 would read, "Behold the Lamb of God, which taketh away the sin of the elect." John 3:16 would read, "For God so loved the elect that He gave His only begotten Son that whosoever of the elect believeth on Him should not perish, but have everlasting life." Second Corinthians 5:19 would read, "God was in Christ, reconciling the elect unto Himself." Hebrews 2:9 would read, "He tasted death for every man comprising the company of the elect." First John 2:2 would read, "He is the propitiation for our [elect] sins: and not for ours only, but also for the sins of those who comprise the world of elect people."

A study of the word "cosmos" has been presented elsewhere.[3] There it was seen that usually this word refers to a satanic system which is anti-God in character, though in a few instances it refers to the unregenerate people who are in the cosmos. Three passages serve to emphasize the antipathy that exists between the saved who are "chosen out of the world" and the world itself: "If the world hate you, ye know that it hated me before it hated you. If ye were of the world, the world would love his own: but because ye are not of the world, but I have chosen you out of the world, therefore the world hateth you" (John 15:18–19); "They are not of the world, even as I am not of the world" (John 17:16); "And we know that we are of God, and the whole world lieth in wickedness" (1 John 5:19). The limited redemptionist, then, is forced to claim that the elect, which the world hates and from which it has been saved, is the world. Shedd points to certain specific passages in an attempt to show that the word "cosmos" can at times refer to the "world" of believers.

> Sometimes it is the world of believers, the church. Examples of this use are: John 6:33, 51, "The bread of God is he which giveth life to the world" [of believers]. Romans 4:13, Abraham is "the heir of the world"

[the redeemed]. Romans 11:12, "If the fall of them be the riches of the world." Romans 11:15, "If the casting away of them be the reconciling of the world." In these texts, "church" could be substituted for "world."[4]

In spite of Shedd's assertion, not one of the passages quoted requires that it be interpreted in any light other than that usually accorded to the satanic system.

2. Passages which are all-inclusive in their scope (Rom. 5:6; 2 Cor. 5:14; 1 Tim. 2:6; 4:10; Titus 2:11).

Again the limited redemptionist points out that in these passages the word *all* is restricted to the elect. Indeed, such passages must be restricted if the cause of the limited redemptionist is to stand—but are these properly so restricted? By the limited redemptionist's interpretation, Romans 5:6 would read, "In due time Christ died for the elect, in their ungodly state." Second Corinthians 5:14 would read, "If one died for the elect, then were the elect dead." First Timothy 2:6 would read, "Who gave himself a ransom for the elect, to be testified in due time." First Timothy 4:10 would read, "Who is the Savior of the elect, especially of those that believe." Titus 2:11 would read, "The grace of God that bringeth salvation hath appeared to the elect."

3. Passages that offer a universal gospel to men (John 3:16; Acts 10:43; Rev. 22:17; etc.). The word "whosoever" is used at least 110 times in the New Testament and always has an unrestricted meaning.

4. A special passage, 2 Peter 2:1, wherein the ungodly false teachers of the last days who bring swift destruction on themselves are said to "deny the Lord that bought them." People are thus said to be ransomed who deny the very ground of salvation and who are destined to destruction.

Two statements may be in order in concluding this section:

a. The limited redemptionist's interpretation of John 3:16 tends to restrict the love of God to those among the unregenerate who are the elect. This interpretation is supported by quoting passages that declare God's peculiar love for His saved people. There is no question but what there is a "much more" expression of the love of God for men after they are saved than before (Rom. 5:8–10), though His love for unsaved men is beyond measure; but to assert that God loves the elect in their unregenerate state more than the nonelect is an assumption without scriptural proof. Some limited redemptionists have been bold enough to say that God does not love the nonelect at all.

b. What if God did give His Son to die for all men in an equal sense so that all might be legitimately invited to gospel privileges? Could He, if actuated by such a purpose, use any more explicit language than He has used to express such an intent?

Conclusion

Again let it be said that to disagree with good and worthy teachers is undesirable, to say the least; but when these teachers appear on both sides of a question, as in the present discussion, there seems to be no alternative. By an inner bent of mind some tend naturally to accentuate the measureless value of Christ's death, while others tend to accentuate the glorious results of the application of His death to the immediate salvation of the lost.

The gospel must be understood by those to whom it is preached and it is wholly impossible for the limited redemptionist, when presenting the gospel, to hide with any completeness his conviction that the death of Christ is only for the elect. And nothing could be more confusing to an unsaved person than to be drawn away from considering the saving grace of God in Christ to contemplating whether or not he is one of the elect. Who can prove that he is of the election? If the preacher believes that some to whom he addresses his message could not be saved under any circumstances, those addressed have a right to know what the preacher believes and in time they will know. Likewise it is not wholly sincere to avoid the issue by saying the preacher does not know whether any nonelect are present. Are they absent from every service? Is it not reasonable to suppose that they are usually present when such a vast majority of humanity will probably never be saved at all? In the preaching of salvation through Christ to lost men, no greater wrong could be imposed than to reduce truths that are throbbing with glory, light, and blessing to mere philosophical contemplation. May the God who loved a lost world to the extent that He gave His own Son to die for that world ever impart that passion of soul to those who undertake to convey the message of that measureless love to men!

CHAPTER 11

The Present Work of Christ in Hebrews

David J. MacLeod

Several years ago a number of writers voiced the concern that attention to the present work of Christ has been "largely neglected" by the systematic theologians of the church.[1] The authors of the New Testament would not have understood such neglect, for Christ's present work is one of their most important themes. The purpose of this article is to examine the work of one of those authors, the writer of the Epistle to the Hebrews, and to outline its contribution to the subject.

There are at least three reasons for such a study. First, to neglect any theme central to apostolic Christianity can impoverish Christians and the church. Second, attention needs to be drawn to some aspects of the subject neglected in earlier studies of Hebrews. Third, it is hoped that the material presented will aid Bible students who teach and write on the Christology of the New Testament.[2]

The Commencement of Christ's Present Ministry

HIS ASCENSION THROUGH THE HEAVENS

Having accomplished His redemptive work on the cross (Heb. 9:12), Jesus was raised from the dead by God the Father (13:20). Subsequently[3] He "passed through the heavens" (διεληλυθότα τοὺς οὐρανούς, 4:14), "a statement which is most important for the theology of Hebrews."[4] The ascension is one of a series of events that marked the beginning[5] of Christ's present ministry. The imagery in 4:14 suggests the Old Testament Day of Atonement when the high priest walked through the outer court into the sanctuary.

HIS ENTRANCE INTO THE SANCTUARY

The Levitical high priest annually entered the earthly holy of holies. Christ, however, at His ascension entered the true holy of holies in heaven (9:24; cf. 6:19; 9:12). The aorist εἰσῆλθεν ("He entered") and the aorist infinitive ἐμφανισθῆναι ("to appear") both speak of Christ's past act of entering and appearing before the face of God, that is, at the time of His exaltation.[6] Just as the high priest entered the holy of holies with blood (9:7), so Christ entered "through (διά) His own blood" (9:12), that is, by virtue of His blood.[7] The use of the title Christ (Χριστός, 9:24) draws attention to His exaltation.[8]

HIS OCCUPATION OF THE PLACE OF HONOR

With the twofold divine accolade of Psalm 110 in mind[9] the author wrote of Christ's formal investiture as High Priest at the time of His entrance into heaven. The first part of the accolade is Yahweh's command (Ps. 110:1) to the Son to take His seat at God's right hand (Heb. 1:3; 8:1; 10:12; 12:2). This act of the Son ("He sat down") holds significance for two reasons.[10] First, it signifies the completion of His work of purification of sins (1:3; 10:12). Unlike the Old Testament high priests, who were always standing because their sacrificial work was never completed (cf. 10:11), Christ sat down because His work was done. Second, it signifies that His present session is one of glory and honor. He whose earthly status was inferior to that of angels is now exalted over all beings (cf. 2:9).[11] The right hand of a king was considered the highest place of honor in the kingdom (1 Kings 2:19).[12] By giving Him this seat God ratified what the Son had accomplished at the Cross.[13]

HIS INSTALLATION AS THE HIGH PRIEST

The second part of the divine accolade (Ps. 110:4) is Yahweh's bestowal of the Melchizedekian priesthood. At Christ's ascension the psalm was fulfilled, and He was designated (προσαγορευθείς) as High Priest (Heb. 5:10). The verb προσαγορεύω, "to call, name, designate,"[14] expresses "the formal and solemn ascription of the title to Him to whom it belongs."[15] Two other aorist participles, γενόμενος ("having become," 6:20; 7:26) and παραγενόμενος ("when [He] appeared," 9:11), are also used by the author to point to the past event when Christ's present priesthood began. The bestowal of the priesthood occurred after Jesus' perfection and as God's response to it (5:10). Presumably all three aorist participles are to be understood in the same way.[16]

HIS ATTAINMENT OF A SUPERIOR MINISTRY

The Son of God has obtained (τέτυχεν) a more excellent ministry (λειτουργίας) than that of the Levitical priests who served the earthly tabernacle (8:5–6). The perfect tense (τέτυχεν) suggests not only that Jesus obtained this ministry in the past but also that He still possesses it.[17] The term λειτουργία is regularly used in the Septuagint of the service of priests, particularly their service at the altar (Num. 16:9; 18:4, 6; 1 Chron. 9:13, 19, 28; 2 Chron. 31:4; 35:16). By using this word the author to the Hebrews highlighted the fact that Christ's ministry is a priestly one.[18] Similarly in 8:2 He is called "a minister (λειτουργός) in the sanctuary,"[19] the term λειτουργός drawing attention to the fact that though His sacrificial work is finished, there is a ministry that continues.[20] It also emphasizes His condescension in serving His people.[21]

The Activities of His Present Ministry

The author of Hebrews wrote of a number of activities presently being performed by Christ as High Priest. Scholars differ over the number of distinct activities and their nature.[22] The following six are closely related and may overlap.

REPRESENTATION

In language drawn from the Day of Atonement ritual in which the high priest entered the holy of holies as the representative of the people (9:7, 25), the author of Hebrews stated that Jesus entered heaven "now to appear in the presence of God for us" (9:24, νῦν ἐμφανισθῆναι τῷ προσώπῳ τοῦ θεοῦ ὑπὲρ ἡμῶν). The term πρόσωπον means "face" or "countenance." The thought is that Christ "is in the immediate presence of God."[23] The aorist infinitive ἐμφανισθῆναι indicates that the purpose of His presence there is to appear openly before God.[24] This purpose is further clarified by the prepositional phrase ὑπὲρ ἡμῶν; He appeared there as the believers' representative[25] ("on our behalf").[26] The point is that in Christ[27] believers become the object of God's favorable regard.[28] The adverb νῦν ("now") sets the ministry of Christ in contrast to that of Aaron. The Levitical priests served a copy, but henceforth (νῦν) Christ serves in the true tabernacle. He initially appeared at His ascension, but the use of νῦν focuses attention on His resultant appearing at the present time.[29]

Incidentally there is no indication that representation involves speech. Just as in Old Testament times the high priest fulfilled his work simply standing before the Lord, so Christ simply appears before God. "No words . . . were spoken [by the priests]. It was enough that man was there according to divine appointment."[30]

In similar fashion in 6:20 the author wrote that Jesus has entered heaven as "a forerunner for us" (πρόδρομος ὑπὲρ ἡμῶν). That He is there "for us" suggests that He entered heaven in the believers' interest, that is, to represent them in the presence of the Father.[31] That He is a "forerunner sets Him apart from the Levitical high priest who entered alone as the people waited outside. Jesus, however, has gone before to open up the way for His people to follow Him."[32] The very title πρόδρομος "denotes the believer's prospect of eventually being where Christ is."[33]

In summary, representation may be defined as that work of Christ for sinners on the basis of a finished sacrifice whereby they have acceptance with God and are favorably regarded by Him. The thought parallels the Johannine doctrine of advocacy (1 John 2:1) in which there is the continuous application of the blood of Christ which cleanses from all sin (1:7). The efficacy of the Son's death is ever available to God's people. This ministry is needed as long as Christ's pilgrim people are still in this life, for during this present life believers are both righteous (justified; cf. Heb. 3:1) and sinners (*simul justus et peccator*; cf. 12:1-2).[34]

INAUGURATION

The second activity of Christ is His inauguration of "a new and living way" into God's presence (10:20). The Christian has παρρησία (v. 19), freedom of access to God.[35] This contrasts dramatically to conditions under the old covenant in which only one man from one tribe could enter the sanctuary once a year. Christians, however, are urged to draw near habitually (προσερχώμεθα, v. 22)[36] in worship, petition, and thanksgiving (4:16; 13:15). They can do this "with a good conscience, not because they are not aware of misdeeds, but because they have been cleansed."[37]

The believers access is along "a new and living way" (ὁδὸν πρόσφατον καὶ ζῶσαν, 10:20). It is "new"[38] in a twofold sense: (1) It is new temporally; before the Cross it was unknown.[39] (2) It is new qualitatively; the right of access never grows obsolete (8:13).[40] This new way is "living" in that it has vital power and is effective.[41] The old way, trodden by the high priest into a typical sanctuary with the blood of lifeless victims, was ineffective. The new way is living, it works; it actually brings the believer into God's presence.[42]

The Christian's παρρησία has been secured "by the blood [i.e., by the death] of Jesus" (10:19). The author added that the "new and living way" was inaugurated—opened up, consecrated, and first used[43] (10:20)—by Jesus the Forerunner (cf. 6:19–20). In "a daring and poetic touch"[44] the author equated Jesus' flesh with the veil of the holy of holies (10:20). Believers, he suggested, follow Jesus into God's presence through (explicit local διά) the veil; they come by means of (implicit instrumental διά) Christ's flesh, that is, His crucified body.[45]

In summary, inauguration may be defined as that work of Christ for His people whereby He has opened up and now keeps open a way of access to God. This way of access was consecrated at the Cross, and it is now always available for those who draw near to God (10:22).

INTERCESSION[46]

The third activity of Christ as High Priest in heaven is that of making intercession for His people (7:25).[47] No act in the ritual of the Day of Atonement prefigured this.[48] The Aaronic high priest offered no prayer of intercession while in the holy of holies.

The verb "to make intercession" (ἐντυγχάνειν) has the meanings "fall in with," "chance upon," "obtain an audience with," "converse with," and so "petition," "appeal to," "entreat."[49] In Hebrews 7:25 it means "to intercede for as a representative," "to make petition." In that the petitions are directed toward God the verb also includes the idea "to pray."

Scholars have discussed extensively the exact nature of Christ's intercession. Some have equated His intercession with His endless self-offering through the eternal Spirit in heaven.[50] Nowhere, however, did the author of Hebrews write that Christ's sacrifice is offered, reoffered, represented, prolonged, or lifted to a celestial continuation through the eternal Spirit.[51] Jesus does not "maintain a kind of continuous liturgical action in heaven"[52]

Others explain intercession as a figurative expression denoting in an abstract way the application of the benefits of the Cross to believers.[53] The author of Hebrews, however, did not seek to comfort his readers with abstractions, instead he focused on the true sufferings and temptations of Jesus (2:18; 4:14–5:9) as equipping Him to give genuine sympathy and help in the concrete situations of life.

Still others equate Christ's intercession with His presence on the throne, that is, they equate it with representation.[54] The word ἐντυγχάνειν suggests, however, not passivity but activity on

Jesus' part, an activity that grows out of His true compassion. The author used it to assure his readers that theirs is not a hopeless situation in helpless isolation.[55]

Another group of writers affirm that intercession is an activity on Christ's part in which He invokes from God the blessings of salvation for His people.[56] Yet because of His exalted, enthroned state, they feel it is repugnant to conceive of intercession as being oral prayer. It is grotesque, they feel, to picture Christ as a suppliant before a reluctant God. In response it has been noted that Christ still has the same human nature in which He performed His priestly sacrifice while on earth.[57] However exalted and glorified that human nature may be, it is still human nature "subsisting in dependence on God and subjection unto Him."[58] In short, in His office as High Priest, Jesus does come as a suppliant to God the Father.

Other scholars are content to understand intercession in a literal way, acknowledging that they have a limited understanding of the manner in which transactions between members of the Godhead are carried out in heaven.[59] They argue that intercession involves prayers to God by Christ on behalf of others for three reasons. (1) Intercession must be *vocalis et realis* because it is made by One who is the glorified God-Man. In other words intercession is made by a Man in heaven for people on earth, and His intercession befits His human nature. (2) The kind of intercession Jesus made while on earth—literal, articulate prayers of entreaty (Luke 22:32; John 14:16; 17:15, 24)—is an index to the nature of His intercession in heaven. (3) God's redemptive program is still in effect, and the distinctive functions performed by the persons of the Godhead are still in effect. If it was not dishonoring to the Son for the Father to send Him into the world to redeem mankind, then it is not dishonoring to Him to say that it is His role now to intercede for the redeemed.

The benefits of Jesus' intercession are twofold: First, His intercession insures the final salvation of believers ("those who draw near," 7:25). In Hebrews the noun "salvation" ($\sigma\omega\tau\eta\rho\iota\alpha$, 1:14) and the verb "save" ($\sigma\omega\zeta\omega$, 7:25) do not mean the initial cleansing that occurs at conversion. They mean something eschatological, something yet to be inherited (1:14).[60] This final deliverance[61] into the promised blessings of the kingdom will occur at Christ's second advent (9:28). Because Christ always lives to make intercession, He is able to bring His people "through all hindrances to that honor and glory designed for them (2:7, 10)."[62] Second, His intercession provides daily help to believers. According to 2:17–18 Jesus is able to help[63] His brethren in their temptations to sin and unbelief. In 4:14–16 the readers are encouraged to draw near to God's throne of grace where they will find a sympathetic High Priest and will receive mercy and grace.[64] The basis or ground of His intercession is threefold. First, the blessing of salvation (7:25) that flows from His heavenly intercession was merited by His work on earth, specifically His obedience to death (5:7–9). Second, the basis of His sympathetic understanding for His people is His own human experience of temptation and suffering (2:18; 4:14–16).[65] Third, the power to help and the uninterrupted nature of His intercession are based on His "indestructible life," that is, His deity (7:16, 24).[66]

The beneficiaries of Christ's intercession are "those who draw near to God through Him" (τοὺς προσερχομένους δι' αὐτοῦ τῷ θεῷ, 7:25). Τοὺς προσερχομένους may include those who come with initial saving faith to Christ.[67] The assumption of the author that his readers are for the most part Christians ("holy brethren," 3:1) suggests, however, that he means not those who draw near initially (at conversion) but those already converted who draw near habitually. Surely Christ's own teaching on intercession had influenced the author.[68] Jesus said that He interceded for believers and not for "the world" (John 17:9). "Those who draw near" are believers, and the present tense of the participle τούς προσερχομένους suggests that they should be continuously, day by day, drawing near to the throne of grace in faith.[69]

In summary, intercession in Hebrews may be defined as the sympathetic appeals and petitions of the ascended, incarnate Son of God[70] to God the Father (on the basis of a finished sacrifice) for the preservation, forgiveness,[71] renovation, and bringing to glory of His people.[72]

MEDIATION

The fourth activity of Christ today as the Christian's High Priest is the mediation of praise and thanksgiving. Believers are described in priestly fashion as those who should continually "offer up a sacrifice of praise to God" (ἀναφέρωμεν[73] θυσίαν αἰνέσεως[74] διὰ παντὸς τῷ θεῷ, 13:15). They may do this, the author affirmed emphatically, "through Him" (δι' αὐτοῦ).[75] Just as they are sanctified through this High Priest (13:12), so also can their sacrifice of praise and thanksgiving be acceptable to God only through Christ.[76]

Not only does Christ mediate the prayers of Christians up to God, but He also mediates the power of God down to them. God equips believers to do His will[77] "through Jesus Christ" (διὰ Ἰησοῦ Χριστοῦ, 13:21). The "power of God in our lives . . . works through the person of Jesus Christ."[78] Διά with the genitive here has the sense of agency by personal means or instrument.[79] In His high priestly work of mediation, then, Jesus Christ is the Agent[80] by whom God's power is communicated to believers.[81]

In summary, mediation may be defined as that present activity in heaven whereby He channels the prayers and praises of believers to God and channels the power of God for daily living to believers.

ANTICIPATION

At His ascension the Son of God "sat down at the right hand of the Majesty on high" (1:3). Many commentators speak of Christ's present session in terms of dominion, authority, and sovereignty, that is, in terms of His present reign as King.[82] This interpretation finds support in the verses that follow 1:3, namely, verses 8–9, 13, in which the Son's throne, scepter, and kingdom—all tokens of power and dominion—are mentioned. Closer examination, however, reveals that Hebrews has no emphasis "on Christ as present ruler of the world. God is the ruler. Christ's session is one of honor and glory, rather than sovereignty."[83]

The expression "He sat down" carries the sense of a finished work of sacrifice (10:12) rather than that of a present reign as King. Christ's role as Heir (1:2) as well as His throne, scepter, and kingdom all describe not His present position, but rather what He shall be in the world to come (2:5).[84] At the present time Christ sits at God's right hand waiting for the day when He shall return to earth to reign (1:6,13; 10:13).

In summary, anticipation may be defined as that quiescent activity of Christ whereby He awaits His return (1:6; 9:28; 10:37), the defeat of His enemies (1:13; 10:13), and His rule as King (1:8–9) over the world to come (2:5).

BENEDICTION

The sixth activity of Christ—an activity that will actually take place at the close of the present session—was prefigured in an event on the Day of Atonement. After the solemn ceremonies in the holy of holies the high priest reappeared to the anxiously waiting people[85] and, in all probability,[86] blessed them. This prefigures the reappearance[87] of Christ at His second coming[88] when He will bring His people their long-awaited salvation (9:28), "the fulfillment of the promise, the long awaited 'rest,' the restoration of the land, and peace and prosperity while dwelling there."[89] In short, Christ's work of benediction in Hebrews[90] is His future return to His people from His heavenly sanctuary and the fulfillment of the promise.

Conclusion

At His ascension Christ was formally installed as High Priest and began His present high priestly work. In the heavenly tabernacle today He represents His people (i.e., He secures their acceptance with God); obtains free access for them into God's presence; intercedes in prayer for them and grants them help; mediates their prayers to God and God's strength to them; anticipates His return to earth to reign; and, at the end of the present session, will bless His people by bringing them deliverance into the kingdom.

CHAPTER 12

The Terms of Salvation

Lewis Sperry Chafer

Outside the doctrines related to the Person and work of Christ, there is no truth more far-reaching in its implications and no fact more to be defended than that salvation in all its limitless magnitude is secured, so far as human responsibility is concerned, by believing on Christ as Savior. To this one requirement no other obligation may be added without violence to the Scriptures and total disruption of the essential doctrine of salvation by grace alone. Only ignorance or reprehensible inattention to the structure of a right soteriology will attempt to intrude some form of human works with its supposed merit into that which, if done at all, must, by the very nature of the case, be wrought by God alone and on the principle of sovereign grace. But few indeed seem ever to comprehend the doctrine of sovereign grace, and it is charitable at least to revert to this fact as the explanation of the all-but-universal disposition to confuse the vital issues involved. The purpose of this chapter is to demonstrate that the eternal glories that are wrought in sovereign grace are conditioned, on the human side, by faith alone. The practical hearing of this truth must of necessity make drastic claims on the preacher and become a qualifying influence in the soul-winning methods employed. The student would do well to bring his message and his methods into complete agreement with the workings of divine grace, rather than attempt to conform this unalterable truth to human ideals.

Salvation by faith begins with those mighty transformations which together constitute a Christian what he is; it guarantees the safe-keeping of the Christian and brings him home to heaven conformed to the image of Christ. The preacher or soul-winner who is able to trace through these limitless realities and to preserve them from being made to depend to any degree on human responsibility other than saving faith in Christ, merits the high title of "a good servant of Jesus Christ, nourished on the words of

. . . faith and of . . . sound doctrine" (1 Tim. 4:6). A moment's
attention to the transforming divine undertakings that enter into
salvation of the lost will bring one to the realization of the truth
that every feature involved presents a task which is superhuman,
and therefore, if to be accomplished at all, must be wrought by
God alone. Such a discovery will prepare the mind for the reception
of the truth, that the only relationship man can sustain to this great
undertaking is to depend utterly on God to do it. That is the
simplicity of faith. However, since moral issues are involved that
have been divinely solved by Christ in His death, He has there too
become the only Savior, and faith must be directed toward Him.
"Whoever believes in Him" shall not perish, but has eternal life
(John 3:16). But even when the supernatural character of salvation
is recognized, it is possible to encumber the human responsibility
with various complications, thereby rendering the whole grace
undertaking ineffectual to a large degree. These assertions lead
naturally to a detailed consideration of the more common features
of human responsibility which are often erroneously added to the
one requirement of faith or belief.

Repent and Believe

Since repentance—conceived of as a separate act—is almost
universally added to believing as a requirement on the human side
for salvation, a consideration of the biblical meaning of repentance
is essential. This consideration may be traced as follows: (1) the
meaning of the word, (2) the relationship of repentance to believing,
(3) the relationship of repentance to covenant people, (4) the
absence of the demand for repentance from salvation Scriptures,
and (5) the significance of repentance in specific passages.

THE MEANING OF THE WORD

In every instance the word μετάνοια is translated "repentance."
The word means "a change of mind." The common practice of
reading into this word the thought of sorrow and heart-anguish is
responsible for much confusion in the field of soteriology. There
is no reason why sorrow should not accompany repentance or lead
on to repentance, but the sorrow, whatever it may be, is not
repentance. "Sorrow worketh repentance" (2 Cor. 7:10, KJV), that
is, it leads on to repentance; but the sorrow is not to be mistaken
for the change of mind which it may serve to reproduce. The son
cited by Christ who first said "I will not go," and afterward

repented and went (Matt. 21:28–30) is a true example of the precise meaning of the word. The New Testament call to repentance is a call not to self-condemnation but to a change of mind that promotes a change in the course being pursued. This definition of the word as it is used in the New Testament is fundamental. Little or no progress can be made in a right understanding of the Word of God on this theme, unless the true and accurate meaning of this word is discovered and defended throughout.

THE RELATIONSHIP OF REPENTANCE TO BELIEVING

Too often, when it is asserted—as it is here—that repentance is not to be added to belief as a separate requirement for salvation, it is assumed that repentance is not necessary to salvation. Therefore it is as dogmatically stated as language can declare, that repentance is essential to salvation and that none could be saved apart from repentance, but it is included in believing and cannot be separated from it. The discussion is restricted at this point to the problem that the salvation of unregenerate persons develops; and it is safe to say that few errors have caused so much hindrance to the salvation of the lost than the practice of demanding of them an anguish of soul before faith in Christ can be exercised. Since such emotions cannot be produced at will, the way of salvation has thus been made impossible for all who do not experience the required anguish. This error results in another serious misdirection of the unsaved, namely, one in which they are encouraged to look inward at themselves and not away to Christ as Savior. Salvation is made to be conditioned on feelings and not on faith. Likewise people are led by this error to measure the validity of their salvation by the intensity of anguish that preceded or accompanied it. In this way sorrow of heart becomes a most subtle form of meritorious work and to that extent a contradiction of grace.

Underlying all this supposition that tears and anguish are necessary is the most serious notion that God is not propitious, but that He must be softened to pity by penitent grief. The Bible, however, declares that God is propitious because of Christ's death for the very sin that causes human sorrow. There is no occasion to melt or temper the heart of God. His attitude toward sin and the sinner is a matter of revelation. To imply that God must be mollified by human agony is a desperate form of unbelief. The unsaved have a gospel of good news to believe, which certainly is not the mere notion that God must be coaxed into a saving attitude

of mind; it is that Christ has died and grace is extended from the
One who is propitious to the point of infinity. The human heart is
prone to imagine that there is some form of atonement for sin
through being sorry for it. Whatever may be the place of sorrow
for sin in the restoration of a Christian who has transgressed, it
cannot be determined with too much emphasis that for the
unsaved—Jew or Gentile—there is no occasion to propitiate God
or to provide any form of satisfaction by misery or distress of
soul. With glaring inconsistency, those who have said that the
unsaved must experience mental suffering before they can be
saved, have completely failed to inform their hearers about how
such required torture may be secured. It should be restated that
since genuine grief of mind cannot be produced at will and since
many natures are void of depression of spirit, to demand that a
self-produced affliction of mind shall precede salvation by faith
becomes a form of fatalism and is responsible for having driven
uncounted multitudes to despair. However, it is true that, from the
Arminian point of view, no greater heresy could be advanced than
this contention that the supposed merit of human suffering because
of personal sins should be excluded from the terms on which a
soul may be saved.

As already stated, repentance, which is a change of mind, is
included in believing. No individual can turn to Christ from some
other confidence without a change of mind, and that, it should be
noted, is all the repentance a spiritually dead individual can ever
effect. That change of mind is the work of the Spirit (Eph. 2:8). It
will be considered too by those who are amenable to the Word of
God that the essential preparation of heart the Holy Spirit
accomplishes in the unsaved to prepare them for an intelligent and
voluntary acceptance of Christ as Savior—as defined in John
16:8–11—is not a sorrow for sin. The unsaved who come under
this divine influence are illuminated—given a clear
understanding—concerning but one sin, namely, that "they do not
believe in Me" (v. 9).

To believe on Christ is one act, regardless of the manifold
results it secures. It is not turning from something; but rather
turning to something from something. If this terminology seems a
mere play on words, it will be discovered, by more careful
investigation, that this is a vital distinction. To turn from evil may
easily be a complete act in itself, since the action can be terminated
at that point. To turn to Christ is a solitary act also, and the joining

of these two separate acts corresponds to the notion that two acts—repentance and faith—are required for salvation. On the other hand turning to Christ from all other confidences is one act, and in that one act repentance is included. Paul stressed this distinction when he wrote, "You turned to God from idols to serve a living and true God" (1 Thess. 1:9). This verse provides no comfort for those who contend that people must first, in real contrition, turn from idols—which might terminate at that point—and afterward, as a second and separate act, turn to God. The text recognizes but one act—"You turned to God from idols"—and that is an act of faith alone.

Those who stress repentance as a second requirement along with believing, inadvertently disclose that in their view the problem of personal sin is all that enters into salvation. The sin nature must also be dealt with; yet that is not a legitimate subject of repentance. Salvation contemplates many vast issues and the adjustment of the issue of personal sin, though included, is but a small portion of the whole. Acts 26:18, sometimes cited in proof of the idea that the unsaved must do various things in order to be saved, rather enumerates various things that are wrought for the believer in the saving power of God.

THE RELATIONSHIP OF REPENTANCE TO COVENANT
PEOPLE

The term "covenant people" is broad in its application. It includes Israel, who are under Jehovah's unalterable covenants and yet are to be objects of another, New Covenant (Jer. 31:31–34), and the church, composed of all believers of the present age, who are also now the objects of that New Covenant made in Christ's blood (Matt. 26:28; 1 Cor. 11:25). A covenant implies a relationship because it secures a right relationship to God in matters with the bounds of the covenant. A covenant that is unconditional, as are the above-named covenants, is not affected by any human elements nor is it changeable even by God Himself.

However, the fact of a covenant and the experience of its blessings are two different things. It is possible to be under the provisions of an unconditional covenant and to fail for the time being to enjoy its blessings because of sin. When sin has cast a limitation on the enjoyment of a covenant and the covenant, being unchangeable, still abides, the issue becomes, not the remaking of the covenant, but the one issue of sin that mars the relationship. It therefore follows that for the covenant people there is need for a divine dealing with the specific sin and a separate and unrelated repentance respecting it. This repentance is expressed by confession to God. Having confessed his sin, David did not pray for his salvation to be restored; he rather prayed for the restoration of "the joy" of his salvation (Ps. 51:12). In like manner, confession restores joy and fellowship to the believer (1 John 1:3–9). When Christ came offering Himself to Israel as their Messiah and announcing that their kingdom was at hand, He, with John the Baptist and the apostles, called on that people to repent in preparation for the proffered kingdom. There was no appeal concerning salvation or the formation of covenants; instead, restoration of the people by a change of mind would lead them to forsake their sins (Matt. 10:6–7). To apply these appeals made to covenant Jews concerning their adjustments within their covenants to individual unregenerate Gentiles, who are "strangers to the covenants" (Eph. 2:12), is a serious error indeed. In like manner, a Christian may repent as a separate act (2 Cor. 7:8–10). While covenant people are appointed to national or personal adjustment to God by repentance as a separate act, there is no basis in either reason or revelation for the demand to be made that an unregenerate person in this age must add a covenant person's repentance to faith in order to be saved.

THE ABSENCE OF THE DEMAND FOR REPENTANCE FROM SALVATION SCRIPTURES

Approximately 115 New Testament passages condition salvation on "believing" and 35 passages condition salvation on "faith," the latter being an exact synonym of the former. These portions of Scripture, about 150 in all, include practically all that the New Testament declares on the matter of human responsibility in salvation; yet each one of these texts omits any reference to repentance as a separate act. This fact, easily verified, cannot but bear enormous weight with any candid mind. In like manner, the Gospel of John, which is written to present Christ as the object of faith unto eternal life, does not even once employ the word "repentance." Similarly, the Epistle to the Romans, which presents a complete analysis of all that enters into the whole plan of salvation by grace, does not use the word "repentance" in connection with the saving of a soul, except in 2:4 where repentance is equivalent to salvation itself. When the Apostle Paul and his companion Silas replied to the jailer concerning what he should do to be saved, they said, "Believe in the Lord Jesus, and you shall be saved" (Acts 16:31). This reply says nothing of the need for repentance in addition to believing. From this overwhelming mass of irrefutable evidence, it is clear that the New Testament does not impose repentance on the unsaved as a condition of salvation. The Gospel of John with its direct words from the lips of Christ, the Epistle to the Romans with its exhaustive treatment of the theme in question, the Apostle Paul, and the whole array of 150 New Testament passages are incomplete and misleading if repentance must be accorded a place separate from and independent of believing. No thoughtful person would attempt to defend such a notion against such odds, and those who have thus undertaken doubtless have done so without weighing the evidence or considering the untenable position they assume.

THE SIGNIFICANCE OF REPENTANCE IN SPECIFIC
PASSAGES

When entering on this phase of the study, it is first necessary to eliminate all portions of the New Testament that introduce the word "repentance" in its relation to covenant people. Likewise some passages employ the word "repentance" as a synonym of believing (Acts 17:30; Rom. 2:4; 2 Tim. 2:25; 2 Peter 3:9), and others refer to a change of mind (Acts 8:22; 11:18; Heb. 6:1–6; 12:17; Rev. 9:20; etc.). Yet again consideration must be accorded three passages related to Israel that are often misapplied (Acts 2:38; 3:19; 5:31). Two verses in Acts refer to John's baptism, which was to repentance (Acts 13:24; 19:4).

Four passages deserve more extended consideration.

Luke 24:47. "And that repentance for forgiveness of sins should be proclaimed in His name to all the nations—beginning from Jerusalem." It will be seen that repentance is not in itself equivalent to believing or faith, though, being included in believing, it is used here as a synonym of the word "believe." Also "forgiveness of sins" is not all that is offered in salvation, though the phrase may serve that purpose in this instance. Above all, the passage does not require human obligations with respect to salvation. Repentance, which here represents believing, leads to divine forgiveness of sins.

Acts 11:18. "And when they heard this, they quieted down, and glorified God, saying, 'Well then, God has granted to the Gentiles also the repentance that leads to life.'" Again repentance, which is included in believing, serves as a synonym for the word "belief." The Gentiles, as always, attain to spiritual life by faith, the all-important and essential change of mind. Also the passage does not prescribe two things necessary for salvation (cf. v. 17).

Acts 20:21. "Solemnly testifying to both Jews and Greeks of repentance toward God and faith in our Lord Jesus Christ." First, though unrelated to this argument, it is important to note that the apostle here placed Jews on the same level with Gentiles, and both are objects of divine grace. Jews with their incomparable background or Gentiles with their heathen ignorance, must each undergo a change of mind respecting God. Until one is aware of God's gracious purpose, there can be no reception of the idea of saving faith. It is quite possible to recognize God's purpose, as many do, and not receive Christ as Savior. In other words repentance toward God could not itself constitute in this case the equivalent of "faith in our Lord Jesus Christ," though it may prepare for that faith. The introduction of the two Persons of the Godhead is significant, and the fact that Christ is the sole object of faith is also most vital. Those who would insist that there are here two human obligations for salvation are reminded again of the 150 portions in which such a twofold requirement is omitted.

Acts 26:20. "But kept declaring both to those of Damascus and also at Jerusalem and then throughout all the region of Judea, and even to the Gentiles, that they should repent and turn to God, performing deeds appropriate to repentance." Again both Jews and Gentiles are addressed as being on the same footing before God. Two obligations are named here, in order that spiritual results may be secured—to "repent and turn to God." The passage would sustain the Arminians' view if repentance were, as they assert, a sorrow for sin; but if the word is given its correct meaning, namely, a change of mind, there is no difficulty. The call is for a change of mind in which a person turns to God. This passage also has its equivalent in 1 Thessalonians 1:9, "You turned to God from idols."

CONCLUSION

An attempt has been made to demonstrate that the biblical doctrine of repentance offers no objection to the truth that salvation is by grace through faith apart from any suggestion of human works of merit. It is asserted that repentance, a change of mind, enters of necessity into the very act of believing on Christ, since one cannot turn to Christ from other objects of confidence without that change of mind. Approximately 150 texts—including all the greatest gospel invitations—limit human responsibility in salvation to believing or to faith. To this simple requirement nothing can be added if the glories of grace are to be preserved.

Believe and Confess Christ

The ambition to secure apparent results and the sincere desire to make decisions for Christ very definite have prompted many preachers in their general appeals to insist on a public confession of Christ on the part of those who would be saved. To all practical purposes and in the majority of instances these confessions are, in the minds of the unsaved, coupled with saving faith and seem based on two passages of Scripture.

SCRIPTURE BEARING ON CONFESSION OF CHRIST.

Matthew 10:32. "Every one therefore who shall confess Me before men, I will also confess him before My Father who is in heaven." This verse, occurring in Christ's kingdom teachings, is part of His instruction to His disciples whom He was sending forth with a restricted message to Israel (cf. vv. 5–7) and which was to be accompanied by stupendous miracles (cf. v. 8). Such instructions were never committed to preachers in the present age, for verse 32 applies primarily to the disciples themselves in respect to their faithful delivery of this kingdom proclamation, and could be extended in its appeal only to the Israelites to whom they were sent. The carelessness that assumes that this Scripture presents a condition of salvation for a Jew or Gentile in the present age is deplorable indeed.

Romans 10:9–10. "That if you confess with your mouth Jesus as Lord, and believe in your heart that God raised Him from the dead, you shall be saved; for with the heart man believes, resulting in righteousness; and with the mouth he confesses, resulting in salvation." This message, falling as it does within the teachings belonging primarily to the way of salvation by grace, is worthy of more consideration. The force of the positive statement in verse 9 is explained in verse 10. Of the word "confess" in verse 10, Authur T. Pierson wrote,

That word means to speak out of a like nature to one another. I believe and receive the love of God. In receiving His love I receive His life, in receiving His life I receive His nature, and His nature in me naturally expresses itself according to His will. That is confession. Alexander MacLaren has said: "Men do not light a candle and put it under a bushel, because the candle would either go out or burn the bushel." You must have vent for life, light, and love, or how can they abide? And a confession of Christ Jesus as Lord is the answer of the new life of God received. In receiving love, you are born of God, and, being born of God, you cry, "Abba, Father," which is but the Aramaic word for "Papa"—syllables which can be pronounced before there are any teeth, because they are made with the gum and lip—the first word of a new born soul, born of God, knowing God, and out of a like nature with God speaking in the language of a child.

The two activities named in these verses are each expanded with respect to their meaning in the immediate context. Of believing it is said, "For the Scripture says, 'Whoever believes in Him will not be disappointed.' For there is no difference between Jew and Greek" (vv. 11–12a). Salvation is promised to both Jew and Greek (though in his case a Gentile) on the one condition that they believe. Such, indeed, shall not be ashamed. Of confession it is said, "For the same Lord is Lord of all, abounding in riches for all who call upon Him; for whoever will call upon the name of the Lord will be saved" (vv. 12b–13). The confession (vv. 9–10) is said to be a calling on the name of the Lord (vv. 11–13). In other words this confession is that unavoidable acknowledgment to God on the part of the one who is exercising saving faith, that he accepts Christ as his Savior. As Abraham amened the promise of God—not a mere responsive believing (Gen. 15:6; Rom. 4:3)—so the trusting soul responds to the promise God offers of salvation through Christ.

TWO CONCLUSIVE REASONS

Two convincing reasons demonstrate why Romans 10:9–10 does not present two human responsibilities in relation to salvation by grace. First, to claim that a public confession of Christ as Savior is required in addition to believing on Christ is to contend that 150 passages in which believing alone appears are incomplete and to that extent misleading. A certain type of mind, however, seems able to construct all its confidence on an erroneous interpretation of one passage and to be uninfluenced by the overwhelming body of Scripture that contradicts that interpretation. Second, to require a public confession of Christ as a prerequisite to salvation by grace is to discredit the salvation of an innumerable company who have been saved under circumstances that precluded any public action.

CONCLUSION

Confession of Christ is a Christian's privilege and duty and may be undertaken at the moment one is saved, but it is not a condition of salvation by grace. Otherwise works of merit intrude where only the work of God reigns.

Believe and Be Baptized

The word βαπτίζω in the New Testament represents two different things—a real baptism by the Spirit of God by which the believer is joined in union to Christ and is henceforth in Christ, and a ritual baptism with water. John distinguished these when he said, "I baptize you in water for repentance; but He who is coming after Me is mightier than I, and I am not even fit to remove His sandals; He Himself will baptize you with the Holy Spirit and fire" (Matt. 3:11). Though this word sustains a primary and secondary meaning and these are closely related ideas, the fact that the same identical word is used for both real and ritual baptism suggests an affiliation between the two ideas with which this word is associated. In fact Ephesians 4:5 declares that there is but one baptism. The contemplation of such facts respecting this word is essential to a right understanding of the theme under discussion. The question naturally arises when it is asserted that one must believe and be baptized, whether a real or a ritual baptism is in view. Two passages demand attention.

MARK 16:15–16

"And He said to them, 'Go into all the world and preach the gospel to all creation. He who has believed and has been baptized shall be saved; but he who has disbelieved shall be condemned.'" In interpreting this passage many have not noted the evidence that the verse refers to baptism by the Spirit, not water baptism. This evidence should at least be weighed for all it is. Should it prove on examination that reference is made to real baptism by the Spirit, which baptism is essential to salvation, the difficulty of a supposed regenerating water baptism is immediately dismissed. Dale has discussed this vital issue in an extended argument.

> All, so far as I am aware, who interpret the language of the Evangelist as indicating a ritual baptism, do so without having examined the

question—"May not this be the real baptism by the Holy Spirit and not ritual baptism with water?" This vital issue has been assumed without investigation, and determined against the real baptism of the Scriptures, without a hearing. Such assumption is neither grounded in necessity, nor in the warrant of Scripture; whether regarded in its general teaching or in that of this particular passage. That there is no necessity for limiting the baptism of this passage to a rite is obvious, because the Scriptures furnish us with a real baptism by the Spirit, as well as with its symbol ritual baptism, from which to choose. There is no scriptural warrant in the general teaching of the Bible for identifying a rite with salvation; nor can such warrant be assumed in this particular passage (which does identify baptism and salvation), because there is no evidence on the face of the passage to show, that the baptism is ritual with water, rather than real by the Spirit. These points must be universally admitted: 1. The passage does not declare a ritual baptism by express statement; 2. It contains no statement which involves a ritual baptism as a necessary inference; 3. The Scriptures present a real and a ritual baptism, by the one or the other of which to meet the exigencies of any elliptically stated baptism; 4. That baptism which meets, in its scriptural passage, must be the baptism designed by such passage. We reject ritual baptism from all direct connection with this passage, in general, because the passage treats salvation and its conditions (belief and baptism). All out of the Papal church admit that ritual baptism has not the same breadth with belief as a condition of salvation, and are, therefore, compelled to introduce exceptions for which no provision is made in the terms of this passage. We accept the real baptism by the Holy Spirit as the sole baptism directly contemplated by this passage, in general, because, it meets in the most absolute and unlimited manner as a condition of salvation the obvious requirement on the face of the passage, having the same breadth with belief, and universally present in every case of salvation. We accept this view in particular: Because it makes the use of "baptized" harmonious with the associate terms, "believeth" and "saved." The use of these terms, as well as "baptized," is elliptical. "Believe" has in the New Testament a double usage; the one limited to the action of the intellect, as "the devils believe and tremble"; the other embraces and controls the affections of the heart, as "with the heart we believe unto righteousness." It is the higher form of "belief' that is universally recognized as belonging to this passage. "Saved," also, is used in the New Testament, with a double application; as of the body, "all hope that we should be saved was taken away"; and of the souls, "He shall save His people from their sins." Again it is this higher salvation that is accepted without question. So, "baptized" is used in a lower and a higher meaning; applied in the one case to the body, as "I baptize you with water"; and in the other case applied to the soul, as "He shall baptize you with the Holy Spirit." By what just reasoning, now, can "believeth," and "saved," be taken in the highest sense, and "baptized," in the same sentence and in the same construction, be brought down to the lowest? We object to such diversity of interpretation as unnatural and without any just support. The only tenable supply of the ellipsis must be, "He that believeth" (with the heart upon Christ), "shall be saved" (by the redemption of Christ). The construction allows and the case requires, that a relation of dependence and unity subsist between "believeth" and "baptized." There is evidently some vinculum binding these words and the ideas which they represent, together. Middleton (Greek article, in loco) says: "In the Complutens. edit. the second participle has the article, which would materially alter the sense. It would imply, that he who believeth, as well as he who is baptized, shall be saved; whereas the reading of the MSS. insists on the fulfillment of both conditions in every individual." This is true; but it is not all the truth. This faith and this baptism must not only not be disjoined by being assigned to different persons, but they must not be disjoined by being assigned to different spheres, the one spiritual and the other physical; and being conjoined, in like spiritual nature, and meeting together in the same person, the whole truth requires, that they shall be recognized not as two distinct things existing harmoniously together, but as bearing to each other the intimate and essential relation of cause and effect, that is to say, the baptism is a consequence proceeding from the belief.[1]

Believing has the influence over the soul, through the power of God in accord with His promise in the gospel, of bringing the one who believes into the estate of salvation with all its values which are received from Christ. The new relationship to Christ of being in Him is wrought by the Holy Spirit's baptism, and it could not be absent in the case of any true salvation. On the other hand all who have been saved have been saved quite apart from ritual baptism. The form of speech which this text presents is common in the Bible, namely, that of passing from the main subject to one of the features belonging to that subject, as "You shall be silent and unable to speak" (Luke 1:20). The word "silent" is amplified by the words "unable to speak." In Mark 16:16 the word "believed" is amplified by the words "and has been baptized."

ACTS 2:38

"And Peter said to them, Repent and let each of you be baptized in the name of Jesus Christ for the forgiveness of your sins; and you shall receive the gift of the Holy Spirit."

A very general impression obtains among informed students of the Scriptures that the translation of this passage is injured by the rendering of two prepositions ἐπί and εἰς by the words "in" and "for." That ἐπί is better translated "on" and εἰς is better rendered "into" would hardly be contested. To this may be added the demand of some worthy scholars that the word "believing" should be supplied, which would give the following rendering: "Repent and let each of you be baptized [believing] in the name of Jesus Christ into the forgiveness of sins." In this way the passage harmonizes with all other Scripture, which, from the interpreter's standpoint, is imperative (2 Peter 1:20); and the remission of sins—here equivalent to personal salvation—is made to depend not on repentance or baptism.

Dale is convinced that real baptism by the Spirit is referred to in Acts 2:38 and also in verse 41. He proposes that the same arguments be advanced to prove that Mark 16:15–16 refers to real baptism by the Spirit serve as valid evidence in Acts 2:38, 41. He feels a particular relief that there is no need, according to this interpretation, of defending the idea that three thousand people were baptized by ritual baptism in what could have been slightly more than half a day and as a surprise necessity for which preparations could not have been made either by the candidates or administrators. Dale contends that to reckon this baptism to have been real and what unavoidably does enter into the salvation of every soul and does not follow after as a mere testimony, is to encounter no insuperable difficulty whatever. Most of all, he points out, by such an interpretation this passage is rescued from the misinterpretation that exalts ritual baptism to the point of being all but essential to salvation.

Significantly the Apostle Peter followed this exhortation contained in Acts 2:38 with a promise regarding the reception of the Holy Spirit. In the disproportionate emphasis that has been placed on ritual baptism—doubtless stimulated by disagreement on its mode—the great undertaking of the Spirit in real baptism, which conditions the believer's standing before God and engenders the true motive for Christian character and service, has been slighted to the point that many apparently are unaware of its existence. Such a situation is not without precedent. At Ephesus the Apostle Paul found certain men who were resting their confidence in "John's baptism," who confessed, "We have not even heard whether there is a Holy Spirit" (Acts 19:2). In other words it is well to note that the truth regarding the baptism with the Spirit is itself more important than the Christian public, led by sectarian teachers, supposes it to be.

CONCLUSION

The above examination of two passages, on which the idea of baptismal regeneration is made to rest, has sought to demonstrate that ritual baptism, however administered, is not a condition to be added to believing as a necessary step in salvation.

Believe and Surrender to God

No intrusion into the doctrine that salvation is conditioned alone on believing is more effective than the added demand that the unsaved must dedicate themselves to do God's will in their daily life, as well as to believe on Christ. The desirability of dedication to God on the part of every believer is obvious, and is so stressed in the Scriptures that many sincere people who are inattentive to doctrine are easily led to suppose that this same dedication, which is voluntary in the case of the believer, is imperative in the case of the unsaved. This aspect of the general theme may be approached under three considerations of it: (1) the incapacity of the unsaved, (2) what is involved, and (3) the preacher's responsibility.

THE INCAPACITY OF THE UNSAVED

The Arminian notion that through the reception of a so-called common grace anyone is competent to accept Christ as Savior if he or she will, is a mild assumption compared with the idea that the unregenerate person, with no common or uncommon grace proffered, is able to dedicate his life to God. The Bible gives overwhelming testimony to the utter inability and spiritual death of the unsaved. They are shut up to the one message that Christ is their Savior; and they cannot accept Him, the Word of God declares, unless illuminated to that end by the Holy Spirit. Saving faith is not a possession of everyone but is imparted specifically to those who do believe (Eph. 2:8). Because this is true, it follows that to impose a need to surrender one's life to God as an added condition of salvation is most unreasonable. God's call to the unsaved is never said to be to the lordship of Christ; it is to His saving grace. With the reception of the divine nature through the regenerating work of the Spirit, a new understanding and a new capacity to respond to the authority of Christ are gained. Those attending such issues in practical ways are aware that self-dedication taxes the limit of ability even for the most devout believer. The error of imposing Christ's lordship on the unsaved is disastrous even though they are not able intelligently to resent it or to remind the preacher of the fact that he, in calling on them to dedicate their lives, is demanding of them what they have no ability to produce.

A destructive heresy was formerly abroad under the name the Oxford Movement, which specializes in this blasting error, except that the promoters of the movement omit altogether the idea of believing on Christ for salvation and promote exclusively the obligation of surrender to God. They substitute consecration for conversion, faithfulness for faith, and beauty of daily life for believing to eternal life. As is easily seen, the plan of this movement is to ignore the need of Christ's death as the ground of regeneration and forgiveness, and to promote the wretched heresy that it matters nothing what one believes respecting the Saviorhood of Christ if only the daily life is dedicated to God's service. A pseudo self-dedication to God is a rare bit of religion with which the unsaved may conjure. The tragedy is that out of such a delusion those who embrace it are likely never to be delivered by a true faith in Christ as Savior. No more complete example could be found today of "the blind leading the blind" than what this movement presents.

WHAT IS INVOLVED

The most subtle, self-satisfying form of works of merit is, after all, found to be an engaging feature in this practice of applying to unbelievers the lordship of Christ. What more could God expect than that the creatures of His hand should by supposed surrender be attempting to be obedient to Him? In such idealism the darkened mind of the unsaved no doubt sees dimly some possible advantage in submitting their lives to the guidance of a Supreme Being—of whom they really know nothing. Such notions are only human adjustments to God and resemble in no way the terms of divine adjustment, which first condemns man and rejects all his supposed merit, and then offers a perfect and eternal salvation to the helpless sinner on no other terms than that one believe on Christ as his or her Savior.

If the real issue in self-dedication to God is stated in its legitimate though extreme form, the possibility of martyrdom is first in evidence. One who is faithful to God is enjoined to be faithful to death (Rev. 2:10). This is a glorious challenge to the devout believer and perhaps many have accepted the challenge and suffered a martyr's death; but would any zealous advocate of the idea that the lordship of Christ must be applied to the unsaved as a condition of salvation, dare to propose to the unsaved that they must not only believe on Christ but be willing to die a martyr's death? The very proposal of such a question serves only to demonstrate the disregard for revealed truth which this error exhibits.

The unregenerate person, because of his condition in spiritual death, has no ability to desire the things of God (1 Cor. 2:14), or to anticipate what his outlook on life will be after he is saved. It is therefore an error of the first magnitude to divert that feeble ability of the unsaved to exercise a God-given faith for salvation into the unknown and complex spheres of self-dedication, which dedication is the Christian's greatest problem.

THE PREACHER'S RESPONSIBILITY

It is the preacher's responsibility, not only to preserve his message to the unsaved from being distorted by issues other than that of simple faith in Christ, but, when speaking to Christians in the presence of the unsaved regarding the issues of Christian character, conduct, and service, to declare plainly that the truth presented has no application to those who are unsaved. Such a reminder, often repeated, will not only preserve unregenerate individuals who are present from the deadly supposition that God is seeking to improve their manner of life rather than to accomplish the salvation of their souls, but will also create in their minds the important impression that in the sight of God they are hopelessly condemned apart from Christ as Savior. God alone can deal with a situation wherein a large percentage of the members of a local church are unsaved, and yet are habitually addressed as though they were saved and on no other basis than that they belong to the church. It is surprising indeed that any unsaved person ever gains any right impression respecting his actual relationship to God, when he is allowed to believe that he is included in all the appeals made to Christians regarding their daily life. If the importance of attention to this wide difference between the saved and the unsaved is not appreciated and respected by the preacher, the fault is nearly unpardonable since the results may easily hinder the salvation of many souls. Next to sound doctrine itself no more important obligation rests on the preacher than that of preaching the lordship of Christ to Christians exclusively, and the Saviorhood of Christ to those who are unsaved.

CONCLUSION

A suggestion born of this theme is that in all gospel preaching every reference to the life to be lived beyond regeneration should be avoided so far as possible. To attend to this is not a deception nor a withholding of the truth from those to whom it applies. It is the simple adjustment to the limitation and actual condition of those to whom the gospel is addressed. Some unsaved individuals, because of the weakness and inability they observe in themselves, may be fearful lest they would not "hold out" as Christians. It is desirable to remind them that in the new relationship to Christ that will exist after they receive Him new abilities will be possessed by which they can live to the glory of God. Such assurance is far removed from the practice of introducing obligations that are exclusively Christian in character and as something to which they must consent in order to be saved. Multitudes of unsaved people have been diverted from the one question of their acceptance of Christ as Savior to other questions regarding amusements and unchristian ways of living. As an unsaved person has no motive or spiritual light by which to face such problems, that person can only be bewildered by these issues. His problem is not one of giving up what in his unsaved state seems normal to him; it is a problem of receiving the Savior with all His salvation.

Believe and Confess Sin or Make Restitution

The Scripture verse employed by advocates of this error applies only to Christians. The passage reads, "If we confess our sins, He is faithful and righteous to forgive us our sins and to cleanse us from all unrighteousness" (1 John 1:9). This declaration, addressed to believers who have sinned, presents the ground on which they may be restored to fellowship with God. The notion that restitution must be made before one can be saved is based on the God-dishonoring theory that salvation is only for good people, and that the sinner must divest himself of evil before he can be saved. In other words God is not propitious respecting sin; He is propitious only toward those who have prepared themselves for His presence and fellowship. Over against this, the truth is ignored that the unregenerate person cannot improve his fallen condition, and if he could, he would be bringing merit to God where merit is wholly excluded to the end that grace may abound and be magnified through all eternity.

The preacher must ever be on his guard to discourage the tendency of the natural man to move along lines of reformation rather than regeneration. All who are serious regarding their lost estate are best helped by that body of truth which declares how

God, through Christ, must save and will save from all sin; that He must and will deal with the very nature which sins; and that He must and will rescue men from their estate under sin. In various ways the natural man proposes to be saved and yet retain his dignity and supposed worthiness, and one of these is the contention that sin must be confessed and restitution made as a human requirement in salvation. It is God "who justifies the ungodly" (Rom. 4:5); it is while individuals are "helpless," "sinners," and "enemies" (5:6, 8, 10) that Christ died for them; and all their unworthiness is accounted for by Christ in His death. There is a duty belonging only to Christians—to set things right after they are saved—and there should be no neglect of that responsibility. It therefore remains true that those who are saved are saved on the one condition of believing on Christ.

Believe and Implore God to Save

None of the errors being considered seems more reasonable than this, and yet none strikes a more deadly blow at the foundation of divine grace. The error includes the claim that the sinner must "seek the Lord," or that he must be pleased with God to be merciful. These two concepts, though nearly identical, should be considered separately.

"SEEK THE LORD"

This phrase in Isaiah 55:6 represents Jehovah's invitation to His covenant people, Israel, who had wandered from their place of rightful blessings under His covenants, to return to Him. It was appointed to that people to "seek the Lord while He may be found" and to "call upon Him while He is near." But the gospel of the grace of God in the present age declares to Jew and Gentile alike that "there is none who seeks after God" (Rom. 3:11), and that "the Son of Man has come to seek and to save that which was lost" (Luke 19:10).

This declaration that in this age there are none who seek the Lord accords with the testimony of the New Testament relative to the incapacity of those who are lost to turn to God. Apart from the new birth the unsaved "cannot see the kingdom of God" (John 3:3), their minds are blinded by Satan (2 Cor. 4:3–4), and they can exercise faith toward God only as they are enabled to do so by the Holy Spirit (Eph. 2:8). In the light of these revelations, there is little ground for the hope that the unsaved will "seek the Lord."

What is far more essential to the right understanding of the way of salvation by grace is that the unsaved are not asked to seek the Lord. If this is true, the unsaved should never be placed in the position of those who must discover God or prevail on Him to be gracious.

BELIEVE AND PRAY

If God is propitious, the unsaved have no need to try to find Him, to wait till He is on "the giving hand," or to implore Him to save. He is propitious to an infinite degree, and the problem confronting the unsaved is one of adjustment to that revelation. The transforming effect of the truth that God is propitious penetrates every phrase of soteriology. His flood tide of blessing—all that is impelled by His infinite love—awaits not the imploring, prevailing appeal that might move one to be gracious, but rather it awaits the simple willingness on the part of individuals to receive what He has already provided and is free to bestow in and through His Son, the Savior.

Salvation is precisely what God's infinite love demands and ordains. Its whole scope and extent is the reflection of that immeasurable love. It embraces all that infinity can produce. The sinner's plight is serious indeed and the benefits he receives in saving grace cannot be estimated; but all this together is secondary compared with the satisfaction which God's great love demands. Two obstacles hinder the satisfaction of divine love—the sin of the creature He loves and the will of that creature. As the Creator of all things, even these obstacles take their place in the divine decree which ordained all things that exist. So, as the only One who could do it, He has met by the sacrifice of His Son the obstacle which sin imposed, and He secures the glad cooperation of the human will. The effect of the death of His Son is to render God righteously free to act for those whom He loves, and that freedom for love to act is propitiation. Therefore it must be again asserted that God is propitious. Infinite love now invites the sinner to eternal glories, and infinite love awaits the sinner's response to that invitation.

With this marvelous revelation in view, there is no place left for the idea that the sinner must "seek the Lord," or that the sinner must plead with God to be merciful and kind. No burden rests on the unsaved to persuade God to be good; the challenge of the gospel is for the unsaved to believe that God is good. Since these great truths are revealed only in the Word of God, the unsaved are enjoined to believe God's Word, and the Scriptures hold a large share in the divine undertaking of bringing men to salvation (John 3:5). It is common, however, for some who, with great passion of soul, attempt to preach the gospel, so to fail in the apprehension of the divine propitiation that they imply that salvation is secured by entreating God, and the value of Christ's mediation on behalf of the sinner if thereby nullified.

The example of the prayer of the publican is usually cited as the best of reasons for urging the unsaved to plead with God for His mercy and salvation. What, it is asked, could be more appropriate than that the unsaved souls pray as did the publican, "God, be merciful to me, the sinner" (Luke 18:13)? The appeal on the part of the publican is assumed to be the norm for all sinners, though in reality it contradicts the very truth of the gospel of divine grace. The incident must be examined carefully. It is essential to note that the publican—a Jew of the Old Testament order and praying in the temple according to the requirements of a Jew in the temple—did not use the word "merciful"—which word is properly associated with the idea of kindness, bigheartedness, leniency, and generosity. Actually the publican said, "God, be propitiated to me, the sinner." The publican used the word ἱλάσκομαι, which means "to make propitiation."

There is a wide difference between the word "merciful" with all its implications and the word "propitiation." By the word "merciful" the impression is conveyed that the publican pleaded with God to be magnanimous. However, by the word "propitiation"—if comprehended at all—the impression is conveyed that the publican asked God to cover his sins in such a way as to dispose of them; yet at the same time to do this in a way that would protect His own holiness from complicity with his sins. If the publican did as Jews were accustomed to do in his day when they went into the temple to pray, he left a sacrifice at the altar. It is probable that he could see the smoke of that sacrifice ascending as he prayed. What he prayed was strictly proper for a Jew of his time to pray under those circumstances. However, his prayer would be most unfitting on this side of the cross of Christ. With reference to the world "merciful," it was not in the publican's prayer nor would it be a proper word for the penitent to use, on either side of the Cross. God cannot be merciful to sin in the sense that He treats it lightly, whether it be in one age or another. But with reference to the word "propitiation" and its implications, that word was justified in the age before Christ died and when sin was covered by sacrifices the sinner provided. It was suitable for the publican, having provided his own sacrifice, to ask that his sacrifice be accepted and himself absolved. Yet, on this side of the Cross when Christ has died and secured propitiation and it is established perfectly forever, nothing could be more an outraging of that priceless truth on which the gospel rests than to implore God to be propitious. Such prayers may be enjoined through ignorance, but the wrong is immeasurable. When this prayer is made, even for God to be propitious, there is a direct assumption expressed that God is not propitious, and to that extent the petitioner is asking God to do something more effective than the thing He has done in giving His Son as a sacrifice for sin.

A moment's consideration discloses the immeasurable wrong that is committed when God is asked to be propitious, when, by the infinite cost of the death of His Son, He already is propitious. The truth that God is propitious constitutes the very heart of the gospel of divine grace, and the one who does not recognize this and sees no impropriety in the use of the publican's prayer today has yet to comprehend what is the first principle in the plan of salvation through Christ. People are not saved by asking God to be good, or merciful, or propitious; they are saved when they believe God has been good or merciful enough to provide a propitiating Savior. The sinner is saved, not because he prevails on God to withhold from him the blow of judgment that is due him for his sin, but because he believes that that blow has fallen on his Substitute. If it is thought that all this is but a mere theological distinction and that after all God is love and the sinner will be treated in love, consideration should be given to the fact that it was for the very purpose of providing a righteous ground for salvation of sinners that the Son of God became incarnate, that He died, and that He arose from the dead. To imply that all this—and there is no salvation apart from it—is only a theological speculation, is to reject the whole plan of salvation through a Savior and to assume to stand before God, who is consuming fire, without shelter, shield, or surety.

Summary

In consummating this article on human terms that condition the salvation of soul, the following summary statements may be made.

First, every feature of man's salvation from divine election in past ages and on through successive steps—the sacrifice of the Savior, the enlightenment by the Spirit, the immediate saving work of God in its manifold achievements, the keeping work of the Father, the Son, and the Spirit, the delivering work of the Spirit, the empowering work of the Spirit, and the final perfecting and presenting in glory—is all a work so supernatural that God alone can effect it. Therefore the only relationship man can sustain to it is to trust God to do it. Such a dependence is not only reasonable, but is all and only what God requires on the human side for the eternal salvation of a soul. This human trust acknowledges that according to revelation God can deal righteously with sinners on the ground of the death of His Son for them. The sinner thus trusts in the Saviorhood of Christ.

Second, the primary divine purpose in saving a soul is the satisfying of infinite divine love for that soul and the exercise of God's attribute of sovereign grace. Should the slightest human work of merit be allowed to intrude into this great divine undertaking, the purpose of manifesting divine grace would be shattered. It therefore follows that, of necessity, people are saved by believing apart from any form of human worthiness.

Third, the New Testament declares directly and without complication in about 150 passages that men are saved on the sole principle of faith. In this connection it has been demonstrated that it is not a matter of believing and repenting, of believing and confessing Christ, of believing and being baptized, of believing and surrendering to God, of believing and confessing sin, or of believing and pleading with God for salvation, but it is believing alone. Such belief is apart from works (Rom. 4:5); it is a committal of oneself to Christ (2 Tim. 1:12); and it is a definite turning—an act of the will—to God from every other confidence (1 Thess. 1:9). This is well summarized in Paul's work to the Philippian jailer, "Believe in the Lord Jesus Christ, and you shall be saved" (Acts 16:31).

CHAPTER 13

The Role of the Holy Spirit in Conversion

Robert A. Pyne

The process of conversion is a familiar battleground in soteriology, particularly when theologians describe the nature of human ability and the necessity of divine initiative. Is mankind able to choose salvation apart from divine intervention? Does God extend the same gracious initiative to all persons? If not, what does He do differently with regard to the elect? Different positions relative to these issues have a profound effect on methods of evangelism and on one's understanding of the grace of God. Also the fact that differences over such issues divide the body of Christ serves as a constant challenge to consider the questions afresh in the hope that some measure of agreement might be attained.

The Need for the Spirit's Work

One of the fundamental issues relative to conversion is the nature of human ability. To what extent are unregenerate individuals capable of apprehending the gospel? Are they able to understand it and respond to it affirmatively, or must God specifically enable them to do so?

According to Romans 1:18–21, unbelievers are capable of comprehending the truth of God's existence. "For the wrath of God is revealed from heaven against all ungodliness and unrighteousness of men, who suppress the truth in unrighteousness, because that which is known about God is evident within them; for God made it evident to them. For since the creation of the world His invisible attributes, His eternal power and divine nature, have been clearly seen, being understood through what has been made, so that they are without excuse. For even though they knew God, they did not honor Him as God, or give thanks; but they became futile in their speculations, and their foolish heart was darkened."

By the common grace of natural revelation, unbelievers are said to be aware of the truth of God's existence. This forms the basis for what Paul regarded as their just condemnation. They are without excuse because they have been exposed to the truth. What they should have comprehended they have instead suppressed. Cranfield summarizes this point appropriately.

> A real self-disclosure of God has indeed taken place and is always occurring, and men ought to have recognized, but in fact have not recognized, Him. They have been constantly surrounded on all sides by, and have possessed within their own selves, the evidences of God's eternal power and divinity, but they have not allowed themselves to be led by them to a recognition of Him.[1]

When considering the more specific revelation of the gospel, it is obvious from experience that unbelievers are capable of articulating the terms of the gospel without embracing it. As with their rejection of natural revelation in Romans 1, the problem is not one of comprehension, but of acceptance. The truth is evident, but it is wrongly thought to be foolishness.

This interpretation suggests that unbelievers will not come to actual faith in Christ apart from the intervention of the Holy Spirit. Only by the Holy Spirit is the wisdom of God properly evaluated and apprehended, for it must be "spiritually appraised" (1 Cor. 2:14).

Several conclusions about the ability of the unregenerate person can be drawn from Romans 1 and 1 Corinthians 2. First, he is able to comprehend divine revelation. That is, he is able to understand what is being said. On the other hand he is not able to evaluate that revelation properly so as to regard it as accurate and personally relevant. To the mind controlled by sin, God's truth seems foolish. The rejection that follows from this improper assessment of God's Word causes further hardness of heart and further ignorance in a cycle of futility (Eph. 4:18–19) that can be interrupted only by the Holy Spirit.

The Ministry of Reproof

In John 16:8–11 Jesus described one aspect of the Spirit's evangelistic work. As part of the Upper Room Discourse, in which the Lord comforted the disciples and gave them instructions before His death, He told them they should be encouraged, for it was to their benefit that He was leaving. The reason this is true is that His departure would result in the coming of the Holy Spirit

(14:16–17; 16:7), who would comfort them, teach them, and help them in their evangelistic mission through His ministry of reproof.

John 16:8–11 poses several problems for the interpreter, particularly concerning the nature and purpose of the Spirit's work. The central verb is ἐλέγχω, and its meaning is important in seeking to understand what the Holy Spirit is doing.

THE MEANING OF ἐλέγχω

In the Septuagint ἐλέγχω is used in three ways. First, it describes an act of reproof regarding some wrong committed. In Genesis 21:25 the verb is used of Abraham's complaint to Abimelech, and in 2 Samuel 7:14 it describes the discipline of the Lord for Solomon's sin (cf. Lev. 19:7; Job 5:17). This is the sense in which the word is used in the Book of Proverbs to speak of godly reproof, which is welcomed by the wise but disregarded by the fool (Prov. 3:11–12; 9:7–8; 15:12; 19:25; 28:23; 30:6).[3]

Second, ἐλέγχω is used to describe an act of judging, either between persons (as in Gen. 31:37) or against an individual or nation (as in Gen. 31:42; cf. 1 Chron. 12:17; 2 Chron. 26:20; Isa. 11:3–4; Amos 5:10; Mic. 4:3; Hab. 1:12). Third, the word is used in 1 Chronicles 16:21–22 to describe reproof in the sense of a warning or command regarding a wrong not yet committed.

So the verb ἐλέγχω in the Old Testament means "to reprove," "to bring a charge against," or "to judge." These classifications accord fairly well with the classical definitions given by Liddell and Scott: (1) to disgrace, put to shame, (2) to question, for the purpose of disproving or reproving, and (3) to accuse, censure.[4] Since the party receiving the judgment or reproof, though always present, does not always welcome it, the idea of "convince" or "persuade" is hardly appropriate here.

Moulton and Milligan give several illustrations of the use of ἐλέγχω in the papyri of the New Testament era.[5] They translate the word with "make an inquiry" in one example and "give evidence" or "supply proof" in two more. Two other examples are more legal in nature, in which the term means "charge," "convict," or "prosecute," depending on the context. Some continuity may be observed between these illustrations and the Old Testament usage as described earlier. Most notably, the idea of "bring a charge against" or "judge" is certainly present. The idea of "giving evidence" or "supplying proof," however, seems to be a new development.

For the most part, the use of ἐλέγχω in the New Testament is similar to its use in the Old. The most common meaning is "to correct or reprove," pointing out sin and error with the idea of bringing about repentance.[6] The verb is used in Matthew 18:15 to describe the correction of a sinning believer, and in Luke 3:19 it refers to John the Baptist's reproof of Herod's adultery (cf. 1 Cor. 14:24–25; 1 Tim. 5:20; 2 Tim. 4:2; Titus 1:9, 13; 2:15; Heb. 12:5; Jude 22 [variant]; Rev. 3:19). In addition, Jude 15 uses ἐλέγχω in the sense of the judgment of persons, a condition that may be either corrective or final.

James 2:9 fits either in this category or in one of two separate categories—legal trial and conviction, or "exposure." Here the passive form of the verb is used to describe what happens to a person through the Law when he shows partiality, and that could mean either "reprove," "convict," or "expose."[7]

The idea of exposure is seen more clearly in Ephesians 5:11, 13, where the deeds of the individual are in view, and Paul told believers to "expose" these unfruitful acts rather than participate in them. He repeated the term in the example of light making unseen things visible.

Outside of John's writings, then, the New Testament authors used ἐλέγχω most often to speak of reproof that is intended to bring about repentance, and in one or two places to speak of exposing evil. The meanings found in the papyri of "giving evidence" or "making an inquiry" are not found here, and the Old Testament idea of judgment may occur in one text, but it is in any case much less common. In these examples one still does not find the idea of "convincing" or "persuading," unless that idea is implied by reproof that seeks to bring about a change of heart. "Reprove" seems to be the best general translation in that it encompasses the ideas of discipline, judgment, and exposure.

John used ἐλέγχω in much the same way as the other New Testament writers. John 3:20 refers to God's light exposing sin in the same metaphorical terms used in Ephesians 5. In John 8:46 Jesus asked, "Who among you convicts Me concerning sin [τίς ἐξ ὑμῶν ἐλέγχει με περὶ ἁμαρτίας]?" This question uses the same words found in 16:8: ἐλέγξει . . . περὶ ἁμαρτίας. Though the idea of conviction may seem appropriate, Jesus' question may just as easily be using ἐλέγχω in the customary sense of "reprove." No one is able to correct Him for any sin, for He has done nothing wrong, but speaks the truth.

In John 16:8 the Holy Spirit is involved in pointing out sin in order to bring about repentance. The legal idea suggested by some[8] seems to have been derived from the use of the term in extrabiblical literature, whereas the biblical writers used ἐλέγχω primarily to describe correction, not prosecution or conviction. If the term denotes reproof here, then the meaning of the term has implications with regard to the extent of the Spirit's ministry as well. As in Proverbs, such reproof is not irresistible; it is welcomed by the wise man but resisted by the fool.

THE OBJECTS OF THE SPIRIT'S REPROOF

Arguing that the world cannot receive the Paraclete (14:17), Brown maintains that the Spirit does not direct this ministry toward the world at all, but proves to the disciples that the world is guilty.[9] However, this idea demands that ἐλέγχω means "to prove wrong about" or "to convict," and this seems unlikely in light of the observations already made. The individual being reproved is usually present, and has freedom to accept or reject the reproof.

Further, as Carson points out, by the promise of the Paraclete, the Lord was assuring the disciples that they would not be alone, particularly in their witness to the world.[10] In this context it seems more than appropriate to describe the nature of the Spirit's ministry to the world. To say that the Holy Spirit has no ministry to the world (while Jesus does) seems odd.

John's use of the word κόσμος reinforces the idea that the Spirit's ministry of reproof is an expression of common grace. First, κόσμος can have reference to the physical world, as in John 1:9–10 and 13:1. Second, it can denote those who live in that world, as in 1:10, 29; 3:16–19; and 4:42. In this category, κόσμος often refers to those who are opposed to Jesus, distinct from the disciples (7:7; 8:23; 12:31; 14:17, 19, 22, 27; 15:18–19; 16:20; 17:6, 9, 14, 16). (However, it should also be noted that the term is not necessarily limited to those who will not believe; 6:33; 12:19.)

In John 17, Jesus affirmed that He came into the world and that God the Father gave the disciples out of the world. As Jesus was leaving the world, He was sending them into it. The world hated Him because He was not of the world, and it hates His disciples because they are not of the world. His aim is that the disciples may be one so that the world may believe that the Father sent Him. It would not be inaccurate to say that the world here is the mission field; the disciples have come out of it, and they are witnessing to it. Far from being written off, the world is the aim of evangelism. As Guhrt writes, "Especially in Paul and John, [κόσμος] designates the place and object of God's saving activity."[11]

As the Light of the world, Jesus exposed the deeds of those in the world. Some responded positively (12:46) and others preferred the darkness (3:19). As with His teaching, this ministry continued only while Jesus was in the world (9:5). When He returned to the Father, the Spirit assumed many of these works in His place (14:16, 25–26; 16:12–15). The Holy Spirit continues to expose the deeds of the world. Those who remain in the world, who prefer the darkness to light, reject the message of Jesus and the light given by the disciples and the Spirit.

The Spirit's ministry of reproof comes to every individual; all are charged with sin. Like the reproof spoken of in Proverbs, it is welcomed by the wise man and rejected by the fool.

THE FOCUS OF THE SPIRIT'S REPROOF

The most difficult issue in the interpretation of John 16:8–11 relates to the function of the ὅτι clauses. Do they provide the reason for the Spirit's reproof in the areas of sin, righteousness, and judgment, or do they function in some other way? For example Bauer, Arndt, and Gingrich classify the use here as "concerning [something], that."[12] Similarly Brown says that "the main emphasis seems to be explicative rather than causative," and translates ὅτι "in that."[13]

Carson has discussed this issue at length, reviewing the options suggested and attempting to fit the pieces together with consistency by maintaining the parallelism of the three ὅτι clauses. He describes the problem in the following way.

> It is easy enough to find a believable interpretation of each case, one that is consistent with Johannine thought, if we forfeit the attempt to insure that such an interpretation will blend harmoniously with the interpretation of the other clauses. We might, for example, find it easy to believe that the Paraclete convicts the world of its sin. Yet we must hesitate before submitting this interpretation because exactly the same structure in the next pair of lines yields the interpretation that the Paraclete convicts the world of its righteousness; and that does not on the face of it appear too coherent. Perhaps these lines mean rather that the Paraclete will convict the world in the realm of the righteousness of Christ. But in that case, we introduce discontinuity: we speak of the world's sin, but of Christ's righteousness. We do this despite the fact that there is no formal mention of "world's" or "Christ's," while there is formal identity of structure.[14]

Carson's own explanation for this problem is that Jesus was speaking of the world's sin, the world's pseudo-righteousness, and the world's wrong judgment concerning Him. Since his explanation does justice to the parallel phrases of verses 9–11, it seems helpful. However, a difficulty arises in the fact that verse 11 does not seem to describe the world's wrong judgment of Christ.

In John 7:24 and 8:15–16, Jesus spoke of the world's false judgment, suggesting the possibility that the judgment in 16:11 should be taken in this way. However, in 12:31 Jesus said, "Now judgment is upon this world; now the ruler of this world shall be cast out." In this passage, Jesus certainly was speaking of God's judgment on the world.[15] If this is the case, then it is likely that the same meaning applies in 16:11, for both passages relate the judgment to the condemnation of the "ruler of the world." The world is judged, beginning with its leader.

If this is correct, the judgment spoken of in 16:11 is God's judgment of the world, not the world's perception of reality. Therefore it seems that a strict parallelism in the three ὅτι clauses (the major presupposition behind Carson's argument) is not necessary.

"Sin" can be understood as the world's sin, about which individuals are reproved because they do not believe in Christ (suggesting unbelief as the essence of sin). "Righteousness" can be understood as the objective standard of righteousness, concerning which the Spirit reproves the world because Christ is no longer there to do so by word and example. "Judgment" can be seen as the judgment that the world will soon receive, the imminence of which has been demonstrated by Satan's judgment at the cross.

The Holy Spirit brings correction (ἐλέγχω) to the world, and does so by revealing sin, directing the way to righteousness, and warning of impending judgment. It is as if He says, "You should not sin, but should pursue righteousness in the face of judgment." All three are aspects of His ministry of correction and reproof.

SUMMARY

According to John 16:8–11, the Holy Spirit shows unbelievers their need for the gospel. The passage does not distinguish between the elect and the nonelect in this aspect of the Spirit's ministry, which is directed toward the entire world.

As an expression of common grace, the Spirit's reproof works alongside the "general" or "external" call of the gospel (Matt. 22:14).[16] Does this constitute a universal remedy for the problem described in 1 Corinthians 2:14? Is it possible through this ministry of the Spirit for all persons to evaluate the gospel message properly and accept it?

If the Spirit's reproof and the universal preaching of the gospel were sufficient to enable unbelievers to accept Paul's message, the argument of 1 Corinthians 2:14 would be invalidated. Paul's point is that those who regard the gospel as foolishness lack the spiritual insight required to see its legitimacy. If they are to come to faith, they are in need of something more.

The Ministry of Effectual Calling

In Romans 8:30 Paul referred to the divine work of "calling": "Whom He predestined, these He also called; and whom He called, these He also justified; and whom He justified, these He also glorified."

THE OBJECTS OF THE CALL

Examining this passage from an Arminian perspective, Guy writes,

> So, in the Pauline language here, "foreknow" means that in every instance "God loves man before man loves God." "Predestine" means that God takes the initiative to remedy the human predicament. "Call" means that God, through the proclamation of the gospel, invites human beings collectively and individually to participate in the actualization of the divine intention for them. "Justify" means that God acts to restore the proper relationship between humanity and deity. "Glorify" means that in the process of salvation God transforms human existence in a way that becomes increasingly evident and is ultimately completed.[17]

By describing these actions in such broad terms, Guy neglects the fact that the individuals involved do more than *potentially* benefit from this divine activity. They *actually* benefit from it. Several observations demonstrate that this work of God[18] is directed toward the elect only. First, the "calling" is clearly limited to those who are "predestined to become conformed to the image of His Son" (v. 29). Since only those who are predestined for salvation are called, and all those who are called are justified and ultimately glorified, it seems obvious that the apostle referred only to the elect.[19]

The idea of God's calling being limited to the elect is consistent with Paul's use of the terms "call," "calling," or "called" elsewhere. He regularly referred to believers as those who are "called" (Rom. 1:6; 1 Cor. 1:9; 7:17–24; Gal. 1:6; Eph. 4:1; 1 Thess. 2:12; 1 Tim. 6:12; 2 Tim. 1:9), highlighting the divine role of summoning individuals to salvation and sanctification.[20]

THE NATURE OF THE CALL

The idea of a "call" in the sense of an invitation is common. The host is the one calling, and the guests are those who are called.[21] When God issues an invitation to salvation, it is in one sense extended to all persons. This is an "external" or "general" calling, which Berkhof describes in the context of gospel preaching.

> External calling . . . comes to all men to whom the gospel is preached, indiscriminately. It is not confined to any age or nation or class of men. It comes to both the just and the unjust, the elect and the reprobate. . . . That the gospel invitation is not limited to the elect, as some hold, is quite evident from such passages as Ps. 81:11–13; Prov. 1:24–26; Ezek. 3:19; Matt. 22:2–8, 14; Luke 14:16–24.[22]

Romans 8, however, is describing a narrower form of divine invitation. As already noted, this invitation is extended only to the elect, to those who have already been predestined to salvation in Christ. If this call is limited to the elect it cannot be rejected. Erickson writes appropriately, "The calling must be efficacious— those who are called are actually saved."[23] This work of God can be referred to as "irresistible grace" in that it is never refused, or "efficacious grace" in that it is always successful in accomplishing its purpose. "By καλεῖν here is meant not just 'call' but 'call effectually.'"[24] In the same way, Dunn comments, "The thought is not of an invitation which might be rejected; God does not leave his purpose to chance but puts it into effect himself."[25]

In "calling" the elect, God actually brings them to conversion. In doing so, He summons individuals to fulfill the holy purpose He has ordained for them.

Just as predestination points toward the ultimate conformity of the elect to the image of Jesus Christ (Rom. 8:29), calling is a summons not just to conversion, but to salvation in all its fullness, with all its responsibilities. That explains why Paul seems to have overlapped God's initiative in his (Paul's) salvation with God's directive in his vocation.[26] For example Paul wrote to Timothy, "Therefore, do not be ashamed of the testimony of our Lord, or of me His prisoner; but join with me in suffering for the gospel according to the power of God, who has saved us, and called us with a holy calling, not according to our works, but according to His own purpose and grace which was granted us in Christ Jesus from all eternity" (2 Tim. 1:9). The calling is related to salvation, even to predestination, and also to the apostle's present responsibilities in ministry.

The fact that believers have been called by God means that He has taken the initiative in providing their salvation, and it also means that He has the prerogative to direct their behavior (Gal. 1:6; Eph. 4:1; 1 Thess. 2:12; 1 Tim. 6:12). As Paul suggested in Philippians 3:12, 14, to attain "the prize of the upward call of God in Christ Jesus" is to "lay hold of that for which also I was laid hold of by Christ Jesus." To fulfill one's calling is not simply to come to faith; it is to fulfill God's divine purpose in salvation. Ultimately that means becoming fully conformed to the image of Christ through glorification (Rom. 8:30; 2 Cor. 3:18).

THE TIMING OF THE CALL

Though the elect are called to much more than a simple "decision" for Christ, Paul seems to have in focus that moment of conversion when he referred to calling in Romans 8:30. Here God's call is the bridge between predestination and justification. That is why Dunn describes it as "divinely accomplished conversion."[27] Calling and faith seem to be two sides of the same coin, emphasizing the divine and human aspects of conversion respectively.[28] For example 1 Corinthians 7:17–24 looks back on conversion as the moment when one was "called," while Romans 13:11 speaks of conversion as "when we believed." Both terms point to a single event.

At the same time, in a logical *ordo salutis,* calling seems to precede faith, because of the necessity of divine initiative in conversion.[29] As Morris writes, Paul's use of "calling" as a summons to salvation "reminds us of the priority of the divine call in salvation. Men do not choose God. He chooses them."[30] Cranfield suggests this same order when he writes, "When God thus calls effectually, a man responds with the obedience of faith."[31]

THE FUNCTION OF THE CALL

Since God's efficacious calling bridges the gap between predestination and justification by faith, it is appropriate to regard this work as the means by which He brings the elect to faith. As

Erickson summarizes, "Special calling means that God works in a particularly effective way with the elect, enabling them to respond in repentance and faith, and rendering it certain that they will."[32]

It has been argued above that unbelievers are not capable of properly evaluating the gospel message unless they are given insight by the Holy Spirit. On their own, unbelievers have had their minds blinded to the truth about Jesus Christ (2 Cor. 4:4). Since God moves such persons to faith through His effectual calling, this divine work apparently removes the blindness and enables them to see the Cross as their hope of salvation.

Erickson suggests that effectual calling consists "in large measure" of the Holy Spirit's work of illumination, "enabling the recipient to understand the true meaning of the gospel."[33] The idea of illumination is an appropriate metaphor. To grant insight where once it was lacking is like turning on a light or giving sight to the blind. Paul used that comparison in 2 Corinthians 3 and 4 with regard to conversion.

Paul began his development of this metaphor by recognizing that, even though it was temporary, Moses' face shone with the glory of God (2 Cor. 3:7). Since this was true, he argued, how much more does the Spirit's present ministry abound in glory? Moses used to veil his face to prevent the Israelites from beholding its radiance, and the same obstruction continues with the Law to this day.[34] The Law does not enable one to behold the glory of God; it actually inhibits one from doing so (v. 14). Paul then compared this situation to that of believers. "But we all, with unveiled face beholding as in a mirror the glory of the Lord, are being transformed into the same image from glory to glory, just as from the Lord, the Spirit" (v. 18).

By stating that he and other believers were unveiled, Paul emphasized the fact that the obstruction of the Law had been removed. Rather than being prevented from viewing the glory of God, as the Israelites had been, believers enjoy the same sort of unhindered access to God Moses had experienced.

The idea of beholding God's glory "in a mirror" has similar implications. Κατοπτριζόμενοι means to "look at something in a mirror."[35] Hughes suggests that it refers to contemplating something through the dim vision of faith, as in 1 Corinthians 13:12.[36] Kittel argues more specifically that this is a "miraculous mirror in which what is invisible is made visible to prophets and pneumatics."[37] Kittel says Paul relied primarily on rabbinic discussions of Numbers

12:8, which maintained that Moses saw God in a mirror, as did other prophets, but that Paul's mirror was clearer. The argument seems persuasive, and the point is that believers, like Moses, are given a clear vision of the glory of God. This vision, however, is dim compared to what will be revealed to them in the future.

"Those who are perishing" (τοῖς ἀπολλυμένοις) remain "veiled" (2 Cor. 4:3), unable to see "the light of the gospel of the glory of Christ" (v. 4). These are the same persons spoken of in 1 Corinthians 1:18 and (by implication) in 1 Corinthians 2:14. They continue to perceive the gospel as foolishness, for they are incapable of recognizing its truth in their sinful condition. In their inability their minds remain hardened as the veil of legalism remains in place (2 Cor. 3:14–15), and "the god of this world" has blinded their minds (4:4). This condition is addressed by God's work of illumination.

Paul wrote, "God, who said, 'Light shall shine out of darkness,' is the One who has shone in our hearts to give the light of the knowledge of the glory of God in the face of Christ" (2 Cor. 4:6). He had experienced the light of the gospel literally, beholding the exalted Christ on the Damascus Road as "a light from heaven flashed around him" (Acts 9:3). The illumination of the heart is more subtle, but no less spectacular. The blindness of the mind is removed, and the gospel which once seemed foolish is now recognized as the power of God (1 Cor. 1:18). Brought to faith through this act of grace, believers have been granted unhindered access to God and a true knowledge of the glory of Christ.[38]

Chafer writes appropriately, "No soul can be saved apart from this enlightenment, for no other power is sufficient to break through the blindness which Satan has imposed on the minds of those who are lost."[39] Without the effectual call of God bringing illumination to hardened hearts, no one would come to faith. This accords with the first line of the Westminster Confession on effectual calling, which reads,

> All those whom God hath predestinated unto life, and those only, he is pleased, in his appointed and accepted time, effectually to call, by his Word and Spirit, out of that state of sin and death, in which they are by nature, to grace and salvation by Jesus Christ; enlightening their minds, spiritually and savingly, to understand the things of God; taking away their heart of stone, and giving unto them an heart of flesh; renewing their wills, and by his almighty power determining them to that which is good, and effectually drawing them to Jesus Christ; yet so as they come most freely, being made willing by his grace.[40]

Conclusion

Apart from God's specific, gracious intervention no one would come to faith. Unless unbelievers are given particular insight through the Holy Spirit, they are not capable of properly evaluating the gospel message.

The Holy Spirit's work of reproof functions along with the general call of the gospel as a ministry of common grace. However, it is insufficient of itself to bring someone to conversion. If the blindness of the "natural man" is to be removed and the truth about Jesus Christ is to be apprehended, something more must take place.

According to Romans 8:30, the divine work of effectual calling accomplishes that task. Bridging the gap between predestination and justification by faith, God's effectual call brings the elect to faith. This effectual call consists of a divine summons to salvation along with illumination, through which the elect rightly perceive the gospel and inevitably trust in Jesus Christ.

CHAPTER 14

Has Lordship Salvation Been Taught Throughout Church History?

Thomas G. Lewellen

Proponents of lordship salvation frequently employ a historical argument to demonstrate the validity of their view of the gospel. The argument is that the long history of the Christian faith stands in united agreement with their message of salvation. The conclusion usually drawn is that if history is on their side, they must be right.

Examples of this line of reasoning abound. Chantry writes,

> In the central issue of the way of salvation, large segments of Protestantism are engrossed in neo-traditionalism. We have inherited a system of evangelistic preaching which is unbiblical. Nor is this tradition very ancient. Our message and manner of preaching the Gospel cannot be traced back to the Reformers and their creeds. They are much more recent innovations.[1]

Or in answering the charge that his message is a threat to the integrity of the gospel, John MacArthur writes, "That is a grave charge. Is it substantiated by church history? I think not. The truth is, the concept of faith that [Zane] Hodges decries as a modern heresy is exactly what the true church has always believed."[2]

Sometimes the argument from history is brought in as only a passing comment.[3] Often, however, the evidence of history is regarded as having almost decisive value in the debate.[4] With this in mind the validity of this argument should be considered. The issue is not the quality of biblical interpretation that is used by either side. The issue is whether history can be used as substantial evidence confirming either side in the lordship salvation or free grace debate.

To evaluate this line of reasoning two things need to be examined carefully. First, is the argument true? Does history agree with the tenets of lordship salvation? In other words does the history of the Christian church yield unmistakable evidence that the leaders of

Christianity throughout the centuries have substantially agreed on the message of salvation, and that their agreed teaching supports the view of lordship salvation? Second, does it matter? If the leaders of history are united in support of lordship salvation, does that prove that such a view is necessarily correct and that the free grace view is only an incorrect and recent aberration?

What Does History Teach about the Gospel?

The recent disagreement between lordship salvation and free grace does not deal with every area of the doctrine of salvation. There is substantial agreement on both sides regarding the Person of Christ as the God-Man, His virgin birth, His substitutionary atonement, His miraculous, bodily resurrection, and the necessity of regeneration by the Holy Spirit for eternal salvation.

At issue are the nature of faith, the relationship between faith and assurance, and the effect of regeneration. In other words the debate centers around three critical questions: What must a person do to be saved? What must a person do to know he is saved? How will salvation show itself in one's life?

THE NATURE OF SAVING FAITH

Lordship and nonlordship views of salvation differ greatly on the nature of saving faith. In many ways this is the crux of the issue. As Packer has aptly stated regarding this debate, "What is in question is the nature of faith."[5]

Generally speaking, lordship salvation teaches that faith is an *active* response on the part of a sinner, centered in the human *will*, and *including obedience* to the commands of God. For example Stott writes, "We may believe in the deity and the salvation of Christ, and acknowledge ourselves to be sinners in need of His salvation; but this does not make us Christians. We have to make a personal response to Jesus Christ, committing ourselves unreservedly to Him as our Savior and Lord."[6] Or as Packer has written, "Christian faith means hearing, noting, and doing what God says."[7] MacArthur writes, "True faith is never seen as passive—it is always obedient. In fact, Scripture often equates faith with obedience."[8]

Obviously to the teachers of lordship salvation, saving faith is an active response in which the sinner commits himself to Christ as both Lord and Savior. The vital elements of this faith include trust, commitment, *and obedience* to God.

The difficulty is that the nature of saving faith has been debated at every point in church history. In fact many of the leading writers and theologians in the history of the church held a view of faith that is at complete variance with that held by teachers of lordship salvation today. For example Saint Augustine (354–430) said, "Faith is nothing else than to think with assent."[9] Many will disagree with his definition (the present writer certainly does), but that was Augustine's view. Faith, to Augustine, was simply mental assent to understood propositions, and nothing more.

John Calvin, the Swiss Reformer (1509–1564), wrote, "For, as regards justification, faith is something merely passive, bringing nothing of ours to the recovering of God's favor but *receiving* from Christ what we lack."[10] Again, "We compare faith to a kind of vessel; for unless we come empty and with the mouth of our soul open to seek Christ's grace, we are not capable of receiving Christ."[11] By "passive" Calvin apparently did not mean the one coming to Christ does absolutely nothing. Obviously the sinner must trust or rely on Christ for salvation. By "passivity" Calvin meant that the sinner *receives* salvation through simple trust in Christ, that He *gives* nothing in order to possess this salvation.

Some writers have asserted that this was not the true position of Calvin. However, recent works have conclusively demonstrated that in fact Calvin taught that faith is a passive response by which a sinner simply receives the gift of God in Christ. Kendall writes, "What stands out in Calvin's descriptions is the given, intellectual, passive and assuring nature of faith."[12] Bell points out that to Calvin, faith was not a cold speculation abut God or a mental assent that was not connected with a vital trust in His promises. Yet, he says, "Calvin taught that faith is fundamentally passive in nature, is centered in the mind or understanding, [and] is primarily to be viewed in terms of certain knowledge."[13] To Calvin, faith is not obedience or commitment. Obedience, in Calvin's view, flows from faith and is part of the nature of the Christian life.[14] Faith itself is *reliance* on the divine promises of salvation in Christ and nothing more.

Whatever disagreements there may have been between Calvin and the Lutheran theologians of the Reformation, on this topic there seems to have been complete agreement. Philip Melanchthon (1497–1560), the contemporary of Luther and author of *The Augsburg Confession*, defined faith purely as "receptivity."[15] This idea of faith as receiving is so much a part of confessional Lutheran theology today as to be beyond controversy.[16] Francis Pieper, the author of the modern standard theology of confessional Lutheranism wrote, "Saving faith is essentially the *reliance* of the heart on the promises of God set forth in the gospel." Again, "In the preceding characterization of faith, we have stated . . . that justifying faith must be viewed merely as the *instrument or receptive organ* for apprehending the forgiveness of sins offered in the gospel."[17]

In the Puritan era, however, there was a shift in the definition of saving faith. In the generations following the Reformation, some theologians subtly changed the Reformers' definition of faith from a passive receptivity to an active response on the part of the sinner, centered in the will and containing both commitment and obedience.[18] This change is most evident in the writings of the English Calvinists and is embodied in the Westminster Standards.[19] This explains in part why lordship salvation teachers rely most heavily on Westminster theology and the writings of the English Calvinists to validate their position.[20]

This review of history does not claim to be conclusive or exhaustive. The one deduction that can be drawn, however, is that the nature of "saving faith" has a rich and varied history in the Christian church. It is not defensible for proponents of either lordship salvation or free grace to claim that their position is *the* view of church history.

MacArthur's statement, "the view of faith that Hodges decries as a modern heresy is exactly what the true church has always believed,"[21] is simply untrue. What is true, however, is that MacArthur's view *is* embodied in the Westminster Standards and *does* have a long and powerful history in the Christian church. The idea that faith is an active commitment, including obedience, is the view of one strand of church history—English Puritanism— which is of course a powerful strand. One should not confuse that strand, however, with the "true church." Calvin disagreed with it; Lutheran theology has always opposed it; even today some Reformed theologians do not accept it.[22]

On the significant issue of the nature of saving faith it must be concluded that past Christian leaders do not agree on the teachings of lordship salvation. In fact many who espouse a free grace view, and who regard faith as simple trust by which the believer relies solely on the divine promises of forgiveness in Christ, find themselves comfortably aligned with both Calvin and Luther and many of their successors.

THE RELATIONSHIP BETWEEN FAITH AND ASSURANCE

Possibly the greatest distance between the positions of lordship salvation and free grace exists in the area of the nature and source of a Christian's personal assurance of salvation. How can a believer *know* he is the object of God's saving grace and that he possesses eternal life? Like the nature of faith, this issue is at the heart of the debate.

Lordship salvation proponents often leave assurance out of their discussions of the gospel. The reason is that they regard assurance as something that is not necessarily connected with saving faith. It is usually considered a fruit of faith and is to be gathered through self-examination. Boice writes, "It is necessary that we do these good works (as Christians in all ages have), for unless we do, we have no assurance that we are really Christ's followers."[23] Chantry similarly remarks, "Only when God is loved supremely and the spirit of the law kept has a man any reason to believe that he has been truly born of God."[24]

MacArthur writes, "The Bible teaches clearly that the evidence of God's work in a life is the inevitable fruit of transformed behavior. Faith that does not result in righteous living is dead and cannot save. Professing Christians utterly lacking the fruit of true righteousness will find no biblical basis for assurance they are saved."[25] Again, "The fruit of one's life reveals whether that person is a believer or an unbeliever. There is no middle ground."[26]

Proponents of lordship salvation say the grounds of assurance are within the believer. The internal change in direction and feeling that the Holy Spirit produces in the heart of the regenerate person gives him assurance that he is saved. This is also the view of the Westminster Confession, which grounds assurance on three pillars:

> . . . the infallible assurance of faith [is] founded upon the divine truth of the promises of salvation, *the inward evidence of those graces unto which these promises are made,* [and] the testimony of the Spirit of adoption witnessing with our spirits that we are the children of God. . . . This infallible assurance *doth not so belong to the essence of faith,* but that a true believer may wait long, and conflict with many difficulties before he be a partaker of it. . . . And therefore it is the duty of everyone to give all diligence to make his calling and election sure.[27]

This view admits that the promises of salvation made in the bible are a source of assurance. These promises, however, are not conclusive unless they are accompanied by the inward evidence of a changed life.

The basic idea in this view is that assurance is something a believer must gather by deduction from the change that he sees in his life. Salvation *is* promised in the Bible to those who believe. The only way, however, a person can know whether he has truly believed, according to lordship salvation proponents, is by seeing the fruit of the Holy Spirit's work in his life. Therefore the nature of this fruit is an important issue if the believer is to know if he has eternal life. Among the Puritans whole volumes were written to teach how a person may have assurance of salvation, and to contrast false presumption with true assurance.[28] For example John Owen (1616–1683) said of his 650-page *Discourse Concerning the Holy Spirit* that one of his major concerns was to help people determine whether they had truly believed.[29]

Such a preoccupation with the uncertainty of salvation was, however, a peculiarity of the Puritan era. It was most certainly not a fruit of the Reformation. Both Calvin and Luther taught that assurance of salvation is of the very essence of faith. A central tenet of Reformation teaching was that the personal certainty of one's eternal destiny is tied up with what it means to believe the gospel.

Martin Luther wrote that saving faith is "the sort of faith that does not look at its own works nor at its own strength and worthiness, noting what sort of quality or new created or infused virtue it may be. . . . But faith goes out of itself, clings to Christ, and embraces Him as its own possession; and *faith is certain that it is loved by God for His sake.*"[30] And where does this certainty come from? According to Luther it comes from relying on the promise of God's mercy in the gospel, and not from any sense of internal change. "For certainty does not come to me from any kind of reflection on myself and on my state. On the contrary it comes solely through hearing the Word, solely because and in so far as I cling to the Word of God and its promise.[31] Faith is only acceptance of the Word, effective for salvation, and is for Luther the decisive source of certainty.

Pfürtner writes, "Luther placed the certainty of salvation at the very heart of his Reformation message, and made western Christianity begin again to be aware of it. . . . Faith, to Luther, is pure reception and seizure of the message of salvation with the act of which the sinner, falling into despair, yields to God and His forgiving grace."[32] As with the nature of saving faith, contemporary confessional Lutheranism has not swayed far from its source on this issue.[33]

Concerning John Calvin's view of assurance, Bell states, "Without question, Calvin teaches that assurance of one's salvation is of the very essence of faith. Assurance is not an optional extra for the believer."[34] Lane stresses,

> For Calvin, it was not possible to partake of salvation without being sure of it. Assurance is not a second stage in the Christian life, subsequent to and distinct from faith. In the following century some of his followers did separate them in this way and this, together with a departure from Calvin's ground of assurance, led to a widespread loss of assurance.[35]

Calvin defined faith as "a firm certain knowledge of God's benevolence toward us, founded upon the truth of the freely given promise in Christ, both revealed to our minds and sealed upon our hearts."[36] Again, with characteristic plainness, he wrote, "*He alone is truly a believer* who, convinced by a firm conviction that God is a kindly and well-disposed Father toward him, promises himself all things on the basis of his generosity; who, relying upon the promises of divine benevolence toward him, lays hold on an *undoubted expectation of salvation.*"[37]

Teachers of lordship salvation frequently give "tests" by which a believer may know whether he is genuinely saved.[38] These tests are all based on some observable change that one might see in his life as a result of regeneration. Calvin, on the contrary, strictly warned against all attempts to find assurance by an observation of one's works. He says that from one's works, "conscience feels more fear and consternation than assurance."[39] As Lane says of Calvin's view, "Any attempt to base assurance on such works is doomed to failure since the tender conscience will soon see the inadequacy of the foundation. If we maintain assurance on such a basis, it shows that we do not recognize our own imperfection and opens the door to self-trust."[40] To Calvin the ground of assurance does not lie within oneself. Faith includes assurance solely because the object of saving faith is the finished work of Christ as it is offered in the gospel. Faith looks to Christ alone and confidently rests on His saving promise.

True, some Reformed theologians in the centuries following the Reformation took issue with Calvin's understanding of faith and assurance. For example R. L. Dabney, a Southern Presbyterian theologian (1820–1898), was aware of the theological difference between Calvin's teaching and that of the Westminster Standards, and he defended it. He wrote:

> The source of this error is no doubt that doctrine concerning faith which the first Reformers, as Luther and Calvin, were led to adopt from their opposition to the hateful and tyrannical teachings of Rome. . . . These noble Reformers . . . asserted that the assurance of hope is of the essence of saving faith. Thus says Calvin in his commentary on Romans, "My faith is a divine and spiritual belief that God has pardoned and accepted me."[41]

Dabney goes on to assert:

> [Calvin] requires everyone to say, in substance, I believe fully Christ *has saved me*. Amidst all Calvin's verbal variations, this is always his meaning; for he is consistent in his error . . . for as sure as truth is in history, Luther and Calvin did fall into this error, *which the Reformed churches, led by the Westminster Confession, have since corrected.*[42]

The relationship between faith and assurance has long been a debated point in Reformed circles. The "Marrow Controversy" in Scotland in the 1700s is one example.[43] The case of John McLeod Campbell in the 1830s is another.[44] A century ago Horatius Bonar (1808–1889), a hymn writer of that period, taught the essentially passive and assuring nature of faith in Christ's atoning work.[45] Lewis Sperry Chafer (1871–1952), an advocate of free grace, certainly would be placed in this tradition.[46]

Concerning the relationship between faith and assurance of salvation, it must be concluded that contemporary teachers of lordship salvation do not have the united voice of the past leaders of the Christian movement behind them. By regarding assurance of salvation as not being of the essence of faith, but rather as a fruit of faith, and by placing the grounds of assurance within the believer, rather than outside the believer in the Person and work of Christ, lordship salvation on this point is at complete variance with both Luther and Calvin and an entire wing of the Reformed tradition.

The view of assurance of salvation espoused by the proponents of lordship salvation *does* have a long history in the Christian church. It is fair to say that much of Puritanism held this view. It is fair to say that this understanding of faith and assurance is written into the Westminster Standards. It is *not*, however, fair to say that this view is the united voice of the history of the church. Those who propagate the free grace view of salvation and who regard assurance of salvation as being essentially connected with what it means to trust in Christ for salvation have a strong tradition of interpretation and teaching on their side.

THE EFFECT OF REGENERATION

When the Holy Spirit imparts new, spiritual life to the sinner, what is the effect in his character and conduct? If a person is genuinely saved, how will this salvation show itself in his life?

Often this seems to be regarded by proponents of lordship salvation as *the* issue. Quotations are frequently extracted from history to demonstrate that regeneration produces a visible change in a person's character and conduct and that a lack of change is the certain evidence of a lack of salvation.[47]

However, great essential agreement exists between proponents and opponents of lordship salvation. Both sides agree that regeneration, or the impartation of eternal life by the Holy Spirit to a sinner, is required for salvation. Both sides agree that regeneration produces a positional change: a Father-child relationship is established between God and the believing sinner. Both sides also agree that regeneration produces a constitutional change: a person receives the Holy Spirit and eternal life, which is God's quality of life placed within his soul. This constitutional change provides the possibility and the power for a superb transformation of character and conduct. Both sides agree that such transformation is expected, desired, demanded, and possible for the believer.

Both sides also agree that Christians can sin, and sin severely. Both sides agree that sin in a believer is serious and brings on him or her the convicting work of the Holy Spirit and should result in confrontation and discipline by the church. And both sides agree that such disobedience can last for some period of time in a believer.[48]

So the Holy Spirit, by His presence in the believer's life, provides the grounds for a transformation of both character and conduct. But true believers can and do sin. It is out of this tension that all theologies have to formulate their view of sanctification. To attempt to make even a cursory statement of historical views on sanctification is beyond the scope of this paper. It would require an examination of many different theological formulations and is not at the heart of the message of justification by faith.

There has been too much heat and too little light shed on this issue in the contemporary debate about the gospel. The truth is, lordship salvation does *not* teach that every professing Christian who sins is not a true believer.[49] Likewise free grace teachers do *not* affirm the salvation of everyone who claims to be a Christian.[50]

Undoubtedly much of Christian history has taught that
regeneration will produce some outward and visible change and
that no change whatsoever may be evidence of a lack of true
regeneration. But free grace teachers teach the same thing.[51] The
points of disagreement go back to the nature of faith and assurance.
What the free grace position simply will not allow is that the
change produced by regeneration is the grounds of or the evidence
for assurance of genuine salvation. This concern has firm roots in
history. As the Lutheran *Formula of Concord* (1577) states:

> We believe, teach and confess also that notwithstanding the fact that
> many weaknesses and defects cling to the true believers and truly
> regenerate, even to the grave, still they must not on that account doubt
> either their righteousness which has been imputed to them by faith, or the
> salvation of their souls, but must regard it as certain that, for Christ's
> sake, according to the promise and immovable word of the holy Gospel,
> they have a gracious God.[52]

This issue is not whether Christians should produce good works.
The issue is whether those good works have decisive value in
determining whether individuals are saved.

Does Church History Matter?

In church history, views on faith, assurance, and regeneration
were held that differ distinctly from those often presented by
proponents of lordship salvation. In all fairness it must also be
noted that views were held that differ from those held by proponents
of free grace. Does it matter then whether history agrees with
one's interpretation of the Bible? In other words what conclusions
can be drawn from the evidence of history?

The question is not, Does the Christian faith care about history?
The answer to that is a resounding yes. Christianity is a historical
religion. It is rooted in historical events—the Person of Christ, His
miraculous birth by a virgin woman, His atoning death, and
bodily resurrection. Without these truths the Christian faith would
fall. But the history of the church since the first century matters
too. The fact that God's people have existed on the earth for
nearly 2,000 years in gathered communities of believers called
churches speaks of Christ's transforming power. And every
Christian should knowingly root himself in this rich and varied
history. Any believer who recites "The Apostles' Creed"
acknowledges that he is part of the long and formidable history of
God's people.

However, the question, Does church history matter? means, Should believers hold to their faith or their particular doctrinal views because they have been held by others in history? If Christians today are consistently evangelical, the answer must be a most emphatic no. Ultimately one's faith rests solely on the revealed truth of God's Word. Every generation of Christian people must test all the conclusions of history, including those most fundamental to the faith (such as the Trinity, the deity of Christ, the substitionary atonement, and justification by faith alone), by the one standard of God's holy Word.

Christians should not believe something simply because it was taught by Athanasius, Augustine, Luther, Calvin, or any other great Christian leader of history. Believers are not to believe certain things simply because they are written in the notes of a particular study Bible, or found on the pages of a favorite theology or commentary, or taught in a cherished seminary. The Word of God alone reveals both what is to be believed concerning God and what duties God requires. All other people, whether giants or dwarfs in the history of the church, have only given words about the Word. People today can learn from them, they can test them, they can agree with them or disagree with them; but the Bible alone "matters" when it comes to doctrine.

A simple illustration demonstrates that this attitude toward the Word of God was that of at least one of the prominent leaders of the Christian movement of the past. The established church of the 1500s charged that the Reformers were teaching doctrines that were new, unknown, and uncertain. John Calvin wrote the *Institutes of the Christian Religion* to provide a systematic defense of the Reformation teaching. In the preface, addressed to King Francis I of France, Calvin sought to answer these charges. He said that none of their opponents' charges were true, since the Reformers' teachings were rooted in God's revelation in the Bible. He wrote that God's "sacred word does not deserve to be accused of novelty."[53]

In the following section, answering the misleading claim that the church fathers did not teach what the Reformers were teaching, Calvin brought forth evidence from some of the Fathers that directly opposed the practices and teachings of the established church of his day. But that is not the evidence he relied on. Even if the Reformation teachings were not in agreement with the writings of the Fathers, that would not have mattered, Calvin asserted.

Sometimes the Fathers disagreed among themselves; often they erred.

> Then with a frightful to-do, they overwhelm us as despisers and adversaries
> of the fathers! But we do not despise them; in fact, if it were to our
> present purpose, I could with no trouble at all prove that the greater part
> of what we are saying today meets their approval. Yet we are so versed
> in their writings as to remember always that all things are ours, to serve
> us, not to lord it over us, and that we belong to the one Christ, whom we
> must obey in all things without exception. He who does not observe this
> distinction will have nothing certain in religion, inasmuch as these holy
> men [the church fathers] were ignorant of many things, often disagree
> among themselves, and sometimes even contradicted themselves.[54]

What does this mean? Simply that history serves believers and
that they serve Christ alone as He reveals Himself in His Word.
"He who does not observe this distinction," between the
authoritative Word and the subservient role of history, says Calvin,
"will have nothing certain in religion." History may teach, it may
warn, it may comfort, it may guide. But only the Word of God has
final authority.

It is surprising that the same line of argument advanced against
the Reformers is used by lordship salvation teachers today. They
claim to be in the "mainstream,"[55] to have history on their side,
and that the view of free grace is a recent innovation—new,
unknown, and uncertain. Such an argument is startling. Perhaps
the argument Calvin used ought also to be advanced today by both
sides, namely, What does the Word of God say?

Does it matter what history teaches about the gospel? Yes,
because from history many lessons can be learned. From history,
believers should learn *humility*. This is not the only generation to
search the Word of God and to attempt to apply its teachings.
From history believers should learn *piety*. Others have died for
their faith and their example can be emulated. From history
believers may gain *wisdom*. History can make Christians aware of
different lines of interpretation that they need to pursue and
consider, lest they become narrow and stilted.

But the greatest lesson to be learned from history, and from the
great Christians leaders of the past, is that believers must constantly
return to the Word of God. It is only in the Bible that God Himself
"opens His own most hallowed lips."[56] And it is only there that the
ideas presented in history can be tested. For it is not about history
but about the Scriptures that Isaiah wrote, "The grass withers, the
flower fades, but the word of our God stands forever" (Isa. 40:8).

CHAPTER 15

The Significance of Pentecost

Charles C. Ryrie

B
y anyone's standards Pentecost was a significant day. It is the purpose of this article to treat the significant aspects of the day in relation to certain major areas of theological studies.

Significance in Relation to Typology

Typology has suffered a great deal at the hands of both its friends and its enemies, since for many the study of types is still an uncertain science. Some, it is true, have found types in everything, while others in their reaction against this give little or no place for typological studies. A type is "a divinely purposed illustration which prefigures its corresponding reality." This definition not only covers types which are expressly designated so by the New Testament (e.g., 1 Cor. 10) but also allows for types not so designated (e.g., Joseph as a type of Christ). Yet in the definition the phrase "divinely purposed" should guard against an allegorical or pseudo-spiritual interpretation of types which sees chiefly the resemblances between Old Testament events and New Testament truths to the neglect of the historical, geographical, and local parts of those events. While all things are in a sense divinely purposed, not all details in all stories were divinely purposed illustrations of subsequently revealed truth. Pentecost is a good example of this, for although there is a clear type-antitype relationship, not all the details of the Old Testament feast find a corresponding reality in the events recorded in Acts 2.

As the antitype of one of the annual feasts of the Jews Pentecost has significance. This feast (Lev. 23:15–21) was characterized by an offering of two loaves marking the close of harvest. The corresponding reality of this ceremony was the joining on the day of Pentecost by the Holy Spirit of Jew and Gentile as one loaf in the one body of Christ (1 Cor. 12:13). Pentecost is sometimes called the feast of weeks because it fell seven (a week of) weeks after Firstfruits. No date could be set for the observance of Firstfruits, for that depended on the ripening of the grain for harvest. However, when the time did arrive a small amount of grain was gathered, threshed, ground into flour, and presented to the Lord as a token of the harvest yet to be gathered. The corresponding reality is, of course, "Christ the firstfruits" (1 Cor. 15:23). The 50-day interval between the two feasts was divinely purposed the Old Testament type and finds exact correspondence in the New Testament antitype.

Significance in Relation to Theology

The theological significance of Pentecost concerns chiefly the doctrine of the Holy Spirit. The third Person of the Trinity, not Peter, played the leading role in the drama of that day; He is the power of Pentecost; and in a very special sense the era which followed is His age. Obviously the Spirit of God has always been present in this world, but He has not always been a resident as one who permanently indwells the church. This was a new relationship which did not obtain even during the days of Jesus' earthly ministry, for He said to His disciples concerning the Spirit, "He abides with you, and will be in you" (John 14:17).

THE EVIDENCES OF HIS COMING (ACTS 2:1–4)

Wind. A sound as of a rushing mighty wind was the first evidence of the Spirit's coming. It came suddenly so that it could not be attributed to any natural cause, and it came from heaven, which probably refers both to the impression given of its origin and also to its actual supernatural origin. It was not actually wind but rather a roar or reverberation, for verse 2 should be literally translated "an echoing sound as of a mighty wind borne violently." It filled all the house, which means that all of the 120 (1:15) would have experienced the sensation since so many people would of necessity have been scattered throughout the house. This was a fitting evidence of the Spirit's coming, for the Lord had used this very symbol when He spoke of the things of the Spirit to Nicodemus (John 3:8).

Fire. The audible sign, wind, was followed by a visible one, fire. Actually the tongues which looked like fire divided themselves over the company, a tongue settling on the head of each one. This, too, was an appropriate sign for the presence of the Holy Spirit, for fire had long been to the Jews a symbol of divine presence (Ex.

3:2; Deut. 5:4). The form of the original text makes one doubt the presence of material fire though the appearance of the tongues was clearly as if they had been composed of fire.

Languages. Each of the Eleven began to speak in a real language which was new to the speaker but which was understood by those from the various lands who were familiar with them. This was the third piece of evidence, and though some have assumed that this miracle was wrought on the ears of the hearers, this certainly forces the plain and natural sense of the narrative. These tongues were evidently real languages (vv. 6–8) which were spoken, and the imperfect tense, "was giving" (v. 4), indicates that they were spoken in turn, one after another.

THE EFFECTS OF HIS COMING (ACTS 2:5–13)

Baptism. The most important effect of the Spirit's coming at Pentecost was the placing of men and women into the body of Christ by His baptism. Just before His ascension Jesus spoke of this baptizing work of the Holy Spirit (Acts 1:5), and it is clear from His words that this was a ministry of the Spirit thus far unknown even to those to whom He had said, "Receive the Holy Spirit" (John 20:22). If the baptism of the Holy Spirit was not something new to men until the day of Pentecost, then the Lord's words in Acts 1:5—and especially the future tense of the verb "you shall be baptized"—meant nothing. Although it is not specifically recorded in Acts 2 that the baptism of the Spirit occurred on the day of Pentecost, it is recorded in Acts 11:15–16 that this happened then, and Peter stated there that what happened at Pentecost was the fulfillment of the promise of Acts 1:5. However, Paul explained what this baptism (not to be confused with what is meant in Acts 2:38) accomplishes. "For by one Spirit we are all baptized into one body, whether Jews or whether Greeks, whether slaves or free, and we were all made to drink of one Spirit" (1 Cor. 12:13). In other words, on the day of Pentecost men were first placed into the body of Christ and that occurred by the baptism of the Holy Spirit. Since the church is the body of Christ (Col. 1:18), the church *could not* have begun until Pentecost. Furthermore, since no reference to the baptism of the Spirit is found in the Old Testament, since all references in the Gospels are prophetic, and since in all prophecies of the future kingdom age there is no reference to the Spirit's baptism, one may conclude that this work of His is peculiar to this dispensation and peculiar to the church (which, it follows, must also be limited to this dispensation) in forming it and uniting the members to the body of Christ forever.

Bewilderment. Certain visible effects of the Spirit's coming were evident in the crowd which gathered as a result of the phenomena connected with His coming. At first the people (including Eastern or Babylonian Jews, Syrian Jews, Egyptian Jews, Roman Jews, Cretes, and Arabians) were amazed. Literally the text says they stood out of themselves with wide-open astonishment (v. 7). This is a mental reaction showing that their minds were arrested by what they observed. Next they were perplexed (v. 12). This is a strong compound word from an adjective that means *impassable* and hence the word comes to mean *to be wholly and utterly at a loss.* This was mental defeat. "The amazement meant that they did not know. The perplexity meant that they knew they did not know."[1] Not knowing is always a blow to man's pride; consequently this crowd, driven to find an answer to what they had seen and heard, replaced their ignorance with criticism (v. 13). These are merely normal reactions of satanically blinded minds to which the things of God are foolishness (2 Cor. 4:4; 1 Cor. 2:14) and should not be surprising if they occur today. The offense of the Cross has not ceased.

Its Significance in Relation to Homiletics

THE SERMON (ACTS 1:14–36)

Introduction: Explanation. Peter, spokesman for the Eleven, seized the opportunity for a witness by answering the charge of drunkenness which had been leveled at the apostles. He thus wisely introduced his sermon by using the local situation, and taking what was uppermost in his hearers' thoughts. He formulated his introduction as an explanation of what they had just seen and heard (v. 15). Strangely enough he did not introduce his message with a story or joke. Nothing in the situation seemed to remind Peter of a certain story. Peter's mind was full of Scripture, not stories; Peter's concern was for the people, not pleasantries. The disciples could not be drunk, he told them, for it was only nine o'clock in the morning. Pentecost was a feast day, and the Jews who were engaged in the services of the synagogues in Jerusalem would have abstained from eating and drinking until at least 10 A.M. and more likely noon.

From this categorical denial of the charge of drunkenness Peter passed easily and naturally to the explanation of what the phenomenon was. Not wine but the Holy Spirit was causing these things, and to prove this Peter quoted Joel 2:28–32. This is a very definite prophecy of the Holy Spirit's being poured out when Israel will again be established in her own land. The problem here is not one of interpretation but of usage only. Clearly Joel's prophecy was not fulfilled at Pentecost, for (a) Peter did not use the usual scriptural formula for fulfilled prophecy as he did in Acts. 1:16 (cf. Matt. 1:22; 2:17; 4:14); (b) the original prophecy of Joel will clearly not be fulfilled until Israel is restored to her land, and is converted and enjoying the presence of the Lord in her midst (Joel 2:26–28); (c) the events prophesied by Joel simply did not come to pass. If language means anything, Pentecost did not fulfill this prophecy nor did Peter think that it did. The usage need not raise theological questions at all, for the matter is primarily homiletical and any problems should be solved in that light. Peter's point was that the Holy Spirit and not wine was responsible for what these Jews had seen. He quoted Joel to point out that as Jews who knew the Old Testament Scriptures they should have recognized this as the Spirit's work. In other words, their own Scriptures should have reminded them that the Spirit was able to do what they had just seen. Why then, someone may ask, did Peter include the words from Joel recorded in Acts 2:19–20? Why did he not stop with verse 18? The answer is simple. Peter not only wanted to show his audience that they should have known from the Scriptures that the Spirit could do what they had seen, but he also wanted to invite them to accept Jesus as their Messiah by using Joel's invitation "every one who calls on the name of the Lord shall be saved" (v. 21). Thus what is recorded in Acts 2:19–20 is simply a connecting link between the two key points in his argument. "The remainder of the quotation from Joel, verses 19–20, has no bearing on Peter's argument, but was probably made in order to complete the connection of that which his argument demanded."[2]

Theme: Jesus is Messiah. Today it does not mean much to say that Jesus is Christ or Messiah. However, to a Jew of that day this assertion required convincing proof, and it was the theme of Peter's sermon. Peter's proof is built along simple lines. First, he painted a picture of the Messiah from the Old Testament Scriptures. Then from contemporary facts he presented a picture of Jesus of Nazareth. Thirdly, he superimposed these two pictures on each other to prove conclusively that Jesus is Messiah. The center of each picture is the resurrection. In verses 22–24 there is a proclamation of the resurrection of Jesus of Nazareth. Then there follows (vv. 25–31) the prediction of resurrection from Psalm 16:8–11 which Peter applied to the Messiah. Then the Messiah is identified as Jesus whom they crucified and of whose resurrection they were witnesses (Acts 2:32–36). It is important to notice that the truth of Jesus' resurrection was not challenged but was well attested by the conviction of these thousands of people who were in the very city where it had occurred less than two months before.

Conclusion: Application. Peter then challenged his hearers to decide about Jesus, and yet there is really no choice, so conclusive had been his argument. How gracious of God to appeal once again to the very people who had crucified His Son. The application was personal. Peter did not say "whom someone crucified" but "whom you crucified" (v. 36).

THE RESULTS (ACTS 2:37–41)

Conviction. Peter's sermon brought conviction of heart. The word translated "prick" (v. 37, KJV) is a rare one which means "to pierce, stun or smite." Outside the Scriptures it is used of horses dinting the earth with their hoofs. In like manner the hearts of his hearers were smitten by Peter's message as the Spirit of God applied it.

Conversion. To the group of 120 (which included men and women, Acts 1:14) were added three thousand souls (Acts 2:41). They repented or changed their minds, for that is the meaning of repentance. It is not mere sorrow, which is related to the emotions, for one can be sorry for sin without being repentant. Neither is it mere mental assent to certain facts, for genuine repentance involves the heart as well.[3] For the Jews who were gathered at Pentecost it involved a change of relationship toward Him whom they had considered as merely the carpenter's son of Nazareth and an impostor by receiving Jesus as Lord and Messiah.

The Spirit of God must always do the work of enlightening and converting, but believers are still His method of heralding the message. May sermons today be like Peter's—doctrinally sound, homiletically excellent, filled with and explanatory of the Word of God, and aimed at those who are addressed.

Its Significance in Relation to Practical Theology

In the realm of practical theology two things command attention from among the many events of Pentecost and the days that immediately followed.

THE ORDINANCE OF BAPTISM

To the question, "What shall we do?" Peter replied, "Repent and let each of you be baptized." That this refers to the new converts' being baptized by the Spirit is untenable for several reasons. (1) It is doubtful that Peter himself and much less probable that his hearers understood yet the truth concerning the baptism of the Spirit even though it did first occur at Pentecost. (2) If this were referring to that automatic ministry of the Spirit, then there would be no need for the report of verse 41, "So then, those who had received his word were baptized." (3) What would this audience have understood by Peter's answer? His words meant that they were to submit to a rite performed with water which would be a sign of their identification with this new group. They would have thought immediately of Jewish proselyte baptism which signified entrance of the proselyte into Judaism.[4] They would have thought of John's baptism, submission to which meant identification with John's message in a very definite way; for John was the first person to baptize other people (all proselyte baptisms were self-imposed), which was a striking way to ask people to identify themselves with all that he stood for. They would have realized that they were being asked to identify and associate themselves with this new group who believed Jesus was the Messiah, and Christian baptism at the hands of these disciples signified this association as nothing else could.[5] Even today for a Jew it is not his profession of Christianity nor his attendance at Christian services nor his belief in the New Testament but his partaking of water baptism that definitely and finally excludes him from Judaism and sets him off as a Christian. And there is no reason why it should not be the same line of demarcation for all converts to Christianity, signifying the separation from the old life and association with the new.[6]

THE ORGANIZATION OF BELIEVERS

Its commencement. As already noted, the church as an *organism*, the body of Christ, began on the day of Pentecost. But the church as an organization also began that day as the Lord added three thousand souls.

Its continuance. The power of the early church, humanly speaking, was due largely to the facts recorded in Acts 2:42. There was no rapid falling away from the newly embraced faith. Indeed, just the opposite was true, for membership in the early church involved persevering adherence. They continued in the apostles' doctrine. "The church is apostolic because it cleaves to the apostles. . . ."[7] Teaching had always had a prominent place among the Jews, and it is not strange to find the Christian group appearing as a school. The apostles were the first teachers, and the bulk of their teaching is in the Gospels. It consisted of the facts of the Lord's life as well as His doctrine and teaching. The church today could well afford to emulate the early church in this. Instead of capitalizing on new converts and exploiting them, church leaders should teach them even if that means keeping them in the background for awhile.

Furthermore they continued steadfastly in fellowship, and this is evidently to be understood in the broadest sense of the word, for the text says "the fellowship." This means partnership with God, partnership with others in the common salvation and in the sharing of material goods. They also continued in the breaking of bread, which refers to the Lord's Supper though not isolated but as the climax of the *agape* or love feast. At the very first this was evidently observed daily (v. 46) though afterward it seemed to form the great act of worship on the Lord's Day (20:7). The early church remembered her Lord with great frequency and with great freedom, for it was observed in homes without distinction between ordained clergy and laity (no service of ordination having yet occurred in the church).

Finally the record says that they continued in prayers. Again the definite article is used with this word and probably indicates definite times for prayer. This is a word that is used exclusively for prayer to God and indicates the offering up of the wishes and desires to God in the frame of mind of devotion.[8]

Its characterization. The early organization was characterized by fear (v. 43), favor (v. 47), and fellowship (vv. 44–46). Fear kept coming on this new group as signs and wonders kept on being done through the apostles (both verbs are in the imperfect tense). This fear was not alarm or dread of injury but a prevailing sense of awe in the manifest presence of the power of God. Favor was also their portion with the people at this time though times changed quickly. Fellowship in spiritual things demonstrated itself in fellowship of goods and worship. No doubt many of the pilgrims to the feast of Pentecost lingered in Jerusalem after their conversion to learn more of their new faith, and this created a pressing economic need. Providing for them through the sale and distribution of goods was God's way of meeting this emergency. The necessity for this was probably short-lived though the saints in Jerusalem remained a poor group.

This is the significance of Pentecost—the type fulfilled, the Holy Spirit baptizing men for the first time into the body of Christ, the sermon built on the fact of Jesus' resurrection and bringing conviction and conversion, and the young church marked off and established in the Word and ways of the Lord.

CHAPTER 16

The Purpose of the Law

J. Dwight Pentecost

W hat is the purpose of the Law? The Apostle Paul faced his readers with this question in the third chapter of Galatians as he taught them the doctrine of sanctification by faith in Jesus Christ. Paul was discussing the problem as to how a believer is sanctified, or how he attains experientially the promises and blessings that are his in Christ. The Galatians had been led to believe that sanctification comes by the Law and that through keeping the Law believers obtain the promises given them by God. To show the fallacy of this interpretation, the apostle cited the experience of Abraham. Abraham was given promises by God (Gen. 12) which were repeated (Gen. 13) and ratified by a blood covenant (Gen. 15). All that Abraham obtained was by faith in the promises of God. Such teaching would be incontrovertible since no Law had been given in Abraham's time. Therefore Abraham could realize God's promises only by faith.

The error propagated among the Galatians was that though Abraham attained God's blessing by faith alone, the giving of the Law altered the basic plan by which God dealt with men, so that Abraham's descendants subsequent to the giving of the Law must attain God's blessings by keeping the Law rather than by faith in the promise of God. To dispel this error, Paul wrote that the Law, which came four hundred and thirty years after, does not invalidate a covenant previously ratified by God, so as to nullify the promise (Gal. 3:17). Paul then wrote in verse 19 that rather than nullifying God's promises, the Law was added (literally, added alongside) the existing promise to serve a specific function. There is no basic conflict between the Law and the promises of God; the two can coexist (v. 21). Anticipating certain objections or questions in the minds of his readers, Paul faced the question specifically. "Why the Law then?" (v. 19). This is the question addressed in this chapter.

Many who lived under the Law had the deepest reverence, respect, and love for the Law. The psalmist frequently reflected this attitude in Psalm 119. "O how I love Thy law! It is my meditation all the day" (v. 97). "Thy law is my delight" (v. 77). "How sweet are Thy words to my taste! Yes, sweeter than honey to my mouth! From thy precepts I get understanding" (vv. 103–104a). "Consider how I love Thy precepts" (v. 159). In contrast with much current antinomianism, which treats the Law as a worthless worn-out garment to be discarded, the Apostle Paul wrote, "The Law is holy, and the commandment is holy, and righteous and good." The Law, loved, revered, and respected by Old and New Testament writers, must have served a worthy function.

The Law of Moses was given to a redeemed people. The writer to the Hebrews said of Moses, "By faith he kept the Passover and the sprinkling of the blood so that He who destroyed the firstborn might not touch them. By faith they passed through the Red Sea as though they were passing through dry land" (Heb. 11:28). On the night of the Passover in Egypt, Israel was redeemed by blood. By faith they began a walk through the wilderness toward the land of promise. On the basis of that blood redemption God could say to the nation, "But now thus says the Lord your creator, Do not fear for I have redeemed you, I have called you by name; you are Mine!" (Isa. 43:1). The nation that was redeemed by faith through blood was brought to Mount Sinai. Though that nation had been redeemed, it was a nation in spiritual immaturity. They recognized a responsibility to the Redeemer which they did not know how to discharge.

The fact of Israel's infancy at the time of the giving of the Law is recognized by the Apostle Paul, who wrote in Galatians 3:23–26, "But before faith came, we were kept in custody under the Law, being shut up to the faith which was later to be revealed. Therefore the Law has become a tutor to lead us to Christ, that we are no longer under a tutor. For you are all sons of God through faith in Christ Jesus." Or again in Galatians 4:1–5, "Now I say, as long as the heir is a child, he does not differ at all from a slave although he is owner of everything, but he is under guardians and managers until the date set by the father. So also while we were children, we are in bondage under the things of the world. But when the fullness of the time came, God sent forth His Son, born of a woman, born under the Law, in order that He might redeem

those who were under the law, that we might receive the adoption
as sons." Paul viewed those living under the Law as children in a
state of immaturity, and he viewed the Law as a pedagogue, a
child trainer or overseer whose responsibility it was to supervise
every area of the life of the child committed to its care. Because of
her immaturity Israel needed the Law. Thus the Law was given as
a gracious provision by God to meet the needs of a redeemed
people who were in a state of spiritual infancy.

The Scriptures reveal a number of reasons why the Mosaic
Law was given to the nation Israel. First, it was given to reveal the
holiness of God. Peter wrote in 1 Peter 1:15, "But like the Holy
One who called you, you yourselves also be holy in all your
behavior, because it is written, 'You should be holy; for I am
holy.'" The fact that God is a holy God was made clear to Israel in
the Law of Moses. Perhaps the primary function of the Law was to
reveal to Israel the fact of the holiness of God and to make Israel
aware of the character of the God who had redeemed them from
Egypt. All the requirements laid on the nation Israel were in light
of the holy character of God as revealed in the Mosaic Law.

Second, the Mosaic Law was given to reveal or expose the
sinfulness of man. Paul wrote of this: "It [the Law] was added
because of transgressions . . . until the seed should come to whom
the promise had been made. But the Scripture has shut up all men
under sin, that the promise by faith in Jesus Christ might be given
to those that believe" (Gal. 3:19, 21). The holiness of God as
revealed in the Law became the test of man's thoughts, words,
and actions, and anything that failed to conform to the revealed
holiness of God was sin. Paul had this in mind when he wrote in
Romans 3:23, "For all have sinned and fall short of the glory of
God." God finds His highest glory in His own holiness. Sin is lack
of conformity to the Law but it is also lack of conformity to the
holiness of God, of which the Law is a revelation. Consequently
the holiness of God becomes the final test of sin rather than the
Law which is the reflection of that holiness. Because all Abraham's
descendants were born in sin, the Law was given by which Israel
might readily determine their sinfulness before a holy God. The
Law made very specific the requirements of divine holiness so
that even children in spiritual infancy could determine whether
their conduct was acceptable to a holy God.

Third, the Law was given to reveal the standard of holiness
required of those in fellowship with a holy God. Israel had been

redeemed as a nation. They were redeemed in order to enjoy fellowship with God. As these redeemed ones faced the question of what kind of life was required of those who walk in fellowship with their Redeemer, the Law was given to reveal the standard God required. "Who may ascend into the hill of the Lord? And who may stand in His holy place? He who has clean hands and a pure heart, who has not lifted up his soul to falsehood and has not sworn deceitfully. He shall receive a blessing from the Lord and righteousness from the God of his salvation" (Ps. 24:3–5). Those who were redeemed to enjoy the Redeemer, and the Law made clear the kind of life God required if they were to walk in fellowship with Him.

Fourth, another purpose of the Law is stated in Galatians 3:24. "Therefore the Law has become our tutor, our schoolmaster . . . to Christ." The word "tutor" ("schoolmaster," KJV) refers to a slave selected by the father to be responsible to supervise the total development of the child, physically, intellectually, and spiritually. The child was under the pedagogue's constant supervision till he would move out of childhood into adulthood. Similarly the Law served to supervise physical, mental, and spiritual development of the redeemed Israelites till they came to maturity in Christ. The psalmist reflected this same concept in Psalm 119:71–72. "It is good for me that I was afflicted; that I may learn Thy statutes. The law of Thy mouth is better to me than thousands of gold and silver pieces." The psalmist confessed that through the Law he learned of God's requirements.

Fifth, the Law was given to be the unifying principle that made possible the establishment of the nation. Exodus 19:5–8 reads, "'Now, then if you will indeed obey My voice and keep My covenant, then you shall be My own for all the earth is Mine; and you shall be to Me a kingdom of priests and a holy nation.' These are the words that you shall speak to the sons of Israel. So Moses came and called the elders of the people, and set before them all these words which the Lord had commanded him. And all the people answered together and said, 'All that the Lord has spoken we will do.'"

In response to the instruction given by Moses as to what God had revealed, the nation voluntarily submitted themselves to the authority of the Law. Apart from voluntary submission to a uniting principle there could have been no nation. So the people redeemed out of Egypt by blood, who had begun a walk by faith, were constituted a nation when they voluntarily submitted themselves to the Law. This same truth is reaffirmed in Deuteronomy 5:27–28. From the divine viewpoint Israel was constituted a nation at the time they voluntarily submitted themselves to the Law.

The Prophet Jeremiah warned Judah that because they had abandoned the Law God would deliver them into the hand of the Gentiles. The Babylonian Captivity, by which Israel lost their national identity, came about because of their failure to observe the Law. In Deuteronomy 28 Moses had made it clear that if the people abandoned the Law, God would deliver them into the hands of the Gentiles (vv. 49–52). And it is not without significance that until Israel submits to the authority of the law of her Messiah-King she will not be fully recognized by God as a nation again.

Sixth, the Law was given to Israel to separate her from the nations so that they might become a kingdom of priests. "Speak to the sons of Israel, saying, 'You shall surely observe My sabbaths, for this is a sign between Me and you throughout your generations, that you may know that I am the Lord who sanctifies you'" (Ex. 31:13). Israel was sanctified (set apart) to become "a kingdom of priests" (Ex. 19:6), that is, a nation that mediated the truth of God to the nations of the earth. The Law became a hedge separating Israel from the nations of the earth. The Law separated and preserved the nation and kept them intact. In order that Israel might function as a light to the world, they were given the Law.

Seventh, the Law was given to a redeemed people to make provision for forgiveness of sins and restoration to fellowship. God instituted five offerings for the nation (Lev. 1–7). While Israel as a nation was preserved before God because of the annual offering of the blood of atonement, individuals in the nation were restored to fellowship, received forgiveness for specific sins through the use of the offerings God provided. The God who had redeemed the nation by faith through blood provided that the redeemed could walk in fellowship with Him. The same Law that revealed their unworthiness for fellowship also provided for restoration to fellowship. This was one of the primary functions of the Law.

Eighth, the Law was given to make provision for a redeemed people to worship. A redeemed people will be a worshiping people, and a people who walk in fellowship with God will worship the God with whom they enjoy fellowship. Israel was expected to observe a cycle of feasts annually (Lev. 23). These feasts were the means by which Israel as a redeemed people worshiped God. In the feasts her attention was directed backward to the redemption out of Egypt and forward to the final redemption to be provided through the Redeemer according to God's promise.

Ninth, the Law provided a test as to whether one was in the kingdom or the theocracy over which God ruled. As Israel stood on the border of the Promised Land, Moses revealed in Deuteronomy 28 the principle by which God would deal with the nation. The first portion of the chapter outlines the blessings that would come on the nation for obedience. A great portion of that extensive chapter deals with the curses that would come on the nation because of disobedience. Even though the nation as a whole entered the Promised Land, because not all had believed God, not all were eligible to receive the blessings promised to those in the land. The Law, then, revealed whether a person was rightly related to God. Those who submitted to and obeyed the Law did so because of their faith in Him, which produced obedience. Those who disobeyed the Law did so because they were without faith in God. Lack of faith resulted in disobedience. Whether an Israelite obeyed the Law or not, then, became the test as to whether he or she was rightly related to God or in God's kingdom.

Tenth, the New Testament shows that the Law was given to reveal Jesus Christ. The great truths concerning the Person and work of the Lord Jesus Christ are woven throughout the Law, and the Law was given so that it might prepare the nation for the coming Redeemer King. Because of this the Lord on the Emmaus Road could expound to His companions great truths concerning the Messiah that had been revealed in the Law and the Prophets (Luke 24:44). Israel, through the Law, was being prepared for the coming Messiah.

These 10 reasons show that the Law was both revelatory and regulatory. It was revelatory in that it revealed the holiness of God. This aspect of the Law was permanent. Holiness does not change from age to age, and that which revealed the holiness of God to Israel may still be used to reveal His holiness to people today. At the same time the Law reveals mankind's unholiness today. Because of this revelatory function Paul said the Law is "holy and righteous and good" (Rom. 7:12).

The Law was also regulatory in that it regulated the life and worship of the Israelites. This regulatory aspect of the Law was temporary, and has been done away. Paul wrote, "But we know that the Law is good, if one uses it lawfully" (1 Tim. 1:8). How can the Law be used lawfully in the present Church Age when the Law had been abolished? The answer is by revealing the holiness of God, the unholiness of mankind, and the Person and work of Christ. On the other hand one who attempts to use the regulatory portions of the Law which were "only until Christ" is using the Law unlawfully. While one sings, "Free from the law, oh happy condition," one still recognizes that the Law is "holy and righteous and good."

CHAPTER 17

The Mediatorial Kingdom from the Acts Period to the Eternal State

Alva J. McClain

The Mediatorial Kingdom in the Period of the Book of Acts

Two mistakes have been made in approaching the Book of Acts. At the one extreme are a few who see nothing there but the kingdom; while at the other extreme are those who insist that Acts concerns the church alone. As in the Gospels, the Book of Acts must be interpreted historically, that is, in accord with the movement of events. To do otherwise will result in serious problems, both in eschatology and ecclesiology.

In spite of all Jesus' teaching before Calvary, the disciples had failed to harmonize the fact of His death with their hopes concerning the kingdom. "We hoped," they said, "that it was he who should redeem Israel" (Luke 24:21, ASV). The solution of their problem was His resurrection, of course, as He reminded them. "Ought not Christ to have suffered these things, and [after that] to enter into his glory?" This would have been clear to them had they not been "slow of heart to believe *all* that the prophets have spoken" (Luke 24:25–26). That the kingdom has not been abandoned is evidenced by the question of His chosen apostles, asked at the close of 40 days of teaching by the risen King Himself on the subject of the "kingdom of God." They said, "Lord, wilt thou at this time restore again the kingdom of Israel?" The crucial point of this question is not whether there ever would be such a restoration, but rather when it would take place. Not *will* this be done but *when*? This is clearly indicated by the order of the words in the original: "Lord, *at this time*, wilt thou restore again the kingdom to Israel?" As Alford observes, any other explanation of the question "would make our Lord's answer irrelevant" in the next verse: "It is not for you to know the times or the seasons" (Acts 1:3–7). However, although the time element is to remain hidden, there is no indication that the kingdom may not be restored within the lifetime of the apostles. We tend to read 19 centuries into these biblical passages.

Peter's sermon on the day of Pentecost suggests that the day of the Lord may be near at hand, and also powerfully argues the right of the risen Jesus to the throne of David. The effect on the audience, composed wholly of Jews from all over the known world, was startling: three thousand were convinced, and their so-called "communism" suggests that they were looking for the great social changes of the kingdom immediately (Acts 2:5–45).

But perhaps the best key to the historical situation in the Book of Acts is found in the third chapter where Peter, speaking to Israel from the temple porch with all the authority of one to whom Christ had committed the "keys" of the kingdom, makes an official reoffer of that kingdom (Acts 3:12–21). Peter's words here are unmistakable: even their rejection and crucifixion of the King have not utterly lost for Israel her opportunity. If they will repent and turn again, their sins will be blotted out, and Jesus Christ will be sent from heaven to restore all the things spoken of by the Old Testament prophets. And in confirmation of the bona fide character of this reoffer of the kingdom, early in the Acts period are many of the miraculous signs and wonders like those associated with the Lord's own original offer of the kingdom. This is at least one explanation of why some things are found here which are not being exactly duplicated today.

This is not to suggest that there are no miracles in the present age, but rather that they are now of a different character; there are no great public demonstrations designed to compel recognition (Acts 4:16), as in this early part of the Christian era. The very Greek terms used are indicative of the special nature of these miracles: they were "signs" and "wonders" to a nation that by divine prophetic sanction had a right to expect such signs in connection with the promised kingdom. Consider, for example, the outpouring of the Spirit tangible to both sight and hearing (2:1–4), special miracles of healing the sick (3:1–10; 19:11–12), great physical wonders (4:31; 8:39; 16:26), immediate physical judgment on sinners (5:1–11; 12:23; 13:11), miraculous visions (7:55; 9:3, 10; 11:5), visible angelic ministry (5:19; 10:3; 12:7), and instant deliverance from physical hazards (28:5).

But once again the authenticating "signs" failed to convince the nation of Israel, though now these signs became even more impressive by reason of the historical fulfillment of the death and resurrection of the King. For the problem was spiritual and moral rather than intellectual, and throughout the Book of Acts one can trace the same growth of Jewish opposition to a definite crisis of official rejection, as in Jesus' ministry. It came this time, not in Jerusalem, but in the great metropolis of Rome where Paul, now a political prisoner, gathered together the influential leaders of Israel into "his own hired" dwelling. They came in great numbers, and for an entire day he spoke with them, "testifying the kingdom of God, and persuading them concerning Jesus, both from the law of Moses and from the prophets" (Acts 28:23–29). But there was no agreement, and after quoting once more the terrible prophecy of Isaiah, which Jesus had quoted on a former and similar occasion, the Apostle Paul turned definitely and finally to the Gentiles. Again the nation of Israel had been faced with a decision, a moral and spiritual decision, and once more they made it the wrong way. Thus the historical die was cast, their holy city was shortly destroyed, they were scattered throughout the nations, to abide "many days without a king, and without a prince, and without a sacrifice" (Hos. 3:4), until they are ready to receive their promised King as He comes down from heaven to save them in their last great extremity.

To summarize briefly: The period of the Acts is therefore transitional in character, and its preaching and teaching had a twofold aspect. First, there is the continued proclamation of the coming kingdom as an immediate possibility, depending on the attitude of the nation of Israel. But at the same time the church, begun on Pentecost, became the spiritual nucleus of the coming kingdom. Second, as the tide of Jewish opposition grew, there seems to have been a change of emphasis in the preaching. The period had opened with the kingdom in first place, the church having almost no distinguishable separate identity. As history unfolded, the church began to assume first place, with a glory of its own, while the future kingdom became more remote.

The Mediatorial Kingdom in the Present Church Age

Does the mediatorial kingdom exist in any sense during the present era; and if so, what is the relationship of the church to this kingdom? "Church" here refers of course to the spiritual body of Christ, the true church, not that abnormal thing called "Christendom." The promise of God to all believers of the present era is that believers will "reign with Him" in the coming kingdom.

This body of true believers constitutes the royal family, the ruling aristocracy of the kingdom. It would not be improper, therefore, to speak of the kingdom as now existing on earth, but only in the restricted sense that today God is engaged in selecting and preparing a people who are to be the spiritual nucleus of the established kingdom. Thus believers actually enter the kingdom before it is established on earth, something so remarkable that it is spoken of as a translation (Col. 1:13).

Jesus set forth this peculiar aspect of the kingdom in a series of parables which refers to the "mysteries" of the kingdom. The present era is a time of seed-sowing, of mysterious growth, mixed growth, and abnormal growth; a period of spreading error; a period that will come to the crisis of a harvest; yet out of this period, even apart from the harvest, there will come a pearl of great price (the church), and a treasure (the remnant of Israel purified and regenerated). Thus at the present time while God is forming the spiritual nucleus for the coming kingdom, He is also permitting a parallel development of righteousness and evil in the world; and both shall be brought to a harvest when good and bad will be separated, and the kingdom established on earth in power and righteousness at the second coming of the mediatorial King.

If I understand the words of certain premillenarian writers, they have made *two* kingdoms out of the one kingdom of Old Testament prophecy; one a purely spiritual kingdom, established at Christ's first coming; the second, a visible kingdom to be established at His second coming. In the interest of clearer understanding and discussion, it would be much better to say that at His first coming Jesus *laid the spiritual basis* for the kingdom that will be at His second coming.

In support of this view, its adherents have pointed to the fact that so late as the history recorded in Acts 28 the Apostle Paul was engaged in "preaching the kingdom of God" (v. 31), which seems to be regarded as proof that a kingdom of God of some kind had already been established. This, however, is a non sequitur. The Old Testament prophets, 2,500 years ago, preached the kingdom. But there is one thing about the kingdom which seems to be completely absent from all the recorded preaching of the present church era; that is the preaching of the "gospel" of the kingdom. According to the biblical records, the preaching of this "good news" was strictly limited to John the Baptist, Jesus, the Twelve, and the Seventy; all specially accredited messengers. What was this gospel of the kingdom? Fortunately, Mark tells exactly what it was: "The *time* is fulfilled, and the kingdom of God is at hand; repent ye and believe the gospel" (1:13). That there was sometime to be a mediatorial kingdom was no particular news to the Jewish people; they had always firmly believed in that. What they did not know had to do with the "time"; and the good news preached by the Lord was that at last the time had come when God was ready to establish the long-expected kingdom. The church today may indeed "preach the kingdom of God," and should preach it; but to assume to preach the *gospel* of the kingdom today would involve a knowledge of the "times and seasons" certainly not possessed by any of the wisest theologians.

The Mediatorial Kingdom in the Millennial Age

This "age to come" will be ushered in by the exercise of Jesus' immediate power and authority. He *has* "all power" now; He will take this power and *use* it to the full when He comes down from heaven. The age-long "silence" of God, the perennial taunt of unbelief, will be broken first by the resurrection and translation of the church; then by the unloosing of divine judgment long withheld; then by the personal and visible appearance of the mediatorial King Himself; followed by the complete establishment of His kingdom on the earth for a period specified (Rev. 20:1–6). The description of this period, as set forth in Revelation 20, is brief with few details. If any should ask the reason for this extreme brevity, the answer is at hand: The Old Testament prophets had already revealed these details in rich profusion, and the reader is presumed to know them. There should be no serious complaint on this point, except by those who do not take the prophets seriously or by those who misinterpret their writings.

During this glorious period every aspect of the mediatorial kingdom of prophecy will be realized on earth—truly the "Golden Age" of history. Children are born, life goes on, men work and play; but under ideal conditions, the only limitations being those involved in the sinful nature and mortality which will still obtain among the earthly subjects of the kingdom. The period will close with a brief rebellion of unsaved humanity; and then the final judgment, its subjects being the "dead," not the living. Before that great white throne will appear only those who have chosen death rather than life. Those who have trusted in Christ have already passed out of death into life, and cannot come into judgment for sin.

The Mediatorial Kingdom in the Eternal State

When the last enemy is put down by the Lord as the mediatorial King, when even death itself is abolished and complete harmony is established, then the purpose of His mediatorial kingdom will have been fulfilled. Then the Son will deliver up His kingdom to God the Father, to be merged into the eternal kingdom, thus being perpetuated forever, but no longer as a separate entity (1 Cor. 15:24–28).

This does not mean the end of the rule of the Lord Jesus Christ. He only ceases to reign as the mediatorial King in history. But as the only begotten Son, very God of very God, He shares with the other Persons of the Triune God the throne of the eternal kingdom. In that final and eternal city of God, the center of a redeemed new heaven and earth, there is but *one* throne. It is called "the throne of *God* and of the *Lamb*" (Rev. 22:3). "And His servants shall serve Him: and they shall see His face; and His name shall be in their foreheads. And there shall be no night there; and they need no candle, neither light of the sun; for the Lord God giveth them light: and they shall reign forever and ever . . . these sayings are faithful and true" (Rev. 22:3b-6a).

CHAPTER 18

The Theological Context of Premillennialism

John F. Walvoord

The charge that premillennialism is only a dispute over the interpretation of Revelation 20 is both an understatement and a serious misrepresentation. Opponents of premillennialism delight to point out that the reference to the thousand years is found only in Revelation 20. Warfield observes in a footnote, "'Once, and only once,' says the 'Ency. Bibl.,' 3095, 'in the New Testament we hear of a millennium.'"[1]

The issues of premillennialism, however, cannot be so simplified. The issues are neither trivial nor simple. Premillennialism is a system of theology based on many Scriptures and with a distinctive theological context. The reckless charge of Landis that European premillennialism is based only on Ezekiel 40–48 and that American premillennialism is based only on Revelation 20:1–7 is as unfair as his more serious charge that "actually their bases are both contra-Biblical," and that premillennialism "is a fungus growth of first-century Pharisaic rabbinism."[2] Most opponents of premillennialism have enough perspective to see that premillennialism has its own biblical and theological context and that its origin in the early church as well as its restoration in modern times is based on biblical and theological studies. It is the purpose of this phase of the study of premillennialism to examine the general features of premillennial theology in contrast to opposing views. Premillennialism involves a distinctive principle of interpretation of Scripture, a different concept of the present age, a distinct doctrine of Israel, and its own teaching concerning the second advent and millennial kingdom.

Principles of Premillennial Interpretation

The literal, grammatical-historical method applied to eschatology. The debate between premillenarians and others hangs to a large extent on the principles of interpretation of Scripture which each group employs. This is commonly recognized by all parties. Amillenarian Pieters states,

> The question whether the Old Testament prophecies concerning the people of God must be interpreted in their ordinary sense, as other Scriptures are interpreted, or can properly be applied to the Christian Church, is called the question of spiritualization of prophecy. This is one of the major problems in biblical interpretation, and confronts everyone who makes a serious study of the Word of God. It is one of the chief keys to the difference of opinion between Premillenarians and the mass of Christian scholars. The former reject such spiritualization, the latter employ it; and as long as there is no agreement on this point the debate is interminable and fruitless.[3]

The premillennial position is that the Bible should be interpreted in its ordinary grammatical and historical meaning in all areas of theology unless contextual or theological reasons make it clear that this was not intended by the writer. Amillenarians use the literal method in theology as a whole but spiritualize Scripture whenever its literal meaning would lead to the premillennial viewpoint. This is obviously a rather subjective principle and open to manipulation by the interpreter to sustain almost any system of theology. The conservative amillenarian claims to confine spiritualization to the field of prophecy and interpret other scriptural revelation literally. Thus a conservative amillenarian would accept literally passages teaching the deity of Christ, the substitutionary atonement, the resurrection of Christ, and similar doctrines. They, like Origen, the father of amillenarianism, would denounce as heretics anyone who would tamper with these fundamental doctrines. Conservative amillenarians would, however, feel perfectly justified in proceeding to spiritualize passages speaking of a future righteous government on earth, of Israel's regathering to Palestine, and of Christ reigning literally on the earth for a thousand years. Their justification for this approach is that these doctrines are absurd and impossible and that therefore they must be spiritualized. The wish is father of the interpretation, therefore, and amillennial interpretation of Scripture abundantly illustrates this.

While professing to confine spiritualization to prophecy, actually amillenarians invade other fields. For instance they tend to spiritualize Israel to mean the church and to make David's throne the throne of God in heaven. They hold up to ridicule as extremists those who want to interpret references to Israel literally. As Allis writes with considerable inaccuracy, "Carrying to an almost unprecedented extreme that literalism which is characteristic of Millenarianism, they [the Brethren Movement] insisted that Israel must mean Israel, and that the kingdom promises in the Old Testament concern Israel and are to be fulfilled to Israel literally."[4] In his zeal to load premillenarians with an extreme position, Allis finds it convenient to forget that the postmillennial Charles Hodge and the amillennial William Hendricksen both interpret references to Israel in Scripture as pointing to God's ancient people, Israel, and not to a Gentile church.

Premillenarians, on the other hand, insist that one general rule of interpretation should be applied to all areas of theology and that prophecy does not require spiritualization any more than other aspects of truth. They hold that this rule is the literal, grammatical-historical method. This means that a passage should be taken in its literal sense, in keeping with the grammatical meaning of the words and forms. History is history, not allegory. Facts are facts. Prophesied future events are just what they are prophesied. Israel means Israel, earth means earth, heaven means heaven.

Problems of the literal method. Those who attack premillennialism delight to show that premillenarians do not always interpret Scripture literally either. Landis asks, "How literal are the literalists?"[5] Allis confuses typical with spiritual interpretation and charges that the premillennial use of typology destroys the literal principle. He writes, "While Dispensationalists are extreme literalists, they are very inconsistent ones. They are literalists in interpreting prophecy. But in the interpreting of history, they carry the principle of typical interpretation to an extreme which has rarely been exceeded by the most ardent allegorizers."[6]

True typical interpretation, of course, always involves literal interpretation first. In drawing typical truth from the Old Testament sacrifices, for instance, the interpreter takes for granted the historical existence of the sacrifices. If Joseph is taken as a type of Christ, his historical life is assumed. It is surprising that a scholar of Allis's caliber should be confused on such a simple hermeneutical distinction. The dispute highlights, however, some of the problems in the use of the literal method.

Premillenarians recognize that all Scripture cannot be interpreted literally. All areas of theology are sometimes revealed in Scripture in symbolic terms. Such passages, however, are usually clearly identified. For instance, the "rod out of the stem of Jesse" and the

"Branch" which "shall grow out of his roots" is understood by all to refer symbolically to Christ. But when the verse states that this "Branch" is the one who "shall smite the earth with the rod of his mouth, and with the breath of his lips shall he slay the wicked," it is clear from the context that a literal prophecy of judgment on the wicked in the earth at the Second Advent is intended even though some of the expressions are figurative. While the expression "rod of his mouth" is clearly figurative, a simple expression such as "earth" in the context of Isaiah 11 cannot be spiritualized on the same grounds. One is not free to make "earth" arbitrarily an equivalent for heaven as many amillenarians do, nor does the regathering of Israel "from the four corners of the earth" (Isa. 11:12) mean the conversion of Gentiles and the progress of the church. While the expression "four corners" is figurative, the word "earth" is not. In other words figures of speech that are clearly identified as such give no warrant whatever to spiritualize words and expressions that can be taken in their ordinary meaning.

The literal method sustained by literal fulfillment. The literal method of interpreting prophecy has been fully justified by the history of fulfillment. The most unlikely prophecies surrounding the birth of Christ, His Person, His life and ministry, and His death and resurrection have all been literally fulfilled. The prophetic vision of Daniel, however couched in symbols and dreams, has had the most concrete fulfillment down to the present hour in the history of Gentile nations. Hundreds if not thousands of prophecies have had literal fulfillment. A method that has worked with such success in the past is certainly worthy of projection into the future.

The interpreter of prophecy has therefore no more warrant to spiritualize prophecy than any other area of theology. If the details of the virgin birth, the character of the miracles of Christ, His very words on the cross, His form of execution, the circumstances of His burial, and His resurrection from the dead could be explicitly prophesied in the Old Testament, certainly there is no a priori reason for rejecting the literal interpretation of prophecy concerning His future righteous government on earth. The literal method is the method recognized in the fulfillment of prophecy and is the mainspring of the premillennial interpretation of the Scriptures.

The question of relative difficulty of interpreting prophecy. Admittedly there are problems in the interpretation of prophecy that are peculiar to this field. While the problems differ in character from the interpretation of history or theological revelation, they do not call for a choice of spiritual or literal interpretation. It is not so much a question of whether the prophecy will be fulfilled, but rather concerning the unrevealed details of time and circumstance. While premillenarians have sometimes been guilty of making prophetic interpretation seem too simple a process, amillenarians have erred in the other direction. After all, interpreting Scripture on such subjects as predestination, the decree of God, the doctrine of the Trinity, the Person of the incarnate Christ, the sufferings of Christ on the cross, and similar doctrines is certainly difficult even though they are in the realm of specific revelation and historic fulfillment. The theologian should no more turn to spiritualization of Scripture to solve the doctrinal difficulties in these areas than he should spiritualize prophecy to fit a denial of a millennial kingdom on earth. Difficulty or even seeming contradiction is not sufficient justification for spiritualization. If the incongruous elements of the human and the divine in Christ can be accepted literally in spite of their seeming contradiction, the elements of prophecy that may seem confusing should not be sacrificed on the altar of spiritualization to remove the problem that arises from literal interpretation.

A general principle guiding the interpretation of prophecy is quite clear in the Scriptures. This principle is that the whole doctrine of prophecy should be allowed to be the guide for the interpretation of details. The main elements of prophecy are far more clear than some of the details. Difficult passages are often solved by a study of related Scriptures. The Book of Revelation, while admittedly difficult to interpret, draws many of its symbols from other portions of Scripture, and many questions of interpretation can be answered within the larger context of the entire Bible.

The problem of the time element in prophecy. One of the problems of interpretation of prophecy is that it involves time relationships. Events widely separated in fulfillment are often brought together in prophetic vision. Thus the first and second comings of Christ are pictured in the same scriptural context. Isaiah 61:1–2 as quoted in part by Christ in Luke 4:16–19 is an illustration of this. In Luke, Christ quoted only the first part of the Isaiah passage, stopping just before the elements that dealt with the Second Coming. Therefore Old Testament prophecy spans the present age with no inkling of the millenniums that separate the first and second advents. On the other hand, when time elements are included, they are intended to be taken literally. Hence, Daniel's "70 weeks" are subject to literal interpretation even though the interval between the 69th and the 70th weeks is only hinted at by Daniel himself. The rule does not justify spiritualization of that which is specifically revealed.

The problem of partial fulfillment. This in a word is the partial fulfillment of a prophecy first, followed by the complete fulfillment later. In Luke 1:31–33, for instance, there was fulfillment of the first part of the prophecy in the Incarnation, but the prediction that Christ would rule over Israel on the throne of David forever has had no fulfillment. Amillenarians have succumbed to the temptation to spiritualize the throne of David. Such an interpretation violates the very integrity of Scripture. Mary certainly understood the prediction to refer to the literal kingdom on earth prophesied in the Old Testament. A spiritual throne in heaven, God's own throne, in no wise fulfills this prediction.

Premillennial principles of literal interpretation justified, the general features of premillennial interpretation are therefore evident. Its method is literal interpretation except for figures plainly intended as symbols. Prophecies are therefore to be taken literally, the exact interpretation following the pattern of the law of fulfillment established by prophecies already fulfilled. Time relationships in prophecy are seen to include the literal interpretation of time elements when given, and at the same time prophetic visions present events widely separated in time in the same revelation. Prophecies fulfilled in part are found to sustain the principle of literal fulfillment, with a partial fulfillment first and complete literal fulfillment to follow. Prophecy in general must follow the same hermeneutical principles of interpretation that govern other areas of theology.

The Premillennial Concept of the Present Age

The practical importance of premillennial interpretation can be seen at once in the comparison of concepts of the present age advanced by the various millennial views. Postmillennialism usually interprets the prophecies of the coming kingdom of righteousness on earth as being subject to a somewhat literal fulfillment in the period just preceding the Second Advent, a period still future from the contemporary viewpoint. This interpretation has almost vanished among contemporary conservative theologians, being continued only in the evolutionary principle of continued world improvement to which some still resolutely cling in spite of trends to the contrary. Amillenarians on the other hand regard the kingdom prophecies as being fulfilled in the present age either on earth or in heaven or both. The premillennial interpretation denies both the postmillennial and amillennial views, affirming that the kingdom on earth will follow, not precede the Second Advent of Christ.

The premillennial concept of the present age views the interadvent period as unique and unpredicted in the Old Testament. The present age is one in which the gospel is preached to all the world. Relatively few are saved. The world becomes, in fact, increasingly wicked as the age progresses. The premillennial view holds no prospects of a golden age before the Second Advent, and presents no commands to improve society as a whole. The apostles were notably silent on any program of either political, social, moral, or physical improvement of the unsaved world. Paul made no effort to correct social abuses or to influence the political government for good. The program of the early church was one of evangelism and Bible teaching. It was a matter of saving souls out of the world rather than saving the world. It was neither possible nor in the program of God for the present age to become the kingdom of God on earth.

Central to the purpose of the present age in the premillennial view is the formation of the church, the body of Christ. This body of believers is quite distinct from Israel in the Old Testament and is not simply a revamped Judaism. The truth regarding the church as a body of Christ is declared to be a mystery, that is, a truth not revealed in the Old Testament. Composed of Jews and Gentiles on an equal basis, and resting on New Testament promises of grace and salvation in Christ, the new entity is a new creation of God, formed by the baptism of the Holy Spirit, indwelt by the Spirit of God, and united to Christ as the human body is united to its head. Almost all premillenarians regard the church as having begun at Pentecost, having its program and formation in the present age, and a prophetic future all its own, not to be confused with Israel or Old Testament saints.

The Premillennial Concept of Israel

There have been, in the main, three interpretations of the theological concept of Israel in Protestant theology. One of these, which can be identified with John Calvin, is the idea that the church is the true Israel and therefore inherits Israel's promises. This is the viewpoint advocated by amillenarians. Allis considers it the only possible amillenarian position. It considers Israel nationally and individually set aside forever and His promises of blessings transferred to the church. Under this concept there is no future hope whatsoever for Israel.

Some amillenarians such as William Hendricksen and some conservative postmillenarians such as Charles Hodge hold that Israel's promises of blessings will be fulfilled to those of Israel in the flesh who come to Christ and become part of the church. The promises are to be fulfilled, then, to Israel, but to Israel in the church. Hodge takes this as a final triumph of the gospel and even envisions some regathering of Israel for this purpose. Under both of these forms of interpretation, no postadvent kingdom is required to fulfill Israel's promises. All will be fulfilled in the present age.

It is clear, however, that many of the promises cannot be literally applied to present earth conditions. Two expedients are followed by the amillenarian and postmillenarian interpretations. Some promises are canceled as having been conditional in the first place. Others are spiritualized to fit the pattern of the present age. This interpretation is based on a somewhat contradictory set of principles. One view is that the promises to Israel were never intended to be taken literally and hence are rightly spiritualized to fit the church. The other is that they were literal enough, but were canceled because of Israel's sin. The concept of Israel prevailing among amillenarians and postmillenarians is therefore confused and inherently contradictory. There does not seem to be any norm or central consistency except in their denial of a political and national future for Israel after the Second Advent. What unity exists in their system rests on this denial.

The premillennial view concerning Israel is quite clear and simple. The prophecies given to Israel are viewed as literal and unconditional. God has promised Israel a glorious future and this will be fulfilled after the Second Advent. Israel will be a glorious nation, protected from her enemies, exalted above the Gentiles, the central vehicle of the manifestation of God's grace in the millennial kingdom. In the present age, Israel has been set aside, her promises held in abeyance, with no progress in the fulfillment of her program. This postponement is considered no more difficult than the delay of 40 years in entering the Promised Land. God's promises may be delayed in fulfillment but not canceled. All concede that a literal interpretation of Israel's promises in the Old Testament present just such a picture. Again it is a question of literal interpretation. The preservation of Israel as a racial entity and the resurrection of Israel as a political entity are twin miracles of the 20th century, which are in perfect accord with the premillennial interpretation. The doctrine of Israel remains one of the central features of premillennialism.

The Premillennial Concept of the Second Advent

The general facts concerning the premillennial viewpoint of the Second Advent are well known. Premillenarians hold to a literal, bodily, visible, and glorious return of Christ to the earth, fulfilling the many scriptural prophecies of this event. They hold that this event is the occasion for the deliverance and judgment of Israel, the downfall and judgment of the Gentiles, and the inauguration of the kingdom of righteousness on earth. In contrast to both amillennialism and postmillennialism, premillenarians hold that the coming of Christ will occur before the millennium. Satan will be bound at that time. The curse of sin will be lifted from the material world. Righteousness, peace, and prosperity will become the rule. Jerusalem will become the capital for the whole world. The kingdom will continue for one thousand years and then will be merged into eternity, attended by catastrophic events—the destruction of the present earth and heavens, the judgment of the wicked dead who will be raised at that time, and the establishment of the saints of all ages in the new earth and new heavens. All these events are interpreted literally by premillenarians and constitute the blueprint of things to come.

Premillenarians often distinguish between the Second Advent and the rapture of the church. Usually Scripture is interpreted to sustain the teaching that the rapture comes before the tribulation time, separated from the second advent by a period of about seven years. Some few hold that the rapture comes in the middle of the tribulation, the midtribulation theory. Others hold to the posttribulation view, which identifies the rapture with the Second Advent proper.

Conclusion

It should be clear from this survey of the field that premillennialism is a distinct system of theology. Opponents of premillennialism are right in part when they charge that premillennialism is essentially different from other forms of theology. The chief differences arise in ecclesiology, eschatology, and hermeneutics. Opponents of premillennialism are wrong, however, when they claim that premillennialism is new, modern, or heretical. Even partisans in the millennial argument usually agree that premillenarians are evangelical, true to biblical doctrines, and opposed to modern defections from evangelical doctrine.

Chapter Notes

Chapter 1

1. Robert L. Dabney, *Lectures in Systematic Theology* (1878; reprint, Grand Rapids: Zondervan, 1972), p. 715.
2. Charles Hodge, *Systematic Theology*, 3 vols. (1871; reprint, Grand Rapids: Eerdmans, 1975), 3:692.
3. Charles Hodge, *Princeton Sermons* (1879; reprint, Edinburgh: Banner of Truth, 1979), p. 292.
4. John Calvin, *Institutes of the Christian Religion*, trans. Henry Beveredge, 2 vols. (Grand Rapids: Eerdmans, 1970), III. 20, p. 146.
5. Philip Schaff, *The Creeds of Christendom*, 3 vols. (Grand Rapids: Baker, 1977), 3:698.
6. Hodge, *Systematic Theology*, p. 708.
7. Hodge, *Princeton Sermons*, p. 291.
8. Hodge, *Systematic Theology*, p. 708.
9. A. A. Hodge, *Evangelical Theology: A Course of Popular Lectures* (1890; reprint, Edinburgh: Banner of Truth, 1976), p. 85.
10. Dabney, *Lectures in Systematic Theology*, p. 716.
11. Hodge, *Princeton Sermons*, p. 294.
12. Ibid., p. 295.
13. Calvin, *Institutes of the Christian Religion*, III. 20, pp. 146–47.
14. Dabney, *Lectures in Systematic Theology*, p. 716.
15. Calvin, *Institutes of the Christian Religion*, III. 20, p. 147.
16. A. A. Hodge, *Evangelical Theology*, p. 91.
17. Hodge, *Systematic Theology*, p. 709.
18. Calvin, *Institutes of the Christian Religion*, III. 20, p. 148.
19. Robert C. Sproul, "Does Prayer Change Things?" *Tenth: An Evangelical Quarterly* 6 (July 1976):53.
20. Ibid., p. 55.
21. Dabney, *Lectures in Systematic Theology*, p. 717.
22. Hodge, *Systematic Theology*, p. 700.
23. Calvin, *Institutes of the Christian Religion*, III. 20, p. 147.
24. A. A. Hodge, *Evangelical Theology*, p. 85.
25. Dabney, *Lectures in Systematic Theology*, p. 719.
26. Ibid.
27. A. A. Hodge, *Evangelical Theology*, p. 88.
28. Francois Turrettine, "Instituto Theologiae Elencticae," trans. George

Musgrave Ginger, typewritten manuscript (Princeton, NJ: Princeton Theological Seminary, n.d.), p. 175.
29. Ibid.
30. Sproul, "Does Prayer Change Things?" p. 58.
31. Dabney, *Lectures in Systematic Theology*, p. 718.
32. A. A. Hodge, *Evangelical Theology*, p. 93.
33. Turrettine, "Instituto Theologiae Elencticae," p. 177.
34. Calvin, *Institutes of the Christian Religion*, III. 20, p. 147.

Chapter 2

1. *Baker's Dictionary of Theology* (Grand Rapids: Baker, 1960), s.v. "Foreknowledge," by Lorraine Boettner, p. 225.
2. *International Standard Bible Encyclopedia*, 1939 ed., s.v. "Foreknowledge," by Casper Wistar Hodge, 2:1130.
3. Walter Bauer, William F. Arndt, and F. Wilbur Gingrich, *A Greek-English Lexicon of the New Testament and Other Early Christian Literature* (Chicago: University of Chicago Press, 1957), p. 716.
4. Ibid., p. 584.
5. *Webster's New World Dictionary*, p. 566.
6. *International Standard Bible Encyclopedia*, s.v. "Foreknowledge," by Hodge, 2:1130.
7. Lewis Sperry Chafer, *Systematic Theology*, 8 vols. (Dallas, TX: Dallas Seminary, 1948; reprint [8 vols. in 4], Grand Rapids: Kregel, 1992), 7:25.
8. Ibid., 7:26.
9. A. T. Robertson, *Word Pictures in the New Testament*, 6 vols. (Nashville: Broadman, 1933), 3:29.
10. William F. Arndt, "Studies in First Peter," *Theology Monthly* 9 (February 1929):42.
11. Bauer, Arndt, and Gingrich, *A Greek-English Lexicon of the New Testament and Other Early Christian Literature*, p. 710.
12. Joseph Henry Thayer, *A Greek-English Lexicon of the New Testament* (Grand Rapids: Zondervan, 1962), p. 538.
13. James Moffatt, *The New Testament: A New Translation* (New York: Doran, 1922), p. 291.
14. *International Standard Bible Encyclopedia*, s.v. "Foreknowledge," by Hodge, 2:1130.
15. Ibid.

Chapter 3

1. C. S. Lewis, *Miracles: A Preliminary Study* (New York: Macmillan, 1947), p. 83.

2. Mary Hesse, "Miracles and the Laws of Nature," in *Miracles,* ed. C. F. D. Moule (London: Mowbray, 1965), p. 35.
3. Albert Einstein, "The Meeting Place of Science and Religion," *Has Science Discovered God?* ed. Edward H. Cotton (Freeport, NY: Books for Libraries, 1931), p. 101.
4. Paul Van Buren, *The Secular Meaning of the Gospel* (New York: Macmillan, 1963), p. 100.
5. Hesse, "Miracles and the Laws of Nature," p. 39.
6. David Hume, *An Enquiry concerning Human Understanding* (LaSalle, IL: Open Court, 1955), p. 127, n. 1.
7. Ibid., 126.
8. Hesse, "Miracles and the Laws of Nature," p. 38.
9. Ibid., p. 37.
10. Ibid.
11. Voltaire, *Philosophical Dictionary*, ed. and trans. Theodore Besterman (Baltimore: Penguin, 1971), pp. 6, 272.
12. Walt Whitman, "Miracles," *Leaves of Grass* (Philadelphia, 1900), p. 428.
13. Lewis, *Miracles: A Preliminary Study*, p. 56.
14. D. Elton Trueblood, *The Logic of Belief*, 2d ed. (New York: Harper, 1942), p. 276.
15. Lewis, *Miracles: A Preliminary Study*, p. 99.
16. Ibid., p. 160.
17. John Louis Booth, "The Purpose of Miracles" (Th.D. diss., Dallas Theological Seminary, 1965), p. 8.
18. Henry Clarence Thiessen, *Introductory Lectures in Systematic Theology* (Grand Rapids: Eerdmans, 1949), p. 36.
19. Henry C. Thiessen, "An Outline of Lectures in Systematic Theology," 3d ed. (unpublished class notes, Wheaton College, 1942), p. 9.
20. Lewis, *Miracles: A Preliminary Study*, p. 131.
21. Ibid., p. 201.
22. Lewis Sperry Chafer, *Systematic Theology*, 8 vols., (Dallas, TX: Dallas Seminary, 1948; reprint [8 vols. in 4], Grand Rapids: Kregel, 1992), 4:256.
23. Lewis Sperry Chafer, *Major Bible Themes* (Dallas, TX: Dallas Seminary, 1926), p. 265.
24. Hume, *An Enquiry concerning Human Understanding*, p. 145.

Chapter 4

1. Augustine, *Epistolae* 82. i. 3.
2. Geoffrey W. Bromiley, "Church Doctrine of Inspiration," in *Revelation and the Bible*, ed. Carl F. H. Henry (Grand Rapids: Baker, 1958), 209.

3. John Calvin, *Sermons on Job*, trans. Leroy Nixon (Grand Rapids: Baker, 1952), p. 744.

4. John Calvin, *Institutes of the Christian Religion*, trans. Henry Beveridge, 2 vols. (Grand Rapids: Eerdmans, 1964), 1:149.

5. Johann Michael Reu, *Luther and the Scriptures*, p. 24.

6. Grand Rapids: Eerdmans, 1957.

7. Everett F. Harrison, "The Phenomena of Scripture," in *Revelation and the Bible*, p. 250.

8. J. I. Packer, *'Fundamentalism' and the Word of God* (Grand Rapids: Eerdmans, 1958), p. 95.

9. B. B. Warfield, *The Inspiration and Authority of the Bible*, ed. Samuel G. Craig (Philadelphia: Presbyterian and Reformed, 1948), p. 442.

10. Edward J. Young, *Thy Word Is Truth* (Grand Rapids: Eerdmans, 1957), pp. 108–9.

11. J. K. S. Reid, *The Authority of Scripture* (New York: Harper, 1957), p. 279.

12. Warfield, *The Inspiration and Authority of the Bible*, p. 181.

13. Alan M. Stibbs, "Witness of Scripture to Its Inspiration," in *Revelation and the Bible*, pp. 108–9.

14. A. A. Hodge, *Outlines of Theology* (New York: R. Carter, 1863), p. 67.

15. John Murray, "The Attestation of Scripture," in *The Infallible Word*, ed. N. B. Stonehouse and Paul Woolley (Grand Rapids: Eerdmans, 1953), p. 7.

Chapter 5

1. A. Berkeley Mickelsen, *Interpreting the Bible* (Grand Rapids: Eerdmans, 1963), p. 5.

2. H. C. G. Moule, *Veni Creator: Thoughts on the Person and Work of the Holy Spirit of Promise* (London: Hodder & Stoughton, 1890), p. 63.

3. Joseph Parker, *The Paraclete* (New York: Scribner, Armstrong & Co., 1875), p. 78.

4. Bernard Ramm, *Protestant Biblical Interpretation*, 3d ed. (Grand Rapids: Baker, 1970), p. 13.

5. J. Theodore Mueller, "The Holy Spirit and the Scriptures," in *Revelation and the Bible*, ed. Carl F. H. Henry (Grand Rapids: Baker, 1958), p. 276.

6. Ronald S. Wallace, *Calvin's Doctrine of the Word and Sacraments* (Grand Rapids: Eerdmans, 1957), pp. 128–29.

7. John Calvin, *Commentary on a Harmony of the Evangelists, Matthew, Mark, and Luke*, trans. William Pringle, 3 vols. (reprint, Grand Rapids: Baker, 1981), 3:375.

8. John F. Walvoord, "How Can Man Know God?" *Bibliotheca Sacra* 116 (April–June, 1959):105.
9. Daniel F. Fuller, "Do We Need the Holy Spirit to Understand the Bible?" *Eternity*, January 1959, p. 22.
10. Henry A. Virkler, *Hermeneutics: Principles and Processes of Biblical Interpretation* (Grand Rapids: Baker, 1981), p. 30.
11. Charles Hodge, *Systematic Theology*, 3 vols. (Grand Rapids:. Eerdmans, 1960), 3:403.
12. Geoffrey W. Bromiley, "The Biblical Doctrine of Inspiration," *Christianity Today*, November 23, 1959, p. 139 (italics added).
13. Fred H. Klooster, "The Role of the Holy Spirit in the Hermeneutic Process," paper read at the Chicago Summit Conference II (Oakland, CA: International Council on Biblical Inerrancy, 1982), p. 16.
14. Ramm, *Protestant Biblical Interpretation*, pp. 13–14.
15. John McClintock and James Strong, *Cyclopedia of Biblical, Theological and Ecclesiastical Literature* (reprint, Grand Rapids: Baker, 1959), 4:205.
16. Mickelsen, *Interpreting the Bible*, p. 39.
17. Parker, *The Paraclete*, p. 83.
18. Lewis Sperry Chafer, *He That Is Spiritual* (1918; rev. ed., Grand Rapids: Zondervan, 1967), p 62.
19. Klooster, "The Role of the Holy Spirit," pp. 12–13.
20. Ramm, *Protestant Biblical Interpretation*, p. 17.
21. Ibid.
22. Ibid.
23. Lewis Sperry Chafer, *Systematic Theology*, 8 vols. (Dallas, TX: Dallas Seminary, 1948; reprint [8 vols. in 4], Grand Rapids: Kregel, 1992), 1:6.
24. Cf. Norman L. Geisler, "The Concept of Truth in the Contemporary Inerrancy Debate," *Bibliotheca Sacra* 137 (October–December 1980):327–39.
25. Bernard Ramm, *The Pattern of Authority* (Grand Rapids: Eerdmans, 1957), p. 37.
26. Robert T. Sandin, "The Clarity of Scripture," in *The Living and Active Word of God: Studies in Honor of Samuel J. Schultz*, ed. Morris Inch and Ronald Youngblood (Winona Lake, IN: Eisenbrauns, 1983), pp. 240–41.
27. Klooster, "The Role of the Holy Spirit," p. 14.
28. James Michael Lee, "The Authentic Source of Religious Instruction," in *Religious Education and Theology*, ed. Norma H. Thompson (Birmingham, AL: Religious Educations, 1982), p. 194.
29. Ibid., p. 195.

30. Ibid., pp. 196–97
31. Ibid., pp. 193–94,
32. James Michael Lee, "Toward a New Era: A Blueprint for Positive Action," in *The Religious Education We Need*, ed. James Michael Lee (Mishawaka, IN: Religious Education, 1977), p. 130.

Chapter 6

1. G. C. Berkouwer, *Man: The Image of God* (Grand Rapids: Eerdmans, 1962), p. 12.
2. Stewart C. Zabriskie, "A Critical View of Karl Barth's Approach to the Christian Doctrine of the *Imago Dei*," *Anglican Theological Review* 47 (October 1965):359.
3. *Baker's Dictionary of Theology*, 1960 ed., s.v. "Man," by Carl F. H. Henry, p. 339.
4. Berkouwer, *Man: The Image of God*, p. 35
5. Gordon H. Clark, "The Image of God in Man," *Journal of the Evangelical Theological Society* 12 (Fall 1969):215. James Orr wrote, "It is not too much to say that every crucial question in theology, almost, is already settled in principle in any thorough-going discussion of the divine attributes" (*God's Image in Man* [New York: 1906], p. 7).
6. *The International Standard Bible Encyclopaedia*
7. *Baker's Dictionary of Theology*, 1929 ed., s.v. "God, Image of," by James Orr, 2:1264. "Man," by Carl F. H. Henry, p. 339.
8. Berkouwer, *Man: The Image of God*, p. 66.
9. Cf. also Hebrews 2:6–8, which is based on Psalm 8; Hebrews 1:3 (underscoring the deity of Christ; and Acts 17:26–29 (Paul's address to the Athenians on Mar's Hill). Also note that Psalm 51:6; Romans 1:23; and 2:15 have important implications for the doctrine now considered.
10. Berkouwer, *Man: The Image of God*, p. 43. Today this distinction is held to be invalid. A naturalistic view holds that man was created only in God's image, but gradually evolved into God's likeness. Many have affirmed that the image was basic, to which was added the likeness, called *donum superadditum*. Origen held that Genesis speaks of man's creation in the image, but can obtain the likeness by works. The church fathers made a distinction between image and likeness, but Luther and Calvin refused to follow this tradition. Consensus today rejects a differentiation on both exegetical and theological grounds.
11. Cf. R. G. Crawford, "The Image of God," *Expository Times* 77 (May 1966):233–36. On the position of the Eastern Church, see *Encyclopedia of the Lutheran Church*, (1965), s.v. "Anthropology,"

by Edo Osterloh, p. 83. For the view that the image speaks of the physical and the likeness to the ethical part of man, see *International Standard Bible Encyclopaedia*, 1929 ed., s.v. "Anthropology," by J. I. Marais, 1:145.

12. *A Dictionary of the Bible*, ed. James Hastings, s.v. "Image," by J. Laidlaw, 2 (1899):452.
13. Berkouwer, *Man: The Image of God*, p. 69.
14. Orr, *God's Image in Man*, pp. 41, 46.
15. A. Altmann, "*Homo Imago Dei* in Jewish and Christian Theology," *Journal of Religion* 48 (July 1968):235.
16. Erdman Harris, *God's Image and Man's Imagination,* (New York, (1959), p. 199. Of course this is not meant to remove the distinction between God and man, but rather to assert the unique status of man in comparison with all other creatures; cf. Berkouwer, *Man: The Image of God*, p. 70.
17. Robert Jamieson, A. R. Fausset, and David Brown, *A Commentary, Critical, Experimental, and Practical on the Old and New Testaments*, 6 vols. (London: n.d.), 1:8. It is interesting that Calvin, expounding Ephesians and Colossians, stressed the righteousness of the new creation, thus interpreting the Old Testament by the New (John Calvin, *Institutes of the Christian Religion* i. 15.4).
18. *Theological Dictionary of the New Testament*, s.v. "οἰκών," by Gerhard Kittel, 2:394.
19. R. Payne Smith, "Genesis," in *A Bible Commentary for Bible Students*, ed. Charles John Ellicott (London: n.d.), 1:17. Skinner is surely more correct when, admitting that the image qualifies man for dominion, he affirms that such rule is a consequence, and not the essence of the image of God (John Skinner, *A Critical and Exegetical Commentary on Genesis*, International Critical Commentary [Edinburgh: Clark, 1910], p. 32). Mauser has recently presented a rather novel approach to the question, when, discussing the position of Hempel, he speaks of an anthropomorphous God answering to a theomorphous man. His view may be summarized in this way: "In the book of Hosea the prophet of Israel is depicted in a remarkably theomorphic fashion in that his life story as a man becomes, at least partially, a representation of God by participation in God's condition. Human life is consequently understood as an image of God which in turn presupposes a concept of the divine in which Yahweh is so essentially God for and with Israel that the human is lodged in Him" (Ulrich Mauser, "Image of God and Incarnation," *Interpretation* 24 [July 1970]:336–56, esp. 336 and 342). The introduction into the discussion of so many *tertium quids* can only serve to confuse the issue.

20. Clark, "The Image of God in Man," p. 216.
21. Adam Clarke, *The Holy Bible, Containing the Old and New Testaments* (New York: n.d.), 1:38.
22. C. F. Keil and F. Delitzsch, *The Pentateuch*, vol. 1 of *Biblical Commentary on the Old Testament*, trans. James Martin (Edinburgh: Clark, 1866) pp. 63–64.
23. Lewis Sperry Chafer, *Systematic Theology*, 8 vols. (Dallas, TX: Dallas Seminary, 1948; reprint [8 vols. in 4], Grand Rapids: Kregel, 1992), 1:181, 184.
24. Calvin, *Institutes of the Christian Religion*, i. 15. 3. He concludes, "I retain the principle . . . that the image of God includes all the excellence in which the nature of man surpasses all the other species of animals" (ibid.). Zenos concurs in understanding the image to be that which relates man to God, namely, his personality (Andrew C. Zenos, "Man, Doctrine of," in *A Standard Bible Dictionary*, ed. Melancthon W. Jacobus et al. (1909), pp. 512–13.
25. Altmann, "*Homo Image Dei* in Jewish and Christian Theology," pp. 235–39. In vivid contrast to the Aramaic versions are the Greek, which, apart from Symmachus, translated the text literally (ibid., p. 240).
26. Ibid., pp. 243–44.
27. *Encyclopedia Judaica*, s.v. "Man, The Nature of," by Israel Adler, 11 (1971), pp. 842–46, esp. 843.
28. Altmann, "*Homo-Image Dei* in Jewish and Christian Theology," p. 254. The Jewish writer of Egypt, Saadya Gaon (892–942), however, held that the image referred to man's rule as lord of the earth—Genesis 1:28–30—reasoning from *Elohim* as "rulers," "judges" (ibid., p. 255).
29. Ibid., pp. 244–45.
30. Berkouwer, *Man: The Image of God*, p. 57.
31. Ibid., p. 76.
32. Ibid., p. 88. See also Charles Hodge, *Systematic Theology*, 3 vols. (New York: 1871), 2:96ff.
33. Walter Russell Bowie, "Exposition, The Book of Genesis," in *The Interpreter's Bible*, ed. George Arthur Buttrick, 12 vols. (Nashville: Abingdon, 1952), 1:484–85.
34. Crawford, "The Image of God," p. 234.
35. Berkouwer, *Man: The Image of God*, pp. 51–52.
36. Clarke, *The Holy Bible, Containing the Old and New Testaments*, p. 221. When Barth unfolds his exposition, he makes the image the sexual distinction between man and woman. Clark is to the point when he observes, "Since this distinction occurs in animals

also, one wonders how it can be the image that sets man apart from the lower creation. And since there are no sexual distinctions in the Godhead, one wonders how this can be an image of God at all" (ibid.).

37. Zabriskie, "A Critical View of Karl Barth's Approach to the Christian Doctrine of the *Image Dei*," pp. 360–61. Barth, along with other Christian exegetes, is guilty of reading New Testament doctrine into Old Testament citations, which is an unhappy exegetical procedure.

38. Ibid., p. 376.

39. *A Dictionary of the Bible*, s.v. "Image," by Laidlaw, 2:452–53. Along with John 1:1–3 the passages cited speak of creation and the upholding of the universe as the work of Christ as Word, Image, and Son respectively.

40. C. J. Chereso, "Image of God," *New Catholic Encyclopedia*, s.v. "Image of God," by C. J. Chereso, 7 (1967):369.

41. Altmann, Altmann, "*Homo Imago Dei* in Jewish and Christian Theology," p. 254.

42. Harris, *God's Image and Man's Imagination*, p. 201.

43. *Encyclopedia of the Lutheran Church*, s.v. "Anthropology," by Osterloh, pp. 83–84.

44. Berkouwer, *Man: The Image of God*, p. 133.

45. Orr, *God's Image in Man*, p. 59.

46. There is no need to restrict the image too narrowly to mind, reason, or logic. Man is far too complex for this alone. When the image is too limited to reason, the conclusion may be, "Then in heaven we will not make mistakes even in arithmetic" (cf. Clarke, *The Holy Bible, Containing the Old and New Testaments*, pp. 218, 222).

Chapter 7

1. J. Oswald Sanders, *A Spiritual Clinic* (Chicago: Moody, 1958), p. 57.

2. If the "Adulteress Pericope" (John 7:53–8:11) is not accepted as part of the original manuscript of John's Gospel, then the number of occurrences is 29.

3. The full clause is οὐδὲν γὰρ ἐμαυτῷ σύνοιδα.

4. C. A. Pierce, *Conscience in the New Testament* (London: SCM, 1955), pp. 32, 55.

5. *The Paraphrased Epistles and The New Testament in Today's English Version*.

6. O. Hallesby, *Conscience* (Minneapolis: Augsburg, 1933), pp. 12–13.

7. Sanders, *A Spiritual Clinic*, p. 58.

8. Two examples of this are συλλυπέω ("to grieve within one's

self," Mark 3:5) and with συντηρέω ("to keep within one's self," Luke 2:19).

9. Franz Delitzsch, *A System of Biblical Psychology*, p. 160.

10. Ibid., p. 161.

11. The Old Testament does not have an exact equivalent of συνείδησις, though the thought of a moral awareness or sensitivity is found in the Old Testament and is frequently rendered by the word "heart." For example "David's heart smote him" (1 Sam. 24:5; 2 Sam. 24:10); My heart shall not reproach me" (Job 27:6).

12. *Schaff-Herzog Encyclopedia of Religious Knowledge*, s.v. "Conscience," by C. A. Beckwith, 3:243.

13. Ibid.

14. Quoted in Augustus Hopkins Strong, *Systematic Theology* (Philadelphia: Judson, 1907), p. 501.

15. Pierce, *Conscience in the New Testament*, p. 125.

16. *Baker's Dictionary of Theology*, s.v. "Conscience," by Alfred W. Rehwinkel, pp. 136.

17. *Encyclopaedia Britannica*, 1967, ed., s.v. "Conscience," 6:363.

18. *Baker's Dictionary of Theology*, s.v. "Conscience," by Alfred W. Rehwinkel, pp. 136–39.

19. Strong, *Systematic Theology*, pp. 498–99.

20. Or this verse may be illustrating the function of the conscience as a witness: We should be submissive to higher powers because our conscience tells us it is right to do so.

21. In Romans 2:14–15 the Greek does not equate the conscience with the condemning and approving of thoughts.

22. Strong, *Systematic Theology*, p. 82.

23. Lewis Sperry Chafer, *Systematic Theology*, 8 vols. (Dallas, TX: Dallas Seminary, 1948; reprint [8 vols. in 4], Grand Rapids: Kregel 1992), 7:92.

24. John Calvin, *Institutes of the Christian Religion*, trans. Henry Beveredge, 2 vols. (Grand Rapids: Eerdmans, 1970), II. 91.

25. A. A. Hodge, *Outlines of Theology*, p. 224.

26. Quoted in Pierce, *Conscience in the New Testament*, pp. 47–51.

27. Quoted in Lewis C. Henry, ed., *Best Quotations for All Occasions*, p. 44.

28. Pierce, *Conscience in the New Testament*, p. 45.

29. Ibid., p. 111.

30. Ibid., p. 71.

31. Ibid., p. 51.

32. Ibid., pp. 84, 86–87.

33. Sanders, *A Spiritual Clinic*, p. 60.

34. Ibid.

35. "Just as a bullet will reach the bull's-eye only if the two sights are in correct alignment, so correct moral judgments are delivered only when conscience is correctly aligned with the Scriptures" (Sanders, *A Spiritual Clinic*, p. 60).
36. Hallesby, *Conscience*, p. 26.
37. Joseph Henry Thayer, *A Greek-English Lexicon of the New Testament* (Grand Rapids: Zondervan, 1962), p. 602.
38. Sanders, *A Spiritual Clinic*, p. 63.
39. Sanders illustrates this in the words of a Canadian Indian: "My conscience is a little three-cornered thing inside of me. When I do wrong it turns round and hurts me very much. But if I keep on doing wrong, it will turn so much that the corners become worn off and it does not hurt any more (ibid., p. 59).
40. Martin Luther expressed the necessity of the conscience being aligned with the Word of God. When called on to renounce his position, he affirmed, "My conscience is bound in the Word of God. I cannot and will not recant anything, since it is unsafe and dangerous to act against conscience. Here I stand. I cannot do otherwise. God help me! Amen" (quoted in Hallesby, *Conscience*, p. 36).
41. An automobile driver should align his speed monitor with what the speed limit actually is, not according to the speed he wants it to be.

Chapter 8

1. Ross S. Bennett, ed., *Our World* (Washington, DC: National Geographic Society, 1979), p. 20.
2. Carl Haub and Douglas W. Heisler, comps., "1980 World Population Data Sheet" (Washington, DC: Population Reference Bureau, 1980).
3. Walbert Bühlmann, *The Coming of the Third Church* (Maryknoll, NY: Orbis, 1977), p. 143.
4. C. Peter Wagner, *Stop the World, I Want to Get On* (Glendale, CA: Gospel Light, 1974), p. 5.
5. P. J. Johnstone, *Operation World* (Bromley, England: STL, 1978).
6. Donald A. McGavran, ed., *Eye of the Storm* (Waco, TX: Word, 1972), p. 233.
7. Ralph P. Winter, "The Grounds for a New Thrust in World Mission," in *Evangelical Missions Tomorrow*, ed. Wade Coggins and Edwin Frizen (South Pasadena, CA: Wm. Carey, 1977), pp. 1–26.
8. Edward R. Dayton, *That Everyone May Hear* (Monrovia, CA: MARC, 1979), p. 19.

9. Roger C. Palms, "Three Billion People—Shall They Hear?" *World Evangelization* 20 (September 1980):2.

10. C. Peter Wagner and Edward R. Dayton, eds., *Unreached Peoples '79* (Elgin, IL: David C. Cook, 1978).

11. Barbara I. Grimes, ed., *Ethnologue* (Huntington Beach, CA: Wycliffe Bible Translators, 1974).

12. George Cowan, *The Word That Kindles* (Chappaqua, NY: Christian Herald, 1979), p. 12.

13. Ralph D. Winter, "The Highest Priority: Cross-cultural Evangelism," in *Let the Earth Hear His Voice*, ed. J. D. Douglas (Minneapolis: World Wide, 1975), p. 229.

14. Arthur P. Johnston, "Focus Comment," *Trinity World Forum* 1 (Fall 1975):3.

15. E. O. James, *Christianity and Other Religions* (Philadelphia: Lippincott, 1968), pp. 29, 173.

16. R. Pannikan, *The Unknown Christ of Hinduism* (London: Darton, Longman & Todd, 1968), pp. 51, 137.

17. Clark Pinnock, "Why Is Jesus the Only Way?" *Eternity*, December 1976, p. 32.

18. S. D. F. Salmond, *The Christian Doctrine of Immortality* (Edinburgh: Clark, 1895), p. 672.

19. J. Herbert Kane, *Understanding Christian Missions* (Grand Rapids: Baker, 1974), p. 135.

20. Pinnock, "Why Is Jesus the Only Way?" p. 32.

21. R. C. H. Lenski, *The Interpretation of St. Paul's Epistle to the Romans* (Minneapolis: Augsburg, 1961), p. 92.

22. John Calvin, *Calvin's Commentaries*, trans. Russ Mackenzie (Grand Rapids: Eerdmans, 1960), 8:30.

23. Thomas Chalmers, *Lectures on the Epistles of Paul the Apostle* (New York: Carter & Brothers, 1855), p. 24.

24. Richard W. DeHaan, *The Word on Trial* (Grand Rapids: Zondervan, 1970), p. 14.

25. Donald Grey Barnhouse, *Man's Ruin* (Grand Rapids: Eerdmans, 1952), p. 243.

26. Gleason L. Archer, *The Epistle to the Romans: A Study Manual* (Grand Rapids: Baker, 1959), p. 11.

27. Malcolm H. Watts, "The Case of the Heathen," *Bible League Quarterly* (July–September 1978):149.

28. Robert C. McQuilkin, *The Message of Romans* (Grand Rapids: Zondervan, 1947), p. 29.

29. Archibald T. Robertson, *Word Pictures in the New Testament*, 6 vols. (Nashville: Broadman, 1931), 4:338.

30. James Denny, "St. Paul's Epistle to the Romans," in *The*

Expositor's Greek Testament, 5 vols. (Grand Rapids: Eerdmans, 1974), 2:593.

31. George W. Peters, *A Biblical Theology of Missions* (Chicago: Moody, 1972), p. 89.
32. Kane, *Understanding Christian Missions*, p. 102.
33. J. I Packer, *Evangelism and the Sovereignty of God* (London: InterVarsity, 1961), p. 27.

Chapter 9

1. Walter Bauer, William F. Arndt, and F. Wilbur Gingrich, *A Greek-English Lexicon of the New Testament and Other Early Christian Literature* (Chicago: University of Chicago Press, 1957), p. 646.
2. G. Abbott-Smith, *Manual Greek Lexicon of the New Testament*, 3d ed. (Edinburgh: Clark, 1937), p. 351.
3. Richard C. Trench, *Synonyms of the New Testament* (Grand Rapids: Eerdmans, 1975), p. 280.
4. John F. Walvoord, *Jesus Christ Our Lord* (Chicago: Moody, 1976), p. 147.
5. Charles Hodge, *Systematic Theology*, 3 vols. (Grand Rapids: Eerdmans, 1979), 2:457.
6. Ibid.
7. Robert L. Dabney, *Lectures in Systematic Theology* (Grand Rapids: Zondervan, 1976), p. 471.
8. William G. T. Shedd, *Dogmatic Theology*, 3 vols. (New York: Charles Scribner's Sons, 1889; reprint, Minneapolis: Klock and Klock, 1979), 2:269.
9. Dabney, *Lectures in Systematic Theology*, p. 471.
10. Lewis Sperry Chafer, *Systematic Theology*, 8 vols. (Dallas, TX: Dallas Seminary, 1948; reprint [8 vols. in 4], Grand Rapids: Kregel, 1992), 5:78.
11. Dabney, *Lectures in Systematic Theology*, p. 473.
12. Shedd, *Dogmatic Theology*, 2:334.

Chapter 10

1. W. Lindsey Alexander, *A System of Biblical Theology*, 2 vols. (Edinburgh: Clark, 1888). 2:111.
2. Marshall Randles. *Substitution* (London: J. Grose Thomas, n.d.). p. 10.
3. Lewis Sperry Chafer, *Systematic Theology*, 8 vols. (Dallas, TX: Dallas Seminary, 1948; reprint [8 vols. in 4], Grand Rapids: Kregel, 1992), 2:76–90.
4. W. G. T. Shedd, *Dogmatic Theology*, 3 vols. (Edinburgh: Clark, 1889), 2:479.

Chapter 11

1. John F. Walvoord, *Jesus Christ Our Lord* (Chicago: Moody, 1969), p. 219. Cf. Brian K. Donne, "The Significance of the Ascension of Jesus Christ in the New Testament," *Scottish Journal of Theology* 30 (1977):555; C. George Fry, "A Day to Remember," *Christianity Today*, May 9, 1969, p. 3; Joel Nederhood, "A Christian Holiday You May Have Forgotten," *Eternity*, May 1974, p. 32; David P. Scaer, "Jesus Did Not Leave—He Reigns through Us," *Christianity Today*, May 21,1982, p. 24.

2. On the present ministry of Christ in Hebrews, see B. F. Westcott, *The Epistle to the Hebrews*, 2d ed. (London: Macmillan, 1892), pp. 229–30; Philip Edgcumbe Hughes, *A Commentary on the Epistle to the Hebrews* (Grand Rapids: Eerdmans, 1977), pp. 349–54; idem, "The Present Work of Christ in Hebrews," *Bibliotheca Sacra* 131 (January–March 1974): 26–33; William Milligan, *The Ascension and Heavenly Priesthood of Our Lord*, 2d ed. (London: Macmillan, 1894), 149–65; Arthur J. Tait, *The Heavenly Session of Our Lord* (London: Robert South, 1912), pp. 149–76; Harm Henry Meeter, *The Heavenly High Priesthood of Christ* (Grand Rapids: Eerdmans, 1916), pp. 181–203; Henry Barclay Swete, *The Ascended Christ* (London: Macmillan, 1916), pp. 1–15, 87–115; Aelred Gody, *Heavenly Sanctuary and Liturgy in the Epistle to the Hebrews* (St. Meinrad, IN: Grail, 1960), pp. 192–202; Peter Toon, *The Ascension of Our Lord* (Nashville: Nelson, 1984), pp. 53–71; J. H. Davies, "The Heavenly Work of Christ in Hebrews," *Studia Evangelia* 4 (1968):384–89; John Murray, "The Heavenly, Priestly Activity of Christ," in *Collected Writings of John Murray*, 4 vols. (Edinburgh: Banner of Truth, 1976), 1:44–58.

3. There are two theories as to the time of Jesus' ascension: (1) He ascended 40 days after the resurrection, as described in Acts 1. (2) He ascended on the day of His resurrection, with the subsequent appearances of Acts 1 being visitations from His exalted order. The author of Hebrews does not address this question. For discussion on this issue see F. F. Bruce, *The Book of Acts*, New International Commentary on the New Testament, rev. ed. (Grand Rapids: Eerdmans, 1988), p. 37; George E. Ladd, *I Believe in the Resurrection of Jesus* (Grand Rapids: Eerdmans, 1975), pp. 127–29; Murray J. Harris, *Raised Immortal: Resurrection and Immortality in the New Testament* (Grand Rapids: Eerdmans, 1983), p. 91; and Toon, *The Ascension of Our Lord*, pp. 125–26.

4. *Theological Dictionary of the New Testament*, s.v. "διέρχομαι," by Johannes Schneider, 2:676. J. G. Davies wrote, "The author of the Epistle to the Hebrews is less concerned with testifying to the fact

of the Ascension than with expounding its theological significance; yet, needless to say, the latter rests upon the former" (*He Ascended into Heaven* [London: Lutterworth, 1958], pp. 44–45).

5. The perfect tense (διεληλυθότα) is used here (as in 2:9; 8:6; 12:2) to refer back to the commencement of Christ's present state (cf. J. H. Davies, "The Heavenly Work of Christ in Hebrews," p. 385).

6. Ibid.

7. Cf. F. F. Bruce, *The Epistle to the Hebrews* (Grand Rapids: Eerdmans, 1964), pp. 200–201.

8. *Theological Dictionary of the New Testament*, s.v. "χρίω," by Walter Grundmann, 9:564.

9. J. H. Davies, "The Heavenly Work of Christ in Hebrews," p. 386.

10. Marcus Dods, "The Epistle to the Hebrews," in *The Expositor's Greek Testament*, 5 vols. (London: Hodder and Stoughton, 1910), 4:252; Hughes, *A Commentary on the Epistle to the Hebrews*, p. 47.

11. J. G. Davies, *He Ascended into Heaven*, p. 65.

12. Franz Delitzsch, *The Psalms*, 3 vols. (Edinburgh: Clark, 1871), 3:189.

13. W. E. Vine, *The Epistle to the Hebrews* (Grand Rapids: Zondervan, 1952), p.14.

14. Walter Bauer, William F. Arndt, and F. Wilbur Gingrich, *A Greek-English Lexicon of the New Testament and Other Early Christian Literature* (Chicago: University of Chicago Press, 1957), p. 711.

15. Dods, "The Epistle to the Hebrews," p. 290.

16. J. H. Davies, "The Heavenly Work of Christ in Hebrews," p. 386.

17. Ibid.

18. *Theological Dictionary of the New Testament*, s.v. "λειτουργέω," by H. Strathmann, 4:221–26.

19. Only once in the Septuagint is λειτουργός used in a sacral setting (Isa. 61:6).

20. As Donald Guthrie noted, the fact that Christ is called a Minister in the sanctuary after He sat down draws attention to His continuing work in heaven (*The Letter to the Hebrews* [Grand Rapids: Eerdmans, 1983], p. 171).

21. The term λειτουργός was generally used of one who is the servant of a superior. It suggests a function to be discharged, a necessary service to be rendered (Westcott, *The Epistle to the Hebrews*, pp. 230–32).

22. Hughes listed three categories: representation, benediction, and intercession (*A Commentary on the Epistle to the Hebrews*, p. 349). Westcott also had three: intercession (which includes representation), mediation of prayers, and securing access for His people (*The Epistle to the Hebrews*, p. 229). Gody had three as

well: purification of the sanctuary, appearing before God, and intercession (*Heavenly Sanctuary and Liturgy in the Epistle to the Hebrews*, p. 193). Meeter had three: offering, intercession, and benediction (*The Heavenly High Priesthood of Christ*, pp. 170–203), and Murray had two: sympathy and intercession ("The Heavenly, Priestly Activity of Christ," pp. 48–58).

23. *Theological Dictionary of the New Testament*, s.v. "πρόσωπον," by Eduard Lohse, 6:775–77.

24. Westcott, *The Epistle to the Hebrews*, p. 272. Gottheb Lünemann, on the other hand, interpreted 9:24 to mean that Christ sees God clearly ("The Epistle to the Hebrews," in *Meyer's Critical and Exegetical Handbook to the New Testament*, 6th ed., 11 vols. [New York: Funk & Wagnalls, 1884], 9:624).

25. Martin Luther warned of the difference between those who read Hebrews 9:24 speculatively and those who read it practically. "The former believe that Christ appears in the presence of God in behalf of others, but the latter believe that Christ has appeared in the presence of God in our behalf" (*Lectures on Titus, Philemon and Hebrews* [St. Louis: Concordia, 1968], p. 217).

26. Thomas F. Torrance has argued that Christ's present work is substitutionary as well as representative. As High Priest, Christ vicariously offers prayers and worship for His people (*Space, Time and Resurrection* [Grand Rapids: Eerdmans, 1967], pp. 115–16); cf. also Toon, *The Ascension of Our Lord*, pp. 65–66. The imagery of the Old Testament would suggest, however, that as a sacrifice Christ's death was substitutionary, but as High priest His ministry is representative.

27. It should be noted that the author of Hebrews did not develop the doctrine of the believer's spiritual union with Christ as did Paul. In Hebrews 9:24 the believer is "in Christ" representatively, but not by spiritual union (see Hughes, *A Commentary on the Epistle to the Hebrews*, p. 349).

28. Westcott, *The Epistle to the Hebrews*, p. 272.

29. The νῦν in 9:24 has been taken in two ways. (1) The first rendering is "henceforth." In this view the author wrote of that moment of Christ's exaltation when God "gave a completely new turn to the history of mankind" (*Theological Dictionary of the New Testament*, s.v. "νῦν," by Gustav Stählin, 4:1113). (2) The other rendering is "at the present time," that is, the entire interadvent era (Henry Alford, *The Greek Testament*, 4 vols. [London: Rivingtons and G. Bell and Sons, 1861; reprint, 4 vols. in 2, Chicago: Moody, 1958, 4:180]; and Dods, "The Epistle to the Hebrews," p. 339). The two are not mutually exclusive, and both ideas are probably involved.

30. Westcott, *The Epistle to the Hebrews*, p. 272.
31. Lünemann, "The Epistle to the Hebrews," p. 548.
32. Hughes, *A Commentary on the Epistle to the Hebrews*, p. 236.
33. Homer A. Kent, Jr., *The Epistle to the Hebrews: A Commentary* (Grand Rapids: Baker, 1972), p.123.
34. Hughes, *A Commentary on the Epistle to the Hebrews*, p. 383.
35. James Swetnam speaks of the "right" to enter ("Form and Content in Hebrews 7–13," *Biblica* 55 [1974]:338). The term παρρησία occurs four times in Hebrews (3:6; 4:16; 10:19, 35). It has been understood in two ways. (1) One view sees it subjectively, that is, that it refers to joyous confidence in entering God's presence (KJV, NASB, NIV, RSV; Franz Delitzsch, *Commentary on the Epistle to the Hebrews*, 2 vols. [Edinburgh: Clark, 1871], 2:170; Alford, *The Greek Testament*, 4:194; Westcott, *The Epistle to the Hebrews*, p. 318; Jean Héring, *The Epistle to the Hebrews* [London: Epworth, 1970], p. 90; Hugh Montefiore, *The Epistle to the Hebrews* [London: Black, 1964], p. 172). (2) The second view sees παρρησία objectively, that is, referring to freedom of access (Weymouth, Jerusalem Bible, James Moffatt, *A Critical and Exegetical Commentary on the Epistle to the Hebrews*, International Critical Commentary [Edinburgh: Clark, 1924], p. 142; Bruce, *The Epistle to the Hebrews*, p. 244; Antony Snell, *New and Living Way* [London: Faith, 1959], p. 127; George W. Buchanan, *To the Hebrews* [Garden City, NY: Doubleday, 1971], pp. 167–68; W. C. van Unnik, "The Christian's Freedom of Speech in the New Testament," *Bulletin of the John Rylands Library* 44 [1961–62]:485; *Theological Dictionary of the New Testament*, s.v. "παρρησία," by Heinrich Schlier, 5:884; W. S. Vorster, "The Meaning of ΠΑΡΡΗΣΙΑ in the Epistle to the Hebrews," *Neotestamentica* 5 [1971]:57; G. M. M. Pelser, "A Translation Problem: Heb. 10:19–25," *Neotestamentica* 8 [1974]:46–47). The context favors the second view for two reasons: (1) The author had just described objective privileges procured by the sacrifice of Christ. (2) It is unlikely that the author would say his readers had "confidence" or "assurance" when they needed to be exhorted to draw near.
36. Among other uses in the Septuagint, προσέρχομαι refers to coming before God in sacrifice or worship. In Hebrews the New Covenant believer is able to draw near to God "in a way which far exceeds the prerogative of the high priest [under the old covenant]" (*New International Dictionary of New Testament Theology*, s.v. "Come," by W. Mundle, 1:322; cf. *Theological Dictionary of the New Testament*, s.v. "προσερχομαι," by Johannes Schneider, 2:683).

37. W. C. van Unnik, "The Christian's Freedom of Speech in the New Testament," p. 485.
38. The word "new" (πρόσφατος, 10:20) was originally a sacrificial term, for it combined προς ("before") and φότος ("slaughter") to mean "just slaughtered." It came to mean "recent," "new," "fresh" (fresh meat, fresh water, new snow, etc.). (Henry George Liddell and Robert Scott, comps., rev. and augmented by Henry Stuart Jones, *A Greek English Lexicon* [Oxford: Clarendon, 1940], p. 1529; Dods, "The Epistle to the Hebrews," p. 346). The root meaning has been too much for some popular expositors to resist, however, and they have argued that it is eternally as if just now Jesus had died (William R. Newell, *Hebrews: Verse by Verse* [Chicago: Moody, 1947], p. 344; E. Schuyler English, *Studies in the Epistle to the Hebrews* [Traveler's Rest, SC: Southern Bible, 1955], p. 307; Arthur W. Pink, *An Exposition of Hebrews* [Grand Rapids: Baker, 1954], p. 588).
39. Westcott, *The Epistle to the Hebrews*, p. 319. The author to the Hebrews here implied a severe break with the old Levitical system. The contrast is not between a new, unfrequented path and an old, familiar one, "but rather between a new way and no way at all" (A. B. Bruce, *The Epistle to the Hebrews*, 2d ed. [Edinburgh: Clark, 1899], p. 395).
40. Westcott, *The Epistle to the Hebrews*, p. 319; Hughes, A Commentary on the *Epistle to the Hebrews*, pp. 406–7.
41. The term ζῶσαν ("living," 10:20) has been interpreted in five ways: (1) The character of those who walk in the "living way," that is, loving and trustful (A. B. Bruce, *The Epistle to the Hebrews*, p. 396). The verse, however, speaks of an objective reality and not the subjective feelings of Christians. (2) Its end, that is, it is life-producing (John Owen, *An Exposition of the Epistle to the Hebrews*, 7 vols. [London: Johnstone & Hunter, 1855], 6:505; Lünemann, "The Epistle to the Hebrews," p. 647), a thought that would be more clearly expressed by ζωοποιοῦσαν (Alford, *The Greek Testament*, 4:195). (3) Its imperishability, that is, it is everlasting (F. Bleek, *Der Brief an die Hebräer*, cited by Delitzsch, *Commentary on the Epistle to the Hebrews*, 2:171), a thought that is redundant in light of πρόσφατος. (4) Its intimacy, that is, it consists of fellowship with Christ (Westcott, *The Epistle to the Hebrews*, p. 319; Hughes, *A Commentary on the Epistle to the Hebrews*, p. 407). The point in 10:20 is access to God, however, and not fellowship with Christ, a point made in 1:9. (5) Its power, that is, it is effective (Delitzsch, *Commentary on the Epistle to the Hebrews*, 2:171–72; Alford, *The Greek Testament*, 4:194–95; A.

B. Davidson, *The Epistle to the Hebrews* [Edinburgh: Clark, 1882], p. 211; Moffatt, *A Critical and Exegetical Commentary on the Epistle to the Hebrews*, p. 143).

42. Moffatt, *A Critical and Exegetical Commentary on the Epistle to the Hebrews*, p. 143.

43. (1) The verb ἐνεκαίνισεν ("He inaugurated") in 10:20 has been interpreted in three ways. (1) One meaning is "to open," to make available for use (JB, NEB, NIV, RSV; John Calvin, *The Epistle of Paul the Apostle to the Hebrews and the First and Second Epistles of St. Peter* [Grand Rapids: Eerdmans, 1963], p. 141; Alford, *The Greek Testament*, 4:194; Delitzsch, *Commentary on the Epistle to the Hebrews*, p. 319; Dods, "The Epistle to the Hebrews," p. 346; F. F. Bruce, *The Epistle to the Hebrews*, p. 245; Hughes, *A Commentary on the Epistle to the Hebrews*, p. 406). In favor of this view is the parallel passage 6:19–20 in which Jesus is called "Forerunner." Against this view is the usage of the verb and the tabernacle imagery of 10:19–25 which suggests the dedication of a sanctuary.

(2) Another view is that ἐνεκαίνισεν means "to dedicate" or "to consecrate with solemn rites" (ASV, KJV, NASB; Vine, *The Epistle to the Hebrews*, p. 114; Moffatt, *A Critical and Exegetical Commentary on the Epistle to the Hebrews*, p. 152; Leon Morris, "Hebrews," in *The Expositor's Bible Commentary,* 12 vols. [Grand Rapids: Eerdmans, 1981], 12:103). In light of the Old Testament imagery of the immediate context this interpretation is preferable to the first view.

(3) A third view is that the word means both "to open" and "to consecrate." In the Septuagint the verb can mean "to initiate" (Deut. 20:5) and "to consecrate" (1 Kings 8:63; 2 Chron. 7:5). It is probable that the author includes both views here. True, Christ was Forerunner at His ascension. Yet the present passage says more. The new way was not only opened at His ascension; it was consecrated by His blood (cf. N. A. Dahl, "A New and Living Way," *Interpretation* 5 [October 1951]:403; and G. M. M. Pelser, "A Translation Problem: Heb. 10:19–25," p. 47).

44. Moffatt, *A Critical and Exegetical Commentary on the Epistle to the Hebrews*, p. 143.

45. (1) The phrase τοῦτ᾽ ἔστιν τῆς σαρκὸς αὐτοῦ ("that is, His flesh," 10:20) has caused much discussion. There are, broadly speaking, four interpretations. (1) The phrase τῆς σαπκὸς αὐτοῦ is a genitive of dependence referring back to ὁδόν, so that "flesh" qualifies "way." Thus the meaning is, "a way through the veil, a way consisting in His human nature." In other words the new way

to God has been opened up by Jesus as a human being (Westcott, *The Epistle to the Hebrews*, pp. 319–21; Alexander Nairne, *The Epistle of Priesthood* [Edinburgh: Clark, 1913], p. 381; Héring, *The Epistle to the Hebrews*, p. 91; Guthrie, *The Letter to the Hebrews*, p. 212). The word order undermines this view in that καταπετάσματος ("veil") is closer to "flesh" than "way." Furthermore the phrase τοῦτ᾽ ἔστιν is customarily used in Hebrews to introduce an appositional statement (e.g., 2:14; 7:5; 9:11). It is impossible to connect σαρκός appositionally to ὁδόν in that the former is a genitive and the latter an accusative.

(2) The phrase τῆς σαρκὸς αὐτοῦ is a genitive of dependence referring back to ὁδόν, but "flesh" is understood in the sense of human life offered in sacrifice, not simply human life assumed at Jesus' incarnation (Montefiore, *The Epistle to the Hebrews*, pp. 173–74).

(3) The phrase τῆς σαρκὸς αὐτοῦ is an appositional genitive referring back to καταπετάσματος. This view assumes that διά governs both nouns locally and that the flesh of Christ is a veil that hid His deity and the divine presence (Calvin, *The Epistle of Paul the Apostle to the Hebrews and the First and Second Epistles of St. Peter*, p. 141; Alford, *The Greek Testament*, 4:195). It may be objected, however, that if Christ passed through His human nature, then He must have left it behind. The Bible, however, does not make such a statement. Furthermore it is unlikely that the author thought of Jesus' humanity as hiding the divine presence when he asserted that the Son reveals God (1:3; cf. John 1:14, 18).

(4) The phrase τῆς σαρκὸς αὐτοῦ is an appositional genitive referring back to καταπετάσματος. It is assumed that διά governs both nouns, the first ("veil") locally and the second ("flesh") instrumentally. The flesh is understood not to hide the divine presence but to be an obstacle to it. As Kenneth Wuest remarked, "As the veil in the tabernacle of Israel while it was not [torn], barred man's access to God, so Messiah's humanity, before it was [torn] on the Cross, barred man's access to God. An uncrucified Savior is no Savior [at all]" (*Hebrews in the Greek New Testament* [Grand Rapids: Eerdmans, 1951], p. 179). So also JB, KJV, NASB, NIV, RSV; Moffatt, *A Critical and Exegetical Commentary on the Epistle to the Hebrews*, p. 143; F. F. Bruce, *The Epistle to the Hebrews*, pp. 247–49; Hughes, *A Commentary on the Epistle to the Hebrews*, pp. 408–9; Simon J. Kistemaker, *Exposition of the Epistle to the Hebrews* (Grand Rapids: Baker, 1984, p. 287; Frederic Gardiner, "On Hebrews 10:20," *Journal of Bible Literature* 8 (1888):142, 146; Norman H. Young, "ΤΟΥΤ ᾽ ΕΣΤΙΝ ΤΗΣ ΣΑΡΚΟΣ ΑΥΤΟΥ (Heb. 10:20): Apposition, Dependent or

Explicative," *New Testament Studies* 20 (October 1973):100–104. Joachim Jeremias has noted a parallel between verses 19 and 20. Each verse treats the following elements: (1) the new way, (2) its purpose, and (3) its opening through the death of Jesus ("Hebräer 10:20: τοῦτ ' ἔστιν τῆς σαρκὸς αὐτοῦ," *Zeitschrift für die neutestamentliche Wissenschaft* 62 [1971]: 131).

46. Historically the work of intercession has been understood in a variety of ways: (1) The Arians suggested that intercession proved Christ's inferiority to the Father. The church fathers responded that it proved His love, not His inferiority. (2) The Eastern church regarded the statements about intercession as symbolical representations of Christ's love. (3) The Western church developed the concept of the perpetual offering of the finished sacrifice and identified the intercession with the offering. The churches of the Reformation argued that Christ's offering was completed at the Cross, and therefore they distinguished His intercession from His offering. (4) The Lutherans argued that intercession was the offering of literal, vocal (*vocalis et realis*) petitions. (5) The Reformed (Calvinistic) churches interpreted Christ's intercession as real but not oral and as consisting in Christ's presence in heaven (representation) and not in articulate supplication. (6) The English Reformers allied themselves with the Lutheran view, but in the mid-19th century they shifted to the continental Reformed view (A. J. Tait, *The Heavenly Session*, pp. 149–76; *International Standard Bible Encyclopedia*, 1982 ed., s.v. "Intercession of Christ," by R. S. Wallace, 2:859–60).

47. The discussion on intercession in this article follows, in the main, that of Meeter, *The Heavenly High Priesthood of Christ*, pp. 181–97.

48. Owen, however, saw the fire on the altar, the daily morning and evening sacrifices (Ex. 29:38–42) and the offering of incense, both annually (Lev. 16:12–13) and daily (Ex. 30:7), as typical of Christ's intercession (*An Exposition of the Epistle to the Hebrews*, 5:537–38). Nathaniel Dimock held that the offering of incense was the true type of Christ's intercession (*Our One Priest on High* [London: Longmans, Green, 1910], pp. 73–75). Hughes says the high priest's shoulder pieces and breastpiece (Ex. 39:6–21) are symbolic of the intercessory function of the high priest (*A Commentary on the Epistle to the Hebrews*, p. 351).

49. C. E. B. Cranfield, *A Critical and Exegetical Commentary on the Epistle to the Romans,* International Critical Commentary, 2 vols. (Edinburgh: Clark, 1979);1:423, n. 1; cf. Bauer, Arndt, and Gingrich, *A Greek-English Lexicon of the New Testament and*

Other Early Christian Literature, p. 270; *Theological Dictionary of the New Testament*, s.v. "ἐντυγχάνω," by Otto Bauernfeind, 8:243). The verb is used five times in the New Testament. It is used twice (Acts 25:24; Rom. 11:2) with the meaning "to approach someone with a complaint" against a third person. Once (Rom. 8:27) it is used of the Holy Spirit, and twice of Christ (Rom. 8:34; Heb. 7:25).

50. Milligan, *The Ascension and Heavenly Priesthood of Our Lord*, pp. 160–61; Torrance, *Space, Time and Resurrection*, p. 115.
51. Cf. Leopold Sabourin, *Priesthood: A Comparative Study* (Leiden: Brill, 1973), p.195.
52. Snell, *New and Living Way*, p. 99.
53. E.g., Dimock, *Our One Priest on High*, pp. 70–74.
54. E.g., John Calvin, *The Epistles of Paul to the Romans and Thessalonians* (Grand Rapids: Eerdmans, 1960), p. 186 (on Rom. 8:34); Westcott, *The Epistle to the Hebrews*, p. 229; Morris, "Hebrews," p. 71.
55. *Theological Dictionary of the New Testament*, s.v. "ἐντυγχάνω," by Otto Bauernfeind, 8:243.
56. E.g., Swete, *The Ascended Christ*, p. 95; Meeter, *The Heavenly High Priesthood of Christ*, pp. 183–84; Davidson, *The Epistle to the Hebrews*, p. 142; F. F. Bruce, The *Epistle to the Hebrews*, pp. 154–55.
57. Owen, *An Exposition of the Epistle to the Hebrews*, 5:539–41; John Brown, *Hebrews* (Edinburgh: Oliphant, 1862), p. 352.
58. Owen, *An Exposition of the Epistle to the Hebrews*, 5:539. Brown wrote, "The only begotten of God, though His Father's equal, in the economy of grace is His Father's servant; and all the blessings conferred on Him and His chosen people are conferred by the Father as sustaining the majesty of the Godhead" (*Hebrews*, p. 352).
59. E.g., Delitzsch, *Commentary on the Epistle to the Hebrews*, 1:372; Brown, *Hebrews*, p. 352; A. B. Bruce, *The Epistle to the Hebrews*, pp. 280–81; Thomas Hewitt, *The Epistle to the Hebrews*, (Grand Rapids: Eerdmans, 1960), p. 126. Cf. also H. A. W. Meter, *Critical and Exegetical Hand-Book on the Epistle to the Romans* (New York: Funk & Wagnalls, 1884), p. 341 (on Rom. 8:34); Frederick L. Godet, *Commentary on Epistle to the Romans*, rev. ed. (New York: Funk & Wagnalls, 1883), p. 332; William Sanday and Arthur C. Headlam, *A Critical and Exegetical Commentary on the Epistle to the Romans*, International Critical Commentary (Edinburgh: Clark, 1902), p. 221; *Zondervan Pictorial Encyclopedia of the Bible*, s.v. "Intercession of Christ," by John Murray, 3:294–95.

60. Cf. *Theological Dictionary of the New Testament*, s.v. "σῴζω," by Werner Foerster, 7:996.
61. Jesus "is able to save εἰς τὸ παντελὲς" (7:25). This phrase has been understood in three ways. (1) One view renders it "for all time" or "forever" (NABS, RSV; Moffatt, *A Critical and Exegetical Commentary on the Epistle to the Hebrews*, p. 100; Montefiore, *The Epistle to the Hebrews*, pp. 128–29; F. F. Bruce, *The Epistle to the Hebrews*, p. 153; Buchanan, *To the Hebrews*, pp. 127–28; Guthrie, *The Letter to the Hebrews*, p. 166. This view does fit the immediate context, which emphasizes that Jesus lives forever. (2) A second view translates the Greek phrase "perfectly," "completely," or "to the very end" (ASV, Darby, KJV, NEB, NIV; Delitzsch, *Commentary on the Epistle to the Hebrews*, 1:371; Alford, *The Greek Testament*, 4:143; Westcott, *The Epistle to the Hebrews*, p.191; Héring, *The Epistle to the Hebrews*, p. 62). This view fits the wider context with emphasis on the failure of the Levitical priesthood to do its work completely. (3) A third rendering is "completely" *and* "forever." This ambiguous sense, including the ideas of both views, is defended by Owen (*An Exposition of the Epistle to the Hebrews*, 5:528–29); Vine (*The Epistle to the Hebrews*, p. 74); Hewitt (*The Epistle to the Hebrews*, p. 125); Hughes (*A Commentary on the Epistle to the Hebrews*, p. 269, n. 25); Paul Ellingworth and Eugene A. Nida (*A Translator's Handbook on the Letter to the Hebrews* [New York: United Bible Societies, 1983], p. 157); and *Theological Dictionary of the New Testament*, s.v. "παντελής," by Gerhard Delling, 8:67.
62. Davidson, *The Epistle to the Hebrews*, p. 142.
63. The verb βοηθέω (2:18, βοηθῆσαι, "to come to the aid") originally meant "to run on a call to help," "to hasten to the help of the oppressed." It came to mean simply "to help" (*Theological Dictionary of the New Testament*, s.v. "βοηθέω," by Friedrich Büchsel, 1:628). As to the nature of the help offered in 2:18, commentators have made five suggestions. (1) Jesus' aid is His sympathy for His people in temptation (cf. 4:15). So Alford, *The Greek Testament*, 4:55; Westcott, *The Epistle to the Hebrews*, p. 59; Morris, "Hebrews," p. 30. (2) Jesus' aid is His example of triumph over temptation (cf. 12:2–3). So F. F. Bruce, *The Epistle to the Hebrews*, p. 53, and Neil R. Lightfoot, *Jesus Christ Today: A Commentary on the Book of Hebrews* (Grand Rapids: Baker, 1976), p. 81. (3) Jesus' aid is His empowerment to overcome temptation (4:16; 13:21). So Lünemann, "The Epistle to the Hebrews," p. 446; Davidson, *The Epistle to the Hebrews*, p. 73. (4) Jesus' aid is the forgiveness of sins and the power to overcome

temptation (Hughes, *A Commentary on the Epistle to the Hebrews*, p. 124). (5) Jesus' aid is the continual application of the propitiatory benefits of His sacrifice to the sins of His people (Moffatt, *A Critical and Exegetical Commentary on the Epistle to the Hebrews*, p. 40; Montefiore, *The Epistle to the Hebrews*, p. 69; Geerhardus Vos, "The Priesthood of Christ in the Epistle to the Hebrews," *Princeton Theological Review* 5 [1907]:582). All five suggestions are true to the context of the epistle.

64. In 4:16 "grace" (χάρις) refers to divine assistance given in present or future needs or trials, while "mercy" (ἔλεος) refers to God's pardon of past failures or sins (Westcott, *The Epistle to the Hebrews*, p. 109; Dods, "The Epistle to the Hebrews," 4:284; Héring, *The Epistle to the Hebrews*, p. 36).

65. Bernard L. Ramm, *An Evangelical Christology, Ecumenic and Historic* (Nashville: Nelson, 1985), p. 100.

66. H. P. Liddon rightly drew attention to Christ's deity in discussing His intercession. At the same time Liddon slighted His true human nature (*The Divinity of Our Lord and Savior Jesus Christ* [London: Longmans, Green, 1906], p. 493). The author of Hebrews kept both in balance.

67. Guthrie, *The Letter to the Hebrews*, pp. 166–67.

68. Davidson, *The Epistle to the Hebrews*, p. 142; F. F. Bruce, *The Epistle to the Hebrews*, p. 154.

69. Dods, "The Epistle to the Hebrews," 4:346; *Theological Dictionary of the New Testament*, s.v. "σώζω," by Werner Foerster, 7:996.

70. In his definition of intercession Hughes includes "the work of the Holy Spirit in our midst" (*A Commentary on the Epistle to the Hebrews*, p. 351). This would certainly be valid if one were constructing a definition of the doctrine in the entire New Testament (cf. Rom. 8:26). It is not valid, however, in a definition of the doctrine in Hebrews.

71. There is much similarity between Christ's role as Representative and Intercessor in Hebrews and His role as Advocate in 1 John 2:1. Some, however, have distinguished the roles. W. H. Griffith Thomas, for example, said that intercession referred especially to the prevention of sin, while advocacy referred especially to the cure/forgiveness of sin (*Hebrews: A Devotional Commentary* [reprint, Grand Rapids: Eerdmans, n.d.], p. 95; cf. Alexander Stewart, "Christ: Priest and Advocate," *The Witness*, September 1924, pp. 373–74). While the two terms may not be identical—the one (intercession) having worship overtones, and the other (advocate) having legal overtones—they do overlap (Montefiore, *The Epistle to the Hebrews*, p. 129).

72. James Hastings, *The Great Texts of the Bible*, 20 vols., vol. 18:

Thessalonians to Hebrews (New York: Scribner's Sons, 1914), pp. 359–62.

73. The verb ἀναφέρω was a technical term for the sacrificial system of the Old Testament (Lev. 17:5; Isa. 57:6; Heb. 7:27). In Hebrews 7:27 it is used for both the Old Testament sacrifices and the sacrifice of Jesus (Bauer, Arndt, and Gingrich, *A Greek-English Lexicon of the New Testament and Other Early Christian Literature*, p. 63).

74. Underlying the teaching of Hebrews 13:15 is the ritual described in Leviticus 7:12 (LXX, 7:2). If an Israelite brought a voluntary peace offering he would offer loaves of fine flour to God. This was described as θυσία αἰνέσεως ("a sacrifice of thanksgiving"). See Delitzsch, *Commentary on the Epistle to the Hebrews*, 2:392; and F. F. Bruce, *The Epistle to the Hebrews*, p. 405.

75. Δι ' αὐτοῦ (13:15) is emphatic, appearing at the very beginning of the verse (Westcott, *The Epistle to the Hebrews*, p. 443; Hughes, *A Commentary on the Epistle to the Hebrews*, p. 583).

76. Cf. Meeter, *The Heavenly High Priesthood of Christ*, p. 185.

77. R. C. H. Lenski called this "the blessed concursus of grace." He said, "We are to do, yet all the while God is doing" (*The Interpretation of the Epistle to the Hebrews and the Epistle of James* [Minneapolis: Augsburg, 1966], p. 495).

78. Moffatt, *A Critical and Exegetical Commentary on the Epistle to the Hebrews*, p. 243.

79. James B. DeYoung, "A Grammatical Approach to Hebrews" (Th.D. diss., Dallas Theological Seminary, 1973), p. 243.

80. In the phrase ποιῶν ἐν ἡμῖν ("working in us," 13:21) there is probably an implicit reference to the work of the Holy Spirit (C. E. B. Cranfield, "Hebrews 13:20–21," *Scottish Journal of Theology* 20 [1967]:440). Yet the indwelling, sanctifying work of the Spirit, so explicit in other New Testament writers (John 7:37–39; Acts 2:33; Rom, 8:1–27), remains implicit in Hebrews in that the author sought to keep his readers' attention fixed solely on the mediatorial work of Christ.

81. There is clearly much overlapping in the concepts of mediation and intercession.

82. For example Delitzsch, *Commentary on the Epistle to the Hebrews*, 1:55; Lünemann, "The Epistle to the Hebrews," p. 399; Westcott, *The Epistle to the Hebrews*, p. 16; Dods, "The Epistle to the Hebrews," 4:252; Moffatt, *A Critical and Exegetical Commentary on the Epistle to the Hebrews*, p. 8; Lenski, *The Interpretation of the Epistle to the Hebrews and the Epistle of James*, pp. 41–42; Hughes, *A Commentary on the Epistle to the Hebrews*, pp. 47–48;

Kistemaker, *Exposition of the Epistle to the Hebrews*, p. 31; and J.
G. Davies, *He Ascended into Heaven*, p. 65.

83. J. H. Davies, "The Heavenly Work of Christ in Hebrews," p. 386.

84. Davidson, *The Epistle to the Hebrews*, p. 51.

85. Dods, "The Epistle to the Hebrews," 4:341; cf. Westcott, *The Epistle to the Hebrews*, p. 278.

86. After the first offerings of Aaron following his consecration to office, he blessed the people (Lev. 9:22). The priestly blessing of Numbers 6:24–28 followed regularly after every morning and evening sacrifice, as if it were the fruits of the offering just made (Dimock, *Our One Priest on High*, pp. 78–79).

87. The verb ὁράω, used in 9:28 in the future tense (ὀφθήσεται, "shall appear"), is the usual one for the resurrection appearances (cf. 1 Cor. 15:5–8). It is used here only in the New Testament of the parousia (*Theological Dictionary of the New Testament*, s.v. "ὁράω," by Wilhelm Michaelis, 5:355–61, esp. p. 360). As C. B. Moll suggested, the verb indicates "a visible return" ("The Epistle to the Hebrews," in *A Commentary on the Holy Scriptures*, ed. John Peter Lange, 25 vols. [New York: Scribner, 1880], 22:165).

88. The phrase ἐκ δευτέρου . . . ἀφθήσεται ("shall appear a second time," 9:28) is the one explicit use of the term "Second Coming" in the New Testament (Alexander C. Purdy, "The Epistle to the Hebrews: Introduction and Exegesis," in *The Interpreter's Bible*, ed. George Arthur Buttrick, 12 vols. [Nashville: Abingdon, 1957], 11:698).

89. Buchanan, *To the Hebrews*, p. 155.

90. Some interpreters include the ascended Christ's gift of the Holy Spirit in His work of benediction (e.g., Meeter, *The Heavenly High Priesthood of Christ*, pp. 200–203; Hughes, *A Commentary on the Epistle to the Hebrews*, pp. 350–51). This is certainly mentioned by other New Testament writers (John 7:37–39; 14:16; 15:26; 16:7; Acts 12:33; Rom. 8:11; Eph. 1:13; 4:30). It is not part of the present discussion, however, in that it is not mentioned in Hebrews.

Chapter 12

1. James W. Dale, *Christic and Patristic Baptism*, pp. 392–94 [italics his].

Chapter 13

1. C. E. B. Cranfield, *The Epistle to the Romans,* International Critical Commentary, 2 vols. (Edinburgh: Clark, 1975), 1:116.

2. Frederic R. Howe, *Challenge and Response: A Handbook of Christian Apologetics* (Grand Rapids: Zondervan, 1982), p. 72.

3. *New International Dictionary of New Testament Theology*, s.v. "Guilt," by Hans-Georg Link, 2:141.
4. Henry George Liddell and Robert Scott, *An Intermediate Greek-English Lexicon* (Oxford: Clarendon, 1889), p. 249.
5. James Hope Moulton and George Milligan, *The Vocabulary of the Greek Testament* (Grand Rapids: Eerdmans, 1930), p. 202.
6. Büchsel writes that the term in the New Testament generally means "to show someone his sin and to summon him to repentance" (*Theological Dictionary of the New Testament,* s.v. "ἐλέγχω," by Friedrich Büchsel, 2:474).
7. That is, to expose in the sense of making sin obvious. First Corinthians 14:24–25 may also fit in this "exposure" category.
8. See Paul Enns, "The Upper Room Discourse: The Consummation of Christ's Instruction" (Th.D. diss., Dallas Theological Seminary, 1979), 296–97; and Rudolf Bultmann, *The Gospel of John: A Commentary,* trans. G. R. Beasley-Murray (Philadelphia: Westminster, 1971): 564–65.
9. Raymond A. Brown, *The Gospel According to John (XII–XXI),* Anchor Bible (Garden City, NY: Doubleday, 1970), pp. 711–12.
10. D. A. Carson, "The Function of the Paraclete in John 16:7–11," *Journal of Biblical Literature* 98 (1979): 551–54.
11. *New International Dictionary of New Testament Theology*, s.v. "Earth," by J. Guhrt, 1:524.
12. Walter Bauer, William F. Arndt, and F. Wilbur Gingrich, *A Greek-English Lexicon of the New Testament and Other Early Christian Literature,* 2d ed., rev. F. Wilbur Gingrich and Frederick W. Danker (Chicago: University of Chicago Press, 1979), s.v. "ὅτι," p. 589.
13. Brown, *The Gospel According to John (XII–XXI),* p. 706.
14. Carson, "The Function of the Paraclete in John 16:7–11," p. 548.
15. This treats the phrase as an objective genitive. If the genitive is subjective, Jesus was referring to the world's judgment on Him. But the fact that Satan's condemnation is parallel to this clause strongly suggests some continuity of thought rather than the sharp contrast that would be demanded if this were a reference to Jesus' death.
16. Cf. John Calvin, *Institutes of the Christian Religion,* 3.24.8; Louis Berkhof, *Systematic Theology* (Grand Rapids: Eerdmans, 1941), p. 461.
17. Fritz Guy, *The Grace of God, the Will of Man: A Case for Arminianism,* ed. Clark Pinnock (Grand Rapids: Zondervan, 1989), p. 39.
18. It is a "work of God" in that the implied subject of the sentence is the Father. Verse 30 continues the use of the third person from verse 29, where Jesus is referred to as "His Son," demonstrating in no uncertain terms that the subject is the Father. This is a shift

from verses 26–27 (and perhaps v. 28), where the Spirit functions as the subject. However, in a passage in which there is considerable overlap between the ministries of the Spirit and of Christ (8:9–11), the distinction should probably not be pressed too far. It is likely that the Father's work is accomplished through the Spirit (as it seems to be in John 14:23). Cf. Roger L. Hahn, "Pneumatology in Romans 8: Its Historical and Theological Context," *Wesleyan Theological Journal* 21 (1986): 85–86.

19. Luther Poellot writes, "It is an effectual call Paul speaks of, as the whole tenor of the paragraph manifests" ("The Doctrine of Predestination in Romans 8:29–39," *Concordia Theological Monthly* 23 [1952]: 343).

20. *Theological Dictionary of the New Testament*, s.v. "καλέω," by K. L. Schmidt, 3:488.

21. Ibid., p. 489.

22. Berkhof, *Systematic Theology*, p. 461. Not all Reformed theologians agree. For example Gerstner writes, "The call is to whomever will (the regenerate), and not to whomever will not (the unregenerate). . . . The only ones who do become regenerate are the elect (see John 6:44). So the call is always to the regenerate and never to the unregenerate. It is not even to the elect while unregenerate but only to the elect when regenerate" (John Gerstner, *Wrongly Dividing the Word of Truth: A Critique of Dispensationalism* [Brentwood, TN: Wolgemuth and Hyatt, 1991], p. 117). However, Berkhof's arguments are persuasive, particularly in light of the universal appeals of Paul (Acts 26:19; 28:23–24), John (John 20:31), and Peter (Acts 2:38–39). Cf. Calvin, *Institutes of the Christian Religion*, 3.23.14.

23. Millard J. Erickson, *Christian Theology* (Grand Rapids: Baker, 1985), p. 930.

24. Cranfield, *The Epistle to the Romans*, 1:432.

25. James D. G. Dunn, *Romans 1–8*, Word Biblical Commentary (Dallas, TX: Word, 1988), p. 485.

26. Cf. *Theological Dictionary of the New Testament*, s.v. "κλητός," by K. L. Schmidt, 3:494.

27. Dunn, *Romans 1–8*, p. 485.

28. Cranfield, *The Epistle to the Romans*, 1:432–33.

29. Many theologians, particularly those who are more Reformed, would insert regeneration between calling and faith. While there is clearly a divine work that comes before faith and is directed only toward the elect, it seems better to restrict oneself to more specific terminology in the description of that work. It may be argued (persuasively, in the opinion of this author) that regeneration takes

place through the indwelling of the animating Holy Spirit (Robert A. Pyne, "The Resurrection as Restoration" [Th.D. diss., Dallas Theological Seminary, 1990], pp. 283–315). Since that indwelling comes through faith (Acts 2:38; Gal. 3:2), it seems appropriate to regard regeneration as a consequence of faith, not as its cause. Erickson's comments are worth noting. "The conclusion here, then, is that God regenerates those who repent and believe. But this conclusion seems inconsistent with the doctrine of total inability. Are we torn between Scripture and logic on this point? There is a way out. That is to distinguish between God's special and effectual calling on the one hand, and regeneration on the other. Although no one is capable of responding to the general call of the gospel, in the case of the elect God works intensively through a special calling so that they do respond in repentance and faith. As a result of this conversion, God regenerates them. The special calling is simply an intensive and effectual working by the Holy Spirit. It is not the complete transformation which constitutes regeneration, but it does render the conversion of the individual both possible and certain. Thus the logical order of the initial aspects of salvation is special calling—conversion—regeneration" (*Christian Theology,* p. 933).

30. Leon Morris, *The First Epistle of Paul to the Corinthians,* Tyndale New Testament Commentaries (Grand Rapids: Eerdmans, 1981), p. 112.
31. Ibid., p. 432.
32. Erickson, *Christian Theology,* pp. 930–31.
33. Ibid., p. 931.
34. The veil was not to prevent them from seeing the fact that the glory was fading, but to prevent them from seeing the glory at all (Ex. 34:30–35). Cf. Philip Edgcumbe Hughes, *The Second Epistle to the Corinthians,* New International Commentary on the New Testament (Grand Rapids: Eerdmans, 1962), pp. 108–10.
35. Bauer, Arndt, and Gingrich, *A Greek-English Lexicon of the New Testament and Other Early Christian Literature,* s.v. "κατοπτρίζω," p. 424.
36. Hughes, *The Second Epistle to the Corinthians,* pp. 117–18.
37. *Theological Dictionary of the New Testament,* s.v. "κατοπτρίζομαι," by G. Kittel, 2:696.
38. It is worth noting that the goal of this process is conformity to the glory of Christ, as in Romans 8:29–30. This is the aim not just of salvation, but of creation itself. "Even before creation God ordained that man should be conformed to the image of his Son—the image, that is, which is his Son; for the Son himself is the Image of God. Accordingly, God created man in or after his own image.

Conformity to the Son, purposed before the beginning, is there at the beginning, and for fallen man is redemptively achieved through that same Son who is the divine Image. . . . From eternity to eternity Christiformity is God's purpose for his creature, man" (Philip Edgcumbe Hughes, *The True Image: The Origin and Destiny of Man in Christ* [Grand Rapids: Eerdmans, 1989], p. 27). In Ephesians 1:18 the believer's enlightenment seems to be regarded as a past experience (by the perfect participle πεφωτισμένους). Here the consequence of enlightenment is that the believer would apprehend the hope of His *calling* and the *glory* of His inheritance in the saints.

39. Lewis Sperry Chafer, *Systematic Theology,* 8 vols. (Dallas, TX: Dallas Seminary, 1948; reprint [8 vols. in 4], Grand Rapids: Kregel, 1992), 3:222. The "dispensational" understanding of effectual grace has been labeled "pure Arminianism" by Gerstner because Chafer and other dispensationalists have maintained that regeneration is logically based on faith rather than the other way around (Gerstner, *Wrongly Dividing the Word of Truth,* p. 140). However, Chafer argues that fallen persons are unable to turn to God apart from the divine enlightenment of effectual calling, which comes only to the elect (Chafer, *Systematic Theology,* 3:217, 223). At the same time, he argues from Ephesians 2:8–9 that faith itself is a divine gift (ibid., pp. 216, 223), and he condemns the "Arminian error" of sufficient grace (ibid., p. 217). It has already been observed that Erickson, who is not a dispensationalist, holds a similar position (see n. 29).

40. The Westminster Confession of Faith, 10.1. The next line of the Confession, however, associates the effectual call with regeneration. It reads, "This effectual call is of God's free and special grace alone, not from any thing at all foreseen in man; who is altogether passive therein, until, *being quickened and renewed by the Holy Spirit,* he is thereby enabled to answer this call, and to embrace the grace offered and conveyed in it." It has been suggested, however, that regeneration should be regarded as a distinct concept (see n. 29).

Chapter 14

1. Walter Chantry, *Today's Gospel: Authentic or Synthetic?* (Edinburgh: Banner of Truth, 1970), p. 12. Chantry notes that the more important issue is that modern methods are not rooted in the teaching of the Scriptures.

2. John F. MacArthur, *The Gospel According to Jesus* (Grand Rapids: Zondervan, 1988), p. 222. See similar statements regarding the "true church" on pp. xiv, 221.

3. See, for example, James Montgomery Boice, *Christ's Call to*

Discipleship (Chicago: Moody, 1986), p. 35; and his foreword to MacArthur, *The Gospel According to Jesus*, p. xii. Also see Will Metzger, *Tell the Truth* (Downers Grove, IL: InterVarsity, 1981), pp. 30, 355, 39; Dietrich Bonhoeffer, *The Cost of Discipleship* (New York: Macmillan, 1963), pp. 49–56.

4. For example the second appendix of John F. MacArthur's book, *The Gospel According to Jesus*, is entitled "The Gospel According to Historic Christianity" and is simply a series of quotations from the writings of past leaders in the church. This argument is presented as though it has decisive value in the debate, and it ends with these words: "Thus 'lordship salvation' is neither modern nor heretical but is the very heart of historic Christian soteriology. . . . To teach anything else is to withdraw from the mainstream of church teaching through the ages" (p. 237).

5. J. I. Packer, foreword to MacArthur, *The Gospel According to Jesus*, p. ix.

6. John R. W. Stott, *Basic Christianity*, 2d ed. (Grand Rapids: Eerdmans, 1971), p. 107, f. p. 121.

7. J. I. Packer, *I Want to Be a Christian* (Wheaton, IL: Tyndale, 1983), p. 25.

8. MacArthur, *The Gospel according to Jesus*, p. 32, f. p. 75.

9. Aurelius Augustine *On the Predestination of the Saints* chap. 5, in *The Nicene and Post-Nicene Fathers of the Church*, 28 vols., trans. and ed. Phillip Schaff (Grand Rapids: Eerdmans, 1956), vol. 5: *St. Augustine: Anti-Pelagian Writings*, p. 499.

10. John Calvin, *Institutes of the Christian Religion*, 2 vols., trans. Ford Lewis Battles, ed. John T. McNeil (Philadelphia: Westminster, 1977), III. xiii. 5 (italics added).

11. Ibid., III. xi. 7.

12. R. T. Kendall, *Calvin and English Calvinism to 1649* (Oxford: Oxford University Press, 1979), p. 19. Also see Calvin, *Institutes of the Christian Religion*, III. ii. 36.

13. M. Charles Bell, *Calvin and Scottish Theology: The Doctrine of Assurance* (Edinburgh: Handsel, 1985), p. 8. Also see A. N. S. Lane, "Calvin's Doctrine of Assurance," *Vox Evangelica* 11 (1979):32–54.

14. Calvin, *Institutes of the Christian Religion*, III. ii. 1–20.

15. *Apology of the Augsburg Confession*, IV. 56, 112, 257. Also see *The Formula of Concord, Solid Declaration*, III. 8–14. All citations of the Lutheran Confessions are from *The Book of Concord: The Confessions of the Evangelical Lutheran Church*, trans. and ed. Theodore G. Tappert (Philadelphia: Fortress, 1959), and follow the standard form of reference. Robert D. Preus gives an excellent summary of both Luther's and Melanchthon's views of faith in

"Perennial Problems in the Doctrine of Justification," *Concordia Theological Quarterly* 45 (1981):163–84.

16. See, for example, Edmund Schlink, *Theology of the Lutheran Confessions* (Philadelphia: Fortress, 1961), pp. 95–101; and Holsten Fagerberg, *A New Look at the Lutheran Confessions (1529–1537)* (St. Louis: Concordia, 1971), pp. 155–61.

17. Francis Pieper, *Christian Dogmatics*, 3 vols. (St. Louis: Concordia, 1953), 2:426, 437 (italics added).

18. The works by Kendall, Bell, and Lane all deal at length with this change in the definition of the nature of faith from Calvin to the Puritans.

19. *The Westminster Confession of Faith*, III. viii; XIV. ii (Philadelphia: Orthodox Presbyterian Church, n.d.). The Westminster Standards are the documents produced by the Westminster Assembly convened by the English Parliament from 1643 to 1649. These documents are the *Westminster Confession of Faith*, the *Shorter Catechism*, and the *Larger Catechism*. They form the doctrinal foundation of much of modern Presbyterianism. A slightly modified *Confession*, called the *London Baptist Confession of Faith of 1689*, also forms the doctrinal basis from which many of the modern Baptist churches have grown.

20. For example in MacArthur, *The Gospel According to Jesus*, 10 of the 17 pages of the second appendix, entitled "The Gospel According to Historic Christianity," are quotations from the Westminster Standards and the writing of post-Reformation English Calvinists.

21. MacArthur, *The Gospel According to Jesus*, p. 222.

22. Gordon H. Clark, *Faith and Saving Faith* (Jefferson, MD: Trinity Foundation, 1983), pp. 110–18; R. T. Kendall, *Once Saved, Always Saved* (Chicago: Moody, 1985); Bell, *Calvin and Scottish Theology: The Doctrine of Assurance*.

23. Boice, *Christ's Call to Discipleship*, p. 166. This seems to be the only time he mentions assurance of salvation directly in this book.

24. Walter Chantry, *Today's Gospel: Authentic or Synthetic?* p. 74.

25. MacArthur, *The Gospel According to Jesus*, p. 23.

26. Ibid., p. 178.

27. *Westminster Confession of Faith*, XVIII. ii–iii (italics added).

28. Kendall deals at length with this topic in *Calvin and English Calvinism to 1649*, pp. 52–138.

29. John Owen, *The Works of John Owen*, 16 vols., vol. 3: *A Discourse concerning the Holy Spirit* (1677; reprint, Edinburgh: Banner of Truth, 1965), pp. 45–47, 226–28.

30. *What Luther Says: An Anthology*, comp. Ewald M. Plass, 3 vols. (St. Louis: Concordia, 1959), 1:496 (italics added).

31. Quoted by Stephen Pfürtner, *Luther and Aquinas on Salvation* (New York: Sheed and Ward, 1964), p. 125.
32. Ibid., pp. 29, 35.
33. See Pieper, *Christian Dogmatics*, 2:445–46.
34. Bell, *Calvin and Scottish Theology: The Doctrine of Assurance*, p. 22.
35. Lane, "Calvin's Doctrine of Assurance," pp. 32–33.
36. Calvin, *Institutes of the Christian Religion*, III. ii. 7.
37. Ibid., III. ii. 16 (italics added).
38. For example, see John F. MacArthur, *The Security of Salvation: Why You Can't Lose It: Study Guide on Romans 5:1–11* (Panorama City, CA: Word of Grace Communications, 1983), pp. 55–58. MacArthur lists 12 "tests" of assurance, all of which are highly subjective. For example, "Are you very sensitive to your sin?" "Are you obedient to God's Word?" "Do you experience the inner working of the Holy Spirit?" Interestingly not one of his "tests" asks what the person thinks of the atoning work of Christ or even alludes to the doctrine of justification by faith.
39. Calvin, *Institutes of the Christian Religion*, III. xiv. 20.
40. Lane, "Calvin's Doctrine of Assurance," p. 34. Numerous pastoral frustrations arise from the idea that assurance comes from the subjective inspection of one's life to find evidence of regeneration. The naturally introspective and uncertain person will find no end of sin when he looks inside, and therefore will have no end of uncertainty regarding his salvation. The solution Calvin offers is to point such people to simple faith in the finished work of Christ as the only means of certain acceptance with God. This demonstrates the warm and powerful pastoral concern underlying all of Calvin's works, despite common opinions to the contrary.
41. R. L. Dabney, *Discussions of Robert L. Dabney, D.D., LL.D., Volume I: Theological and Evangelical* (Richmond, VA: Presbyterian Committee of Publication, 1890), p. 173.
42. Ibid., pp. 215–16 (italics his).
43. Bell, *Calvin and Scottish Theology: The Doctrine of Assurance*, pp. 151–80.
44. See John McLeod Campbell, *Reminiscences of John McLeod Campbell* (London: n.p., 1873), chap. 5, "Assurance of Faith and the Universality of the Atonement," pp. 152–80. Bell's work is an extended documentation of this issue among the Scottish theologians from the Reformation through the 19th century.
45. Horatius Bonar, *God's Way of Peace* (London: Evangelical, 1968), p. 58. This work is an evangelistic tract based on Calvin's view of faith and assurance.

46. See Lewis Sperry Chafer, *Salvation* (1917; reprint, Grand Rapids: Zondervan, 1973), pp. 57–62.

47. In *The Gospel According to Jesus*, few of the historical citations are used to validate MacArthur's view of faith and assurance. Most of them seem to make the point that regeneration produces a visible change in a person.

48. This last statement may be questioned by some who hold to lordship salvation. However, the *Westminster Confession of Faith* asserts, "Nevertheless [true believers] may, through the temptations of Satan and the world, the prevalency of corruption remaining in them, and the neglect of the means of their preservation, *fall into grievous sins; and, for a time, continue therein*: whereby they incur God's displeasure, and grieve His Holy Spirit" (XVII. iii, italics added). Those who follow in the tradition of the *Confession* at this point (as lordship salvation teaching generally does) usually assert that a believer may sin seriously for a time, but that assurance of salvation is impossible to one in such a state.

49. Lordship salvation teachers sometimes make extreme statements that imply that *any* sin is an indication of a lack of salvation. For example Boice writes, "And anyone who claims to be following Christ while actually continuing in unrighteousness is deluded. And he or she is not a Christian" (*Christ's Call to Discipleship*, pp. 18–19). The point may depend on the meaning of "continuing," but the statement is nonetheless needlessly hyperbolic. Even the catechism that Boice's church uses asserts that every Christian sins daily in thought, word and deed (*Westminster Shorter Catechism*, Question 82).

50. Free grace teachers generally dislike being confused with the vague decisionism that prevails in much of modern evangelicalism. Terminology such as "pray the sinner's prayer," "make a decision," "ask Jesus into your heart," "come forward," "give your life to Christ," and others are common, but not scriptural. The free grace view of the gospel affirms the sufficiency of the atonement and the necessity of faith in Christ alone for salvation. See, for example, G. Michael Cocoris, *Evangelism: A Biblical Approach* (Chicago: Moody, pp. 79–86; Chafer, *Salvation*, pp. 31–39; and Charles Caldwell Ryrie, *Balancing the Christian Life* (Chicago: Moody, 1969), pp. 169–81.

51. Chafer, *Salvation*, p. 75.

52. *The Formula of Concord, Epitome*, III (Affirmative Theses), 6.

53. Calvin, *Institutes of the Christian Religion*, preface, sec. 4.

54. Ibid.

55. MacArthur, *The Gospel According to Jesus*, p. 237.

56. Calvin, *Institutes of the Christian Religion*, I. vi. 1.

Chapter 15

1. G. Campbell Morgan, *The Acts of the Apostles* (New York: Revell, 1924), p. 39.
2. J. W. McGarvey, *New Commentary on Acts of Apostles* (Cincinnati: Standard, 1892), p. 28.
3. In Roman 2:5 lack of repentance is linked with the heart in the phrase "impenitent heart." "Impenitent" is the negative of the root word "repentance."
4. Alfred Edersheim, *The Life and Times of Jesus the Messiah* (New York: Longmans, Green, 1890), 2:745–47, for a concise discussion of the baptism of proselytes.
5. The language of verse 41 implies that the three thousand converts were all baptized on the same day. There were numerous pools and reservoirs in Jerusalem which would have provided the facilities for this even by immersion. If all the 120 disciples assisted in administering the ordinance it could easily have been done in a very short time. *Life* magazine reported a modern instance in which 34 men immersed 3,381 converts in four hours (August 14, 1950).
6. A. T. Robertson explains the meaning of the words "unto the remission of your sins" (v. 38), and his words are here quoted lest any misinterpret the words of Peter to teach baptismal regeneration. "In themselves the words can express aim or purpose for that use of *eis* does exist as in 1 Corinthians 2:7. . . . But then another usage exists which is just as good Greek as the use of *eis* for aim or purpose. It is seen in Matthew 10:41 . . . where it cannot be purpose or aim, but rather the basis or ground, on the basis of the name of prophet, righteous man, disciple, because one is, etc. It is seen again in Matthew 12:41 about the preaching of Jonah. . . . They repented because of (or at) the preaching of Jonah. The illustrations of both usages are numerous in the N. T. and the *Koine* generally. . . . I understand Peter to be urging baptism on each of them who had already turned (repented) and for it to be done in the name of Jesus Christ on the basis of the forgiveness of sins which they had already received" (*Word Pictures in the New Testament*, 6 vols. [Nashville: Broadman, 1933], 3:35–36).
7. Richard Belward Rackham, *The Acts of the Apostles*, p. 33.
8. J. B. Lightfoot, *Saint Paul's Epistle to the Philippians* (New York: Macmillan, 1890), p. 160.

Chapter 18

1. Benjamin Breckkenridge Warfield, *Biblical Doctrines* (New York: Oxford University Press, 1929), p. 643.

2. Ira D. Landis, *The Faith of Our Fathers on Eschatology* (Lititz, PA: By the author, 1946).

3. Albertus Pieters, "The Leader," September 5, 1931, as cited by Gerrit H. Hospers, *The Principle of Spiritualization in Hermeneutics* (East Williamson, NY: By the author, 1935), p. 5.

4. Oswald T. Allis, *Prophecy and the Church* (Philadelphia: Presbyterian and Reformed, 1945), p. 218.

5. Landis, *The Faith of Our Fathers on Eschatology*, p. 45.

6. Allis, *Prophecy and the Church*, p. 21.